Critical Reflection on Research in Teaching and Learning

Critical Issues in the Future of Learning and Teaching

Series Editors

Britt-Marie Apelgren (*University of Gothenburg, Sweden*)
Pamela Burnard (*University of Cambridge, UK*)
Nese Cabaroglu (*University of Cukurova, Turkey*)
Pamela M. Denicolo (*University of Surrey, UK*)
Nicola Simmons (*Brock University, Canada*)

Founding Editors

Pamela M. Denicolo (*University of Surrey, UK*)
Michael Kompf† (*Brock University, Canada*)

VOLUME 19

The titles published in this series are listed at *brill.com/cifl*

Critical Reflection on Research in Teaching and Learning

Edited by

Nancy E. Fenton and Whitney Ross

BRILL
SENSE

LEIDEN | BOSTON

All chapters in this book have undergone peer review.

The Library of Congress Cataloging-in-Publication Data is available online at http://catalog.loc.gov

Typeface for the Latin, Greek, and Cyrillic scripts: "Brill". See and download: brill.com/brill-typeface.

ISSN 2542-8721
ISBN 978-90-04-43663-3 (paperback)
ISBN 978-90-04-43664-0 (hardback)
ISBN 978-90-04-43665-7 (e-book)

Copyright 2020 by Koninklijke Brill NV, Leiden, The Netherlands.
Koninklijke Brill NV incorporates the imprints Brill, Brill Hes & De Graaf, Brill Nijhoff, Brill Rodopi, Brill Sense, Hotei Publishing, mentis Verlag, Verlag Ferdinand Schöningh and Wilhelm Fink Verlag.
All rights reserved. No part of this publication may be reproduced, translated, stored in a retrieval system, or transmitted in any form or by any means, electronic, mechanical, photocopying, recording or otherwise, without prior written permission from the publisher. Requests for re-use and/or translations must be addressed to Koninklijke Brill NV via brill.com or copyright.com.

This book is printed on acid-free paper and produced in a sustainable manner.

Contents

List of Figures and Tables   VII
Notes on Contributors   VIII

1   Critical Reflection on Research on Teaching and Learning   1
       Whitney Ross and Nancy E. Fenton

PART 1
Critical Explorations through Visual Media

2   Photo-Elicitation: A Powerful and Challenging Strategy for Exploration and Enhancement of Education   15
       Narelle Patton

3   Educating Reflective Practitioners through Video-Elicited Reflection   34
       Minna Körkkö, Outi Kyrö-Ämmälä and Suvi Lakkala

4   Understanding Educational Leadership through Network Analysis: A Critical Reflection on Using Social Network Analysis in a Mixed Methods Study   52
       Cherie Woolmer and Jee Su Suh

PART 2
Critical Explorations through Affect, Voice, and Power Relationships

5   Using Poetic Re-Presentation to Study Trust in Higher Education   75
       Candace D. Bloomquist and Kim West

6   Narratives of Embodied Practice: Using Portraiture to Study Leadership   93
       Jessica Raffoul, Beverley Hamilton and David Andrews

7   Complexity, Negotiations, and Processes: A Longitudinal Qualitative, Narrative Approach to Young People's Transition to and from University   107
    Henriette Tolstrup Holmegaard

PART 3
Clinical Explorations through Dialogue, Collaboration, and Ethics

8   Participatory Action Research: Navigating Nuances   133
    Nicola Simmons

9   Making Learning Visible: Research Methods to Uncover Learning Processes   154
    Klodiana Kolomitro, Corinne Laverty and Elizabeth A. Lee

10 Reflecting on Messy Practice: Action Research on Peer Review of Teaching   173
    Agnes Bosanquet and Rod Lane

11 Concluding Comments   192
    Nancy E. Fenton and Whitney Ross

    Index   203

Figures and Tables

Figures

3.1 The reflective process in teacher education elicited by VEO.   48
4.1 Basic sociogram representing 3 nodes (degree = 3) and 3 ties.   56
4.2 Base network.   62
4.3 Conversations about innovation in teaching and learning.   62
4.4 Conversations about emotional support for teaching and learning.   63
7.1 Drawing by biochemistry student of future self in 3 years.   116
7.2 Drawing by biomedicine student of future self in 3 years.   117
8.1 Navigating potential challenges to participatory action research/SoTL.   148
9.1 Student-generated maps. The first map was created independently by the student and the second map is the same map with additions made by the student at the close of the collaborative dialogue.   167
10.1 The PAR cycle (from Kemmis, McTaggart, & Nixon, 2014, p. 19).   180
10.2 The action research spiral (from Kemmis, McTaggart, & Nixon, 2014, p. 19).   180

Tables

3.1 Participants and data collection methods for VEO trials 2016–2017.   38
8.1 Timelines for action research cycles.   140
8.2 Overview of principal investigator and participant roles.   143
9.1 Rubric created to capture strategies and prompts in solving multiple-choice questions.   159
10.1 Peer review of teaching plan.   177
10.2 Components of the peer review of teaching project.   181
10.3 Structure of the workshop series.   182

Notes on Contributors

David Andrews
is a Professor in Kinesiology at the University of Windsor and teaches in the movement science and applied human performance programs. His disciplinary research in biomechanics and ergonomics focuses on injury prevention and assessing physical demands and injury risk in sport and occupational settings. His teaching and learning interests and research span peer observation of teaching, educational leadership, and student engagement in large classes. Dr. Andrews is a 3M National Teaching Fellow, Past President of the Canadian Society for Biomechanics, former Research and Teaching Leadership Chairs for the Faculty of Human Kinetics, and former Head of the Department of Kinesiology.

Candace D. Bloomquist
is an Assistant Professor in Creighton University's EdD in Interdisciplinary Leadership Program. She holds a BSc in Exercise Science, a MSc in Kinesiology, and a PhD in Kinesiology (Exercise Psychology). She has worked in both the US and Canada as a health educator, a community action specialist, and in the US Army as a medical laboratory technician. She researches cultures of trust, interdisciplinary leadership, and continuous quality improvement in both healthcare and education settings.

Agnes Bosanquet
is the Director, Learning and Teaching Staff Development and an Associate Professor at Macquarie University, Sydney, Australia. She has 20 years experience teaching undergraduate and postgraduate students and developing academics in face-to-face, blended and online learning environments. With a PhD in Cultural Studies, she uses critical theories and creative methodologies to undertake qualitative research in higher education. Her research interests are critical university studies and changing academic roles and identities.

Nancy E. Fenton
is an Assistant Clinical Professor in the Faculty of Health Sciences and Associate Director, Research at the Paul R. MacPherson Institute for Leadership, Innovation and Excellence in Teaching, at McMaster University. Her research interests involve interdisciplinary qualitative health and educational research related to leadership, social networks and policy.

Notes on Contributors

Beverley Hamilton

is the Academic Initiatives Officer in the Provost's office at the University of Windsor. She undertakes research, projects, and policy development to enhance academic practice and the student experience, and works with and offers leadership development to academic leaders navigating a diversity of institutional contexts.

Henriette Tolstrup Holmegaard

is an Associate Professor in Science Education. Her research centres around the inequalities played out in science- and engineering education. She applies a wide range of qualitative methodologies and in particular longitudinal studies to explore children and young peoples' choices and science identities as negotiated over time, and in the transition in between different institutional settings. She is currently involved in research that investigates children and young peoples' science capital and identities over a ten-year period. In her recent publication, she studies young peoples' imagined futures as an interaction of their resources and the narrative repertoires available to them.

Klodiana Kolomitro

is the Director of Education Development, with the Office of Professional Development and Educational Scholarship in the Faculty of Health Sciences, and cross-appointed to the Department of Biomedical and Molecular Sciences, Queen's University, Canada. Her research interests include curriculum development, well-being, anatomical education, and SoTL. She has a PhD in Curriculum and Pedagogy from OISE/University of Toronto, and a MSc in Anatomy and Cell Biology from Queen's University. Klodiana is the recipient of the 2019 Educational Developers Leadership Award from the Educational Developers Caucus of Canada. She is a volunteer with Academics Without Borders, and Associate Editor of *CJSoTL*.

Minna Körkkö

(MEd) works as researcher at the Faculty of Education, University of Lapland. Her research interests include research-based teacher education, reflective practice, teacher professional development and multicultural education. Her doctoral dissertation focuses on the video application called video enhanced observation (VEO) and how it can be used for promoting student teachers' reflection as part of reflective practice. She has published several international articles in the field of teacher education and worked on many relevant international and national projects.

Outi Kyrö-Ämmälä
(PhD) works as a university lecturer in teacher Education at the Faculty of Education, University of Lapland. She is also acting a Vice-Dean responsible for teaching at the faculty. Kyrö-Ämmälä has played an integrative part in developing a research-based teacher education program at the University of Lapland. Her research interest is focused also in inclusive education. During last years, she has participated in several relevant international and national projects concerning inclusive education and the development of teacher education.

Suvi Lakkala
(PhD) is a senior lecturer in general education and teacher education at the University of Lapland. Her research interests cover inclusive education, interprofessional work, educational transitions and teachers' professional development. She has several international and domestic publications in the field of inclusive education. She has worked on many international and national projects concerning inclusive education.

Rod Lane
is an Associate Professor and the Deputy Head of Department leading learning and teaching and in the Macquarie School of Education, Sydney, Australia. He has a PhD in Education, 24 years of experience teaching in secondary and higher education contexts and has an international profile for his research in conceptual change and educational assessment. Dr Lane has played a substantial role in advising Australian State and Federal Governments in pedagogy, curriculum and assessment. He has numerous awards for excellence in learning and teaching including an Australian Learning and Teaching Council (ALTC) Citation for Outstanding Contributions to Student Learning and is Senior Fellow of the Higher Education Academy (SFHEA).

Corinne Laverty
is a research librarian at Queen's University Library in Kingston Ontario. She spent the last five years as Teaching & Learning Specialist at the Queen's Centre for Teaching and Learning where she led a workshop series on educational research. The series is contributing to campus interest and accomplishment around the Scholarship of Teaching and Learning. Her current research projects include approaches to decolonizing post-secondary information literacy development and student perspectives on elements of an inclusive classroom.

Elizabeth A. Lee
recently retired from the faculty of education at Queen's University. Her research interest is individual's conceptualization of learning processes and has

published papers across different domains, language development, library science, special education and literacy. Currently she is examining teachers' perceptions of learning in an Anishinaabemowin immersion program.

Narelle Patton
is the Sub Dean Workplace Learning and Accreditation in the Faculty of Science at Charles Sturt University, Australia. Narelle's teaching, research and leadership philosophy has evolved from her extensive professional, workplace learning, academic, research and leadership experience that has been grounded in a social justice framework and a genuine desire to assist people to reach their full potential in relation to wellbeing and education. Narelle's research interests include professional practice, professional practice capabilities, learning and teaching strategies and workplace learning. Narelle researches in a qualitative paradigm utilising hermeneutics, phenomenology, and visual and creative research strategies to develop new understandings.

Jessica Raffoul
is a Learning Specialist with the Centre for Teaching and Learning at the University of Windsor. In this role, she designs and contributes to research, programs, and curricula that support teaching and learning, with a particular focus on the scholarship of teaching and learning, educational leadership, and reflective practice. She has participated in the organization of multiple national and international conferences, managed a national teaching and learning journal, coordinated programs, developed resources, disseminated research, and taught courses. She holds degrees and certificates in English literature, creative writing, philosophy, and higher education.

Whitney Ross
is an Educational Developer in the Centre for Academic Excellence at Niagara College specializing in inclusivity and culturally responsive teaching. Her research interests include qualitative explorations of equity and inclusion in higher education, change processes and institutional frameworks, and social networks in teaching and learning.

Nicola Simmons
is a faculty member in Educational Studies at Brock University. She has held national and international leadership roles in the Scholarship of Teaching and Learning and as past chair of the Educational Developers Caucus (EDC). Nicola focuses on SoTL and adult learning, development, and meaning-making. She is a 2017 3M National Teaching Fellow and a 2016 inaugural EDC Distinguished

Educational Development Career Award winner. Currently, she holds a Brock Chancellor's Chair for Teaching Excellence.

Jee Su Suh
is a PhD candidate in Neuroscience at McMaster University. Her doctoral research investigates biological indicators of diagnosis and treatment response in major depressive disorder, utilizing techniques in neuroimaging and machine learning. She was employed part-time as a Student Partner at the Paul R. MacPherson Institute for Leadership, Innovation and Excellence in Teaching from 2018-2019, working in partnership with Drs. Cherie Woolmer and Nancy E. Fenton. In addition to her work in biological psychiatry, she is continuing to pursue applications in social network analysis on functional neuroimaging data from healthy subjects.

Kim West
is a Learning & Development Specialist at the University of Saskatchewan. She has a BSc with Honors and a PhD in Earth Sciences. She has worked for nearly 20 years in the field of teaching and learning at the University of Saskatchewan as a coach/mentor of graduate students, instructor and curriculum designer of university teaching courses and programs, and as a sessional lecturer in geography and planning. Her current work supports people leaders at the University of Saskatchewan in the areas of trust, rapport, empathy, diversity, equity, inclusion, and mindful leadership practices.

Cherie Woolmer
is a Postdoctoral Research Fellow based at the MacPherson Institute at McMaster University, Canada and a Fellow of the International Society for Scholarship of Teaching and Learning (ISSoTL). She currently leads the Student Partnership Program at McMaster, involving over 200 faculty and students in projects to enhance teaching and learning. Prior to joining McMaster, Cherie worked in educational development in the United Kingdom, supporting faculty and undergraduate students in interdisciplinary research teams. Her research focuses on faculty-student partnerships is informed by critical pedagogy, socio-cultural approaches to change, and measuring the impact of pedagogical partnerships.

CHAPTER 1

Critical Reflection on Research on Teaching and Learning

Whitney Ross and Nancy E. Fenton

1   Introduction

Research in teaching and learning, often called the Scholarship of Teaching and Learning (SoTL), can take many forms and explore many diverse avenues. In light of this diversity, before beginning an introductory overview of research in teaching and learning, we wish to pause to acknowledge the language that we are using to describe this larger area of research. Numerous discourses exist on the relationship between educational research, educational scholarship, SoTL, and more (for example, Geertsema, 2016; Streveler, Borrego, & Smith, 2007). Within our research contexts, we have often used the broad and inclusive language of research in teaching and learning as an umbrella term to not exclude those that may identify their work with alternative and/or different labels. In this introduction, we wish to provide a brief overview of key features of research in teaching and learning while acknowledging that some practitioners may not identify their work under the banner of SoTL.

Ever since Boyer's (1990) formative work encouraging the expansion of the study of teaching and learning, we have seen research on teaching and learning develop and embark on new horizons. With such rapid development, it is difficult to provide an operational definition of the Scholarship of Teaching and Learning. The very diverse and broad nature of SoTL does not allow always for a precise definition to emerge, but many have identified key criteria and aims of SoTL. Felten's (2013) Principles of Good Practice in SoTL suggest that SoTL is (1) inquiry in student learning, (2) situated in context, (3) methodologically sound (4) conducted in partnership with students, and (5) appropriately public. Scoufis (2013) emphasizes the importance of elevating the 'L' in SoTL and suggests that the Scholarship of Teaching and Learning is an appropriate vehicle for producing evidence for enhanced student learning. Potter and Kustra (2011) offer that SoTL is

> the systematic study of teaching and learning, using established or validated criteria of scholarship, to understand how teaching (beliefs,

behaviors, attitudes, and values) can maximize learning, and/or develop a more accurate understanding of learning, resulting in products that are publicly shared for critique and use by an appropriate community. (p. 2)

With a similar emphasis on dissemination, Kreber and Cranton (2000) describe the Scholarship of Teaching and Learning as "ongoing learning about teaching and the demonstration of such knowledge" (p. 477).

Such a range of interpretations and classifications of the Scholarship of Teaching and Learning is aptly suited to the landscape of teaching and learning from which it emerges. As Fanghanel et al. (2015) note, "This state of affairs, to an extent, mirrors the complexity of teaching and learning, the variety of contexts in which it takes place, and the skepticism among many that teaching and learning is an area worthy of inquiry" (p. 6). It is this operational uncertainty, this richness of diversity, which allows for innovative research inquiries in teaching and learning to flourish.

The diversity of research approaches that are utilized in the Scholarship of Teaching and Learning has been confirmed by surveys of published SoTL literature (Divan et al., 2017). This diversity is influenced in part by the fact that researchers in teaching and learning bring with them their own discipline identity and research approaches (Healey, 2000). Huber and Hutchings (2005) have described the Scholarship of Teaching and Learning as a 'big tent,' an inclusive area of research inquiry into teaching and learning. Fanghanel et al.'s (2015) literature view of SoTL demonstrates the broad range of topics and concepts that SoTL can cover including reflection and inquiry, strategies and best practices for enhancing teaching and learning, evidence-informed and scholarly teaching, and engaging students in research.

In the Scholarship of Teaching and Learning, there is no one right way to ask a question or to answer it and there is not just one type of question to pose. This can be simultaneously empowering and paralyzing for researchers looking to conduct their own investigations of teaching and learning. Indeed, a lack of coherence in the conceptualization of the Scholarship of Teaching and Learning can be challenging to new researchers (Miller-Young & Yeo, 2015). Yet, this diversity can also be fostered to function as a means to accommodate newcomers to the field (Fanghanel et al., 2015).

The broad landscape of teaching and learning surely deserves just as broad a methodological range of research approaches. We believe that one of the most attractive and beneficial features of research in teaching and learning is this methodological uncertainty. The 'big tent' that allows for researchers to utilize diverse and novel methods as they delve deep into investigations of teaching and learning. Methodological pluralism within the Scholarship of Teaching and Learning is something to be celebrated and continually practiced. We view this collection as evidence of just that – the celebration of methodological pluralism that is inherent to the very nature of teaching and learning research.

2   Qualitative Methods and Research in Teaching and Learning

In keeping with the rising interest in educational scholarship in higher education, research on teaching and learning has expanded and grown substantially over the past few decades (Hutchings, Huber, & Ciccone, 2011; Kwo, 2007). In light of such an expansion, researchers are continually seeking new and different ways to ask teaching and learning questions. As appropriately noted by Hutchings (2000), "there is no single best method of approach for conducting the Scholarship of Teaching and Learning" (p. 1). Coupled with the diversity of methods is the broad scope of purpose associated with SoTL investigations.

With such a fertile research playground at hand, the richness of qualitative methods allows us to explore the landscape of teaching and learning in imaginative ways. The "essence of qualitative inquiry [is] a way of understanding, describing, unraveling, illuminating, chronicling, and documenting social life – which includes attention to the everyday, to the mundane and ordinary, as much as the extraordinary" (Leavy, 2014, p. 1). The 'fullness' of qualitative inquiry allows researchers to capture and critically explore the complexities of teaching and learning experiences. In the context of research in teaching and learning, qualitative approaches have been defined as "one[s] that explore a central phenomenon without assigning a quantifiable attribute, permitting a broad view of the participant's experiences" (Divan et al., 2017, p. 18). Capturing this broad view of participant's experiences is essential to the intricacies and subjective contexts that are at the core of teaching and learning.

In 2006, Huber put forward that researchers should continue to step into uncertain and novel terrain as they consider the variety of qualitative methodologies available to them. Such a call has been keenly taken up by researchers in teaching and learning. Consistent with the 'big-tent' notion of the Scholarship of Teaching and Learning, researchers are bringing forth innovative qualitative methods that push beyond the boundaries of the standard semi-structured interview so often associated with qualitative research. From action research, self-study, grounded theory research, to classroom ethnography, and more, a variety of qualitative methods are being utilized to explore pertinent questions emerging within teaching and learning environments (Hubball & Clarke, 2010).

Within this very volume, we have a range of novel methods that include photo-elicitation, social network analysis, poetic re-representation, portraiture, and longitudinal narrative analysis. As researchers draw on different disciplines and epistemologies, we are privy to rich paradigms of qualitative inquiry that explore the experiences of educators and students.

Overall, it is an exciting time to be practicing qualitative research on teaching and learning. Research explorations of teaching and learning continue to expand the important role they can play within institutions of higher education. More and more, teaching and learning research is growing in significance and impact as institutions strategically plan around concepts of academic and teaching quality within higher education (Fanghanel et al., 2015). As such, research in teaching and learning will continue to inform the very practice of teaching and learning in higher education in critical and influential ways.

3 Reflecting on Praxis

In an introduction, it is often apt to tell readers what the book is about. In a similar vein, it is just as prudent to inform you what this book will not be. This volume is less a 'how-to' handbook or compendium of qualitative methods, and more a collection of stories focused on 'the doing of research.' A unique feature of this book is the reflections on praxis that are at the core of each chapter and the method explored. Most books on qualitative research methods will often focus on the logic and/or implementation of research practice whereas this book serves as a reflection of research practice. What special challenges did researchers face when conducting their qualitative research? What changes did they have to make? What sits with them as they look back with the gift of hindsight? This notion of praxis is conveniently suited for research in teaching and learning as it is often described as an aspect of practice and conducted in 'the first person' (Hutchings, 2000). Likewise, Hubball and Clarke (2010) have deemed the Scholarship of Teaching and Learning as a "distinctive form of practice-based research within higher education" (p. 1). By reflecting on praxis, researchers are invited to interrogate their assumptions about research, practice, and teaching and learning itself. As Miller-Young and Yeo (2015) rightly point out, behind any investigation of teaching and learning are one's own views and assumptions about how teaching and learning work. All the contributors in this book were asked to situate their work theoretically and provide detailed descriptions of the qualitative methodological approach they employed within the context of reflection.

This deliberate framing of reflection on praxis provides researchers with space to engage with and embody the sometimes very messy reality of research. It is rare for a qualitative research project to unfold from start to finish exactly as forecasted. Our processes are never linear, but too often we do not have the space and/or time to stop and bring to light the necessary detours and adjustments we had to make. By reflecting on praxis, researchers are allowed to explore the anecdotes that are often scrubbed clean from the polished final product but are always kept in mind when embarking on one's next project.

This emphasis on praxis, as distinguished from a singular focus on theory, provides avenues for researchers to critically explore the complicated nuances, minutiae, challenges, failures, learning and relearning that they encounter while embarking on their research journeys. Each chapter that follows will explore how a specific method was undertaken and the challenges and considerations involved. Authors will not present simple generalized procedures, but will reflect on their own research investigations into aspects of teaching and learning. This reflection of praxis connects the diverse research investigations that follow and produces a rich collection of reflective experiences that readers can, in turn, use as a point of departure to consider and reflect on their own experiences with research in teaching and learning. Through reflexivity, this book serves as a forum to explore the inventive world of qualitative research methods in teaching and learning and enter spaces that often remain uncovered in traditional collections of methodologies.

4   Organization of the Book

For each chapter, the authors were asked to reflect on the special challenges they faced conducting the research they describe and to expose the aspects of their work that might not otherwise fit neatly into a traditional methodology chapter, including technical dilemmas, institutional and disciplinary resistance, and issues they encountered along the way that would be instructive to others in the field. This is a unique ask of our contributors, but we felt it would be essential for shaping and understanding how these critical methods are used in practice. That said, this unique ask also comes with limitations. Given that we asked researchers to authentically reflect on their research experiences, the reflections and discussions produced are subjective to the experiences of these individual researchers. They ultimately reflected on and discussed the certain aspects of their research process that most prominently resonated with them. This means that, at times, not all research considerations for a specific research method and/or study are covered as extensively as others. Emphasis on certain aspects like research ethics, data analysis, and dissemination will vary from chapter to chapter. Our desire to not influence the reflections of our authors meant that we did not provide explicit leading questions or requirements pertaining to their reflections on praxis. The result is a collection of genuine reflections produced by researchers on their own research investigations of teaching and learning.

The contributions begin with a three-chapter part on critical explorations through the use of visual media. Patton gives primacy to the visual and opens opportunities to engage people at the emotional and imaginative levels in Chapter 2, focusing on visibility through photo-elicitation. Patton takes a reflexive journey and implements photo-elicitation strategies to explore students' learning during clinical education experiences. Like Raffoul, Hamilton, and Andrews (see Chapter 6), Patton draws upon critical methodology and the practice of reflexivity as key strategies to attend to issues of power and ethics of photography. Examples drawn from photo-elicitation interviews with researchers and participants resulting in a teaching strategy to enhance students' reflective capabilities, highlight some of the challenges of visual research and bring to light a range of issues, such as image ownership, informed consent, peer acceptance, and publication. Along the way, Patton provides strategies to overcome these challenges by encouraging researchers to join this rapidly evolving field of visual research.

Körkkö, Kyrö-Ämmälä, and Lakkala also write about visual-elicited reflection in Chapter 3, focusing on student teacher self-reflection through video enhanced observation (VEO). They draw upon their experience studying the reflective practice of the primary school teacher education program at the University of Lapland (UoL) since 2016. In this chapter, the authors emphasize that contrary to conventional videos, VEO allows time-stamp live video of lessons with tags, for easy review and retrieval of key moments of classroom activity. Their unique experiences in the field provide insights into how the application is employed and the challenges of using this methodology for the first time. Körkkö, Kyrö-Ämmälä, and Lakkala deftly situate VEO within student-supervision practices. That is, VEO encourages our thinking beyond the traditional focus of supervision – from assessing students – towards supporting their self-reflection.

Like Raffoul, Hamilton, and Andrews (see Chapter 6), Woolmer and Suh experiment with a relatively underutilized research methodology to explore networks of educational leaders. In Chapter 4, Woolmer and Suh describe in-depth the conceptual and analytic processes involved with Social Network Analysis (SNA) and the mixed-method approach to investigate networks of faculty members engaged in a two-year Leadership in Teaching and Learning

(LTL) Fellowship program. They candidly expose both the excitement and challenge of using a new systematic approach by sharing some of the questions that framed their journey – What happens when you use an untried methodological approach? What ethical and logistical challenges will we confront? What if the methods take us out of our methodological comfort zone? Building upon prior LTL research, Woolmer and Suh capture, illustrate, and analyze how networks and conversations about teaching and learning change as fellows progress through the two-year program. While this chapter demonstrates both the challenges and limitations of using SNA, the authors challenge new researchers of this methodology to think further about the intersection between choices of design and analysis and the influence of social context and the implications for praxis.

The second part, which focuses on critical approaches through affect, voice, and power relationships, begins with a chapter involving poetic re-representation. Bloomquist and West challenge us to reflect on trust in higher education, an issue they explore in Chapter 5 using poetic representation to promote dialogue and critical inquiry. The chapter begins will a brief story of why poetic representation helped frame their role as researchers and deep listeners and how poetry shaped their journey as both teachers and researchers. They describe a unique research project from the vantage point of a graduate student (both student and teacher) that combines individual interviews and poetic transcription as a model to create research poems that reflectively constructed through interview themes. The authors argue that research poems capture real-life emotions and experiences that go beyond conventional methods to illuminate the decisions and actions of teachers that create a culture of trust. In the later part of the chapter, Bloomquist and West conclude with a call to action for teachers to engage in discussions about trust and how as researchers we can help foster culture(s) of trust in higher education.

In Chapter 6, Raffoul, Hamilton, and Andrews employ an innovative form of narrative research, called portraiture, to illuminate the subtleties of leadership practice. This novel method blends art and science to capture the complexity, dynamics, and nuances of human experiences. The use of portraiture enabled the researchers to explore the situational, relational, and uncertain nature of leadership, and to uncover some of the fundamental tensions leaders in higher education face. They draw heavily on Meyer and Land's threshold concept work and through story-telling, analysis, and re-storying between leaders and researchers, several thresholds or bottlenecks emerge that ultimately generate an interwoven first-person narrative. The authors highlight some of the challenges of the intensely interactive nature of portraiture and take seriously issues such as trust and power relations. Through their experiences, Raffoul,

Hamilton, and Andrews encourage us to stretch our thinking about how the various senses can be engaged in research by challenging us to listen, to see more broadly, and to feel the traces of leaders' pathways across multiple contexts and endeavors.

In Chapter 7, Holmegaard describes how longitudinal qualitative narrative interviews give access to the complexity of life through dialogue with participants across contexts and time. The author traces the origin and spectra of the methodology and dives into the theoretical background and practical applications of longitudinal narrative interviews. Using examples drawn from two research projects involving students' transition into and out of higher education, Holmegaard discusses how this methodology offers a critical lens to understand the continuous negotiations of the past, present, and future as they evolve in various contexts. The author problematizes such issues as negations, complexity, and processes to avoid rendering the research object as static and reflects upon the strengths and limitations embedded in the method to shine a light on points of consideration for achieving a more nuanced perception of participants' lives. Such work has potential application across a broad spectrum of qualitative methods including ethnography and focus groups to gain a deeper understanding of the cultural contexts of narratives.

As the opening chapter of Part 3 on critical explorations through dialogue, collaboration, and ethics, Simmons introduces participatory action research. In Chapter 8, Simmons explores in-depth the connections between action research, experiential learning, and reflective practice as a generative, theory-building heuristic practice of cycles that can lead to continuous improvement. Simmons argues that such an approach is representative of the way scholars undertake inquiry into teaching and learning. The method described in this chapter highlights how 'joint reflection' between educator and researcher can make for rich dialogue, but can also bring complication to research agendas. Simmons teases apart the roles of researcher and participants in one participatory action research study illuminating how to 'smooth' the research ethics board process, handle the intricacies of the negotiating the shifting roles and responsibilities between the researcher and participant, while at the same time how seductive it is to get side-tracked with shifting goals.

In Chapter 9, Kolomitro, Laverty, and Lee draw upon two novel qualitative methods. In the first case study, narrative research was employed to assess higher-order thinking skills using multiple-choice questions in anatomy. This approach required undergraduate student participants to verbalize their thought process as they solved multiple-choice questions that were crafted at three levels of cognitive functioning, based on the ICE (ideas, connections, extensions) model. Kolomitro, Laverty, and Lee then use one-on-one, think-aloud interviews to identify strategies that students employ while working through the questions. Along the way, the authors illuminate some of the challenges in using this labor-intensive approach. In the second case study, the authors employ an interesting collaborative dialogue and visualization mapping approach to capture graduate students' understanding of the research process by engaging in reciprocal, collective meaning-making. Through the use of visual mapping and think-aloud techniques, Kolomitro, Laverty, and Lee highlight some of the challenges of conducting this collaborative type of research along with the potential impact such research can have on teaching.

In Chapter 10, Bosanquet and Lane reflect upon the unanticipated complexities of conducting action research on the peer review of teaching. They recount the experiences and lessons learned through promoting a culture of ongoing reflection with the intent of improving enhancements in learning, teaching, and curriculum. In contrast to Simmons' chapter, which also engages a participatory action research (PAR) approach, these authors describe in detail the complex, messiness of qualitative work focusing on the ethical, theoretical, practical, and affective issues they encountered. Bosanquet and Lane bring Volkwein's (1999) framework to bear on some of the competing agendas and tensions between peer reviews for improvement versus peer review for accountability. This chapter also highlights how the authors teased apart the diverse range of competing values, expectations, and motivations.

We conclude the book in Chapter 11 with our own reflections on a collaborative autoethnographic research study and explore the themes brought forward by our authors' reflections on praxis to provide concluding thoughts about the nature of qualitative research methods in research in teaching and learning.

As editors, we hope that this unique approach to an edited volume on qualitative research methods presents new opportunities for readers. This includes the opportunity to learn from the challenges, caveats, and qualifications that the researchers in this book had to encounter and embrace through their research studies. As well, we hope that the deeply personal and introspective reflections on praxis provided by these talented researchers serve as an invitation for others to do the same. The reality of research practice is never as neat as the final product that we present and disseminate. The diversity of experiences and reflections of the authors that follow provide opportunities for us to continue to improve and inform our own practices and approaches in research in teaching and learning.

References

Boyer, E. (1990). *Scholarship reconsidered: Priorities of the professoriate.* Carnegie Foundation for the Advancement of Teaching.

Divian, A., Ludwig, L., Matthews, K., Motley, P., & Tomljenovic-Berube, A. (2017). Survey of research approaches utilized in the scholarship of teaching and learning publications. *Teaching & Learning Inquiry, 5*(2), 16–29.

Fanghanel, J., McGowan, S., Parker, P., McConnell, C., Potter, J., Locke, W., & Healey, M. (2015). *Defining and supporting the Scholarship of Teaching and Learning (SoTL): A sector-wide study.* Higher Education Academy.

Geertseema, J. (2016). Academic development, SoTL and educational research. *International Journal for Academic Development, 21*(2), 122–134. doi:10.1080/1360144X.2016.1175144e

Healey, M. (2000). Developing the scholarship of teaching in higher education: A discipline based approach. *Higher Education Research and Development, 19*(2), 169–89.

Hubball, H., & Clarke, A. (2010). Diverse methodological approaches and considerations for SoTL in higher education. *The Canadian Journal for the Scholarship of Teaching and Learning, 1*(1), 1–12. doi:10.5206/cjSoTL-rcacea.2010.1.2

Huber, M. T. (2006). Disciplines, pedagogy, and inquiry-based learning about teaching. In C. Kreber (Ed.), *Exploring research based teaching* (New Directions for Teaching and Learning, Vol. 107, pp. 63–72). Jossey-Bass.

Huber, M. T., & Hutchings, P. (2005). *The advancements of learning: Building the teaching commons. The Carnegie Foundation report on the scholarship of teaching and learning.* Jossey-Bass.

Hutchings, P. (2000). Approaching the scholarship of teaching and learning. In P. Hutchings (Ed.), *Opening lines: Approaches to the scholarship of teaching and learning* (pp. 1–10). Carnegie Publications.

Hutchings, P., Huber, M. T., & Ciccone, A. (2011). Getting there: An integrative vision of the scholarship of teaching and learning. *International Journal for the Scholarship of Teaching and Learning, 5*(1), Article 1.

Kreber, C., & Cranton, P. (2000). Exploring the scholarship of teaching. *Journal of Higher Education, 71*(4), 476–495.

Kwo, O. (2007). SoTL in the commons: Elephant, authenticity and journey. *International Journal of the Scholarship of Teaching and Learning, 1*(2), Article 4.

Leavy, P. (2014). Introduction. In P. Leavy (Ed.), *The Oxford handbook of qualitative research* (pp. 1–21). Oxford University Press.

Miller-Young, J., & Yeo, M. (2015). Conceptualizing and communicating SoTL: A framework for the field. *Teaching and Learning Inquiry, 3*(2), 37–53.

Potter, M. K., & Kustra, E. (2011). The relationship between scholarly teaching and SoTL: Models, distinctions, and clarifications. *International Journal for the Scholarship of Teaching and Learning, 5*(1), 1–18.

Scoufis, M. (2013). Have we lost focus on our students' learning? *International Journal for the Scholarship of Teaching and Learning, 7*(1), Article 3.

Streveler, R. A., Borrego, M., & Smith, K. A. (2007). Moving from the scholarship of teaching and learning to educational research: An example from engineering. *To Improve the Academy, 25*(1), 139–149.

Volkwein, J. F. (1999). The four faces of institutional research. *New Directions for Institutional Research, 104*, 9–19.

PART 1

Critical Explorations through Visual Media

CHAPTER 2

Photo-Elicitation: A Powerful and Challenging Strategy for Exploration and Enhancement of Education

Narelle Patton

Abstract

This chapter is built on a premise that what can be known through oral and written knowledge is a fraction of what can be accessed through engagement with wordless knowledge. The complex and fluid nature of 21st-century society requires an openness to research and education strategies that harness the power of wordless ways of knowing in order to meet contemporary demands. A spirit of imagination, creativity, empathy, and risk-taking is needed to bring this vision to life. Visual research and education strategies are explored in this chapter as powerful, enjoyable, and rewarding ways to investigate educational phenomena and deepen student learning. Teaching and learning as inherently human practices (that is they are experienced, lived through and remembered afterward) can be richly explored and deeply understood through visual research strategies that lift the cloak of invisibility over everyday activities, and allow examination of the familiar with a more critical eye. The power of photo-elicitation to deepen understanding of teaching and learning is explored through a reflexive journey of the author's implementation of photo-elicitation strategies across a range of contexts. Careful alignment of philosophical frameworks with research strategies ensures quality and rigor and generation of trustworthy and rich findings.

Keywords

visual research – photo-elicitation – visual pedagogy

∴

And what is word knowledge but a shadow of wordless knowledge?
KAHLIL GIBRAN (1926)

∴

1   Introduction

Images are ubiquitous in society and are inextricably woven with our personal and professional identities, narratives, lifestyles, and cultures (Patton, Higgs, & Smith, 2009). Visual research gives primacy to the visual and opens opportunities to engage people at emotional and imaginative levels (Patton, Higgs, & Smith, 2011). Increasingly, visual strategies are being used to develop deeper understandings of human worlds through a critical exploration of often taken-for-granted experiences (Prosser, 2007).

Teaching and learning as inherently human practices (that is they are experienced, lived through, and remembered afterward) can be richly explored and deeply understood through visual strategies that lift the cloak of invisibility over everyday activities, and allow examination of the familiar with a more critical eye. Visual research encompasses a wide range of techniques including observation, art, photography, artifacts, video-recording, film, and television (Patton, Higgs, & Smith, 2011). Researchers may use images as data for analysis or to co-construct meanings between researchers and participants. The latter is the focus of this chapter. The power of photo-elicitation to deepen understanding of teaching and learning is explored through a reflexive journey of my implementation of photo-elicitation strategies across a range of contexts. These experiences include exploration of physiotherapy students' learning during clinical education experiences as well as the lived teaching experiences of university academics. In these research projects, careful alignment of philosophical frameworks (philosophical hermeneutics and phenomenology of practice) with research strategies (photo-elicitation) ensured the quality and rigor of the research and generation of trustworthy and rich research findings.

Photo-elicitation effectively engages participants in collaborative, empowering, and enjoyable research where researchers and participants effectively co-create new knowledge as they jointly examine and discuss photographic representations of the phenomenon of interest. This ability to shift research power towards participants is especially relevant in educational settings where academic researchers may hold additional power over student participants.

The range of photographs provided by participants in my research demonstrated their freedom from temporal, physical, and hierarchical constraints, and the ability to represent and discuss matters meaningful to them. Participants' improved memories of their experiences also stimulated rich dialogue during interviews.

Importantly, given the widespread acknowledgment of the centrality of reflection in knowledge construction, photo-elicitation interviews sharpened participants' reflective abilities. This finding, alongside student reports of their enjoyment of the process of reflecting in a visual and dialogical reflective space, led to the development, introduction, and evaluation of photo-elicitation as a teaching strategy to develop students' understandings of complex phenomena as well as their reflective capabilities. My use of photo-elicitation to explore and share post-graduate students' tacit and embodied understandings of professional practice proved to be a powerful and enjoyable pedagogical strategy that engendered deep and memorable learning.

The implementation of photo-elicitation strategies in research and education should only be considered when it is appropriate and beneficial to do so. Ethical issues are of specific concern as researchers and educators need to remain cognizant of the power of photographs to tap into deep emotions and feelings of participants, students, and themselves and be prepared to respond appropriately. Issues of informed consent, anonymity, image ownership, permission, and copyright also require specific consideration. Further, the positioning of visual strategies outside of the mainstream of many disciplines (those that privilege quantitative evidence-based practice), raises challenges for visual researchers around peer acceptance and publication of their work.

Despite the inherent power of visual strategies to enrich qualitative research and student learning, their implementation in research and education remains at the fringe of mainstream practices. This is in part due to the many special challenges raised by the implementation of visual approaches. Strategies to overcome these challenges are discussed throughout this chapter and finally, researchers are encouraged to join the exciting, enjoyable, rewarding, and rapidly evolving field of visual research.

2 Photo-Elicitation

Visual research is frequently used in conjunction with other research strategies such as observation and interviews to incorporate richness into research findings (Banks, 2007). A defining characteristic of visual research is that it gives primacy to what is visually perceived rather than what is spoken, written, or statistically measured (Prosser, 2007). Through the incorporation of images, visual researchers aim to develop deeper and broader understandings of research participants' lived experiences and perceptions through a critical exploration of their often taken-for-granted experiences (Patton, Higgs, & Smith, 2011).

Photo-elicitation techniques, where researchers and participants use images to co-construct data, effectively engage participants (in my experience students, clinical educators, and academics) in collaborative, empowering, and enjoyable research. During photo-elicitation interviews researchers and participants examine photographs together, relieving participants of the stress of being the subject of an interrogation (Collier, 1986). This ability to shift research power towards participants is especially important for educational research where academic researchers may hold additional power over student participants.

The use of photographs in research interviews sharpens participants' memories of their experiences and imbues interviews with authenticity and realistic reconstruction (Patton, Higgs, & Smith, 2011). Photo-elicitation as a research strategy also has the potential to expand the quality and quantity of information collected. This is partly achieved through the expansion of time frames for data collection and partly through the provision of participant control in text construction. As researchers are not required to be present at all stages of data collection, photo-elicitation is a relatively unobtrusive, inexpensive, and non-labor-intensive strategy (Frith & Harcourt, 2007). The inclusion of photo-elicitation enables participants to draw a more detailed and complete picture of their lived experiences while overcoming potential limitations of data collection strategies such as observation and interviews dependent on the researcher's continued presence (Patton, Higgs, & Smith, 2011).

3 Illuminating Workplace Learning through Photo-Elicitation

In my doctoral research (Patton, 2014), a philosophical hermeneutic study that explored physiotherapy students' learning in a clinical education context, I chose to incorporate photo-elicitation as a text construction strategy to expand data collection, evoke understandings not accessible by other means, and to engage participants in a more empowering and meaningful research process. In this research, text construction was enriched as the use of photography expanded time frames for information gathering and provided student participants with freedom to represent factors both within and beyond the immediate workplace that they perceived influenced their learning. Further, participants' viewing of and reflecting on photographs opened up enjoyable spaces for reflection on their experiences and development of more explicit understandings of not only *what* but also *how* they learned while undertaking clinical placement.

3.1   *Physiotherapy Student Perspective*

Physiotherapy undergraduate students who were completing a 3 or 4-week clinical placement block at a large regional health service participated in the photo-elicitation component of my doctoral research (Patton, 2014). During the student photo-elicitation component of this research, which followed an initial period of observation and interview, student participants were provided with a digital camera and were invited to take photographs of places and spaces or things that they felt most influenced their learning while on clinical placement. The students were guided to collaborate with their clinical educators to determine appropriate and convenient times to take photographs and only to take photographs during these mutually agreed times throughout their placement. This was important to ensure that students' participation in the research did not interfere with any planned or serendipitous clinical learning activities or the normal running of clinical workplace activities. The students were asked to provide up to ten photographs. The number of photographs the students were asked to provide was constrained to limit time imposition and the potential to distract them from their clinical learning.

The students were explicitly instructed not to take photographs of people to avoid ethical dilemmas such as the potential for coercion to participate within a vulnerable population of people who are unwell, and the limited ability to guarantee the anonymity of these people. I screened all photographs supplied by students prior to printing to ensure that no identifying data, such as the patient's name on a bed, name on a file, or a person in the background, had been inadvertently included in the photograph. Any photographs containing identifying information were destroyed by the deletion of electronic files, were not printed, and were not included in any research reports. Of the 121 photographs supplied by the students only two included people. Requesting the students not include people in their photographs did not adversely affect the richness of the texts constructed as students had the opportunity to discuss people at subsequent photo-elicitation interviews. The students' photographs regularly included images that represented people and opened opportunities for discussion of the influence of people on their learning during their photo-elicitation interviews. The students creatively represented a range of people who they perceived influenced their learning, for example, hospital beds (patients), meeting tables (inter-professional team), tea rooms (physiotherapy team and other students), water bottles (clinical supervisor), physiotherapy equipment (patients), dining tables (family and friends) and accommodation (other students).

The photo-elicitation interview was undertaken in my academic office, following completion of placement and when students returned to university. Students were comfortable with this arrangement as I had an established academic and research relationship with them. I uploaded the digital photographs from the camera to my computer where they could be viewed, and the students were asked to select a photograph and discuss its significance as reflecting a factor influencing their learning while on clinical placement. This ensured that the students as research participants retained control in the co-construction of knowledge through privileging information that was meaningful to them.

The implementation of photo-elicitation as a text construction strategy in this research was highly successful. The novelty of being provided with a digital camera and being invited to take photographs facilitated student engagement with the research. I experienced no difficulty recruiting student participants in this research, which came as a surprise as I expected to encounter at least some student reticence. Not only were students happy to participate, but they were also very keen to start taking photographs. This was evidenced by students asking me when they would be provided with a camera (while I undertook observation and interviewing components of the research) and describing to me the photographs they were planning to take once they had a camera. This was interesting to me as students' reflective thinking about their learning had been stimulated prior to and in preparation for taking photographs.

Further evidence of the success of the photo-elicitation text construction strategy was the broad range of places and spaces the students represented in their photographs. This evidenced how the use of photography had provided students with the freedom to represent factors within and beyond the immediate workplace that they perceived influenced their learning while on clinical placement. I was surprised and delighted with the range of photographs the students supplied. Some examples of more surprising photographs included those of horses, a pier, a petrol bowser, two-minute noodles, chocolate milk, a teapot, a no-smoking line, and Christmas decorations. These photographs opened up spaces for rich discussions and co-construction of deeper understanding about *what* and *how* students learned during clinical placements.

During the photo-elicitation interview, the students had a measure of control in text construction as they chose the subjects of the photographs they took, and those photographs allowed them to raise topics of importance in subsequent interviews. The photographs also sharpened students' memories and further assisted them to voice their perspectives and contribute to the authenticity and rigor of the research. Beyond sharpening the students' memories, the photographs also acted as a bridge to those memories. This is evidenced in the following student quote:

> They [photographs] do just trigger everything and if you hadn't done that I don't think I would have remembered as much. It's not so much remembering, it's resurfacing those memories. (Shelly)

Finally, the use of photographs in this research stimulated rich dialogue and the emergence of new understandings for the students and myself. Illustrating the development of new understanding for the students, following the photo-elicitation interviews each of the student participants thanked me for providing them with an opportunity to reflect on contextual factors that shaped their learning during clinical placement. Each of the students had developed a more explicit understanding of contextual influences on their clinical learning, as well as strategies to facilitate their learning on future clinical placements.

3.2 *Clinical Supervisor Focus Groups*

Physiotherapists employed by a large regional health service, and who had supervised physiotherapy students undertaking at least one block placement, participated in the photo-elicitation focus group component of my doctoral research (Patton, 2014). The aim of these focus groups was to gain clinical supervisors' perceptions of contextual factors that influenced students' learning while on clinical placement and to identify actions clinical supervisors took (or could take) to construct optimal learning environments.

In these focus groups, student-generated photographs were used as prompts and memory triggers to initiate discussion amongst the clinical supervisors. The photographs (119) were printed on A4 glossy cards and were displayed on tables for the clinical supervisor participants to view prior to commencing the focus group discussion. On arrival, the clinical supervisors were invited to view the photographs and to select up to four photographs that they felt represented factors that influenced student learning during clinical placements. The clinical supervisors were then invited to generate a title for the selected photographs and were advised that the photographs would be used as prompts for the ensuing focus group discussion.

The student photograph display generated wide-ranging conversations amongst the clinical supervisors. As a pre-focus group activity, viewing and selecting pertinent student photographs provided an engaging and enjoyable entry to the focus group topic for the clinical supervisors. The clinical supervisors appeared to enjoy viewing the photographs and quickly identified and titled photographs that resonated with their views. As a result, a broad range of titles was generated for discussion. The titles included clinical themes such as problem-solving, reflection, physiotherapy techniques, equipment, patients, and teamwork; educational themes such as learning space, feedback, and utilization of learning resources; and student-centered themes where the clinical supervisors acknowledged student emotion including stress and anxiety and student diet and accommodation. The focus group discussions commenced with an invitation to share with the group the titles they had given to photographs and the reasons underpinning their photograph selection. Clinical supervisors were then encouraged to discuss their perceptions of their responsibility in relation to constructing clinical learning environments, including areas they felt were important and boundaries to their responsibility for facilitation of students' professional practice capabilities.

The inclusion of photographs in the focus groups also increased all participants' ability to contribute to the conversation, thus ensuring that all views were heard. Interestingly, this ability for all to contribute moved beyond the turn-taking nature of participants' sharing of their views about each photograph. It was further facilitated by the participants' genuine interest in not only viewing each other's photographs, but hearing their titles and the meanings ascribed by each participant to their chosen photographs. This was important in this research, as focus group participants ranged from highly experienced clinicians and clinical supervisors to those with less experience. As the facilitator, it was interesting to note how the photographs acted as a leveler and broke down any existing hierarchies. The discussion was further enriched as the participants described different interpretations of the photographs. Thus, the conversation was rich and wide-ranging.

3.3   *Key Learnings*

Visual research strategies can open up powerful ways to engage participants in collaborative, empowering, and rigorous research. For these reasons, it may be tempting to embrace visual research without due consideration of the appropriateness of the method to the research question or context (Patton, Higgs, & Smith, 2011). The level of congruence achieved between the research paradigm chosen to frame the research, the research question and aims, and the research design is crucial to the generation of credible research (Grbich, 2010). Further, credibility and rigor in interpretive research are in a large part dependent on researchers maximizing opportunities for participants to express their perspectives without constraint (Bowden & Green, 2010). Therefore, as interpretive research explores the views of participants and incorporation of photo-elicitation and other visual strategies enhance participants' ability to represent their views, together they provide a congruent framework and strategy to rigorously and credibly explore the views of others such as clinical supervisors and students.

4   Photo-Elicitation: Transforming Learning and Teaching

My individual teaching philosophy has evolved from my extensive professional, workplace learning, academic, and research experience that has been grounded in a social justice framework and a genuine desire to help people to reach their full potential in relation to wellbeing and education. Throughout my professional career, I have practiced in a person-centered framework and in my academic career have striven to keep students at the center of my practice. Keeping students at the center of teaching and learning means that every student regardless of deportment is really known and helped by an academic staff member (Trump, 1977). I believe that core to student-centered learning is the development of authentic relationships across all learning and teaching activities. Student-centered teaching and learning also requires the visioning and implementation of a complex and dynamic set of teaching approaches. My teaching approaches are also strongly steeped in social constructivist learning theories, e.g. Vygotsky (1978) and Rogoff (1990), who privilege social processes in learning and teaching. The use of photo-elicitation as a pedagogical strategy resonates harmoniously with both my person-centered and social constructivist approaches to learning and teaching.

4.1   *Implementing a Photo-Elicitation Strategy in Higher Education*

Visual strategies such as photo-elicitation are increasingly used in research to enrich data collection and enhance the robustness of the research. In contrast, the use of photo-elicitation as a learning and teaching strategy is underreported. The use of images in teaching represents an exciting and evolving field that provides educational opportunities to creatively imagine new and powerful pedagogies to enhance student learning. To explore and harness the power of photo-elicitation as a learning and teaching strategy, I introduced an online photo-elicitation group activity in a subject within a Graduate Certificate of Learning and Teaching in Higher education program. This activity required students to collaboratively explore and deepen their understanding of professional practice and practice-based education. This section describes the implementation of this photo-elicitation learning and teaching strategy and reports the findings of a qualitative research project that explored how this photo-elicitation activity employed as a learning and teaching strategy shaped students' learning (Patton & Sutton, 2017a).

The photo-elicitation activity was a group assessment task with students allocated to a group of four to six students and each group was provided with a collaborative space on the learning platform (Interact 2) to complete the assessment task. The groups were provided with a choice of interactive tools, such as discussion boards, wikis, and blogs to facilitate student interaction and to complete the assessment task. Each group was required to collaboratively develop their understanding of professional practice and practice-based education and to submit one narrated presentation that demonstrated this understanding. This group assessment task required students to explore and share their individual views of professional practice and practice-based education in relation to individual discipline areas and to then collaboratively develop a new definition of professional practice and practice-based education that encompassed all group members' individual views. Students were also required to maintain individual participation logs that documented their individual level of engagement with the activity as well as reflection on the usefulness of that engagement.

Each group member took at least one photograph that represented professional practice and one photograph that represented practice-based education to them. Using the group allocated space on the Interact 2 site, students shared these photographs alongside a short explanation of how the photographs represented professional practice and practice-based education to them. All group members then commented on each of the photographs and responded to comments of other group members. Consistent with social constructivist learning philosophies, each group collaboratively developed a deeper and richer understanding of professional practice and practice-based education.

This photo-elicitation group activity proved to be a highly engaging and successful learning and teaching activity. I gauged the success of the activity by the high level of student engagement on the Interact 2 group sites, the range and individual nature of photographs uploaded to the sites, high quality of insights demonstrated in the final group presentations, and positive feedback received from students during and at the end of the session. Importantly, students enjoyed taking the photographs and sharing their perspectives to build richer and deeper understandings of professional practice and practice-based education. The power of this activity to elicit student engagement and change in academic staff was evidenced in the unsolicited feedback received from a student in the subject:

Many a teaching conversation has been had because of this subject. Please keep the photo-elicitation exercise. It has been a great catalyst for discussion but more importantly, compels students to engage with the subject from the outset.

4.2 *Researching How Photo-Elicitation Shapes Student Learning*

Reflecting on the success of photo-elicitation as a learning and teaching strategy I wanted to better understand how photo-elicitation used as a teaching strategy shapes student learning. Since the research aimed to deepen understanding based on interpretations and perceptions of students, a qualitative paradigm using hermeneutic strategies was chosen to frame the research (see Patterson & Higgs, 2005). From a range of hermeneutic strategies, philosophical hermeneutics (see Gadamer, 1989) was chosen to guide text construction and interpretation (Patton & Sutton, 2017a).

This research utilized two data collection strategies: (1) an anonymous online survey and (2) semi-structured interviews. The survey provided information about participants' experiences of visual learning and teaching strategies both in general and specifically in relation to the subject where I had introduced the photo-elicitation activity. Interviews provide a uniquely sensitive and powerful method for capturing experiences and lived meanings of participants' everyday world (Kvale, 2007). The semi-structured interviews illuminated participants' unique and varied experiences and provided insight into perspectives that might otherwise be lost resulting in deep and rich understandings of how the use of photo-elicitation learning and teaching activities shaped participants' learning. All texts generated including survey responses, researchers' observations, field notes, and interview transcripts were coded and interpreted within a hermeneutic tradition that included multiple reading of the transcripts and identifying shared understanding, pre-judgments, interests, and assumptions.

The research participants were academics enrolled in a Professional Practice and Practice-Based Education subject in the Graduate Certificate of Learning and Teaching at Charles Sturt University. Participant recruitment spanned two offerings of the subject and deliberately commenced during the second offering of the subject. This strategy harnessed the power of modeling how academics can research their own teaching practices and provided an opportunity to participate in pedagogical research for university academics new to teaching and learning. Researching my own learning and teaching activities in this way presented specific ethical challenges. I took explicit care not to be actively involved in participant recruitment and data collection including sending invitations to participate in the survey and interviews and did not undertake any participant interviewing myself. Instead, all correspondence with participants and interviewing was undertaken by my research colleague who did not have an academic relationship with any of the participants and did not hold a position of power over any of the participants. Further, participants were assured that their decision to participate in the research was voluntary and that participation in the survey was anonymous with neither researcher able to access participant identity. This anonymity was critical to safeguard participants' freedom to provide their perspectives honestly and without coercion and, in so doing, ensure the rigor of the research. My co-researcher undertook all interviews following completion of the subject and finalization of all grades. Participants' confidentiality was further protected through the use of pseudonyms in all transcripts and research reports.

The participants of this research described a range of teaching experience with 12% of participants reporting less than 3 years of teaching experience and 18% reporting more than 10 years of teaching experience. The majority of participants (44%) reported between 3–5 years of teaching experience. Interestingly, congruent with the under-reporting of visual learning and teaching strategies, the majority (81%) of participants had never previously encountered visual teaching strategies either as a student or teacher. This highlights the importance of embedding innovative and effective pedagogical strategies such as photo-elicitation in programs aimed at enhancing academics' learning and teaching such as the Graduate Certificate in Learning and Teaching in Higher Education.

This research revealed that visual pedagogies open up powerful, personal, and enjoyable ways to engage students in meaningful learning (Patton & Sutton, 2017a). Photo-elicitation provided an immediate, tangible, and intimate way of understanding and enhancing students' learning. The photo-elicitation activities prompted students to think both more deeply and broadly about a topic as they chose or took photographs and were exposed to other students' perceptions and viewpoints. Further, the photographs provided an opportunity for students to meaningfully connect topic areas being studied to their lived experiences and interests. It *personalized* student learning. The effectiveness of this connection and consequent deep learning undertaken was evidenced in participants' ability to recall what they had learned up to eighteen months after completing the subject. Finally, the photo-elicitation activity provided a fun way to increase student engagement and group interaction. In these ways, the photo-elicitation activity resonated strongly with my teaching philosophy that is a student-centered practice within a social constructivist framework.

The use of images in teaching represents an exciting and evolving field that provides educational opportunities to creatively imagine new and powerful pedagogies to enhance and personalize student learning.

5 Exploring the Lived Experience of Teaching through Photo-Elicitation

Visual research strategies such as photo-elicitation provide an effective means to develop deep and meaningful understandings of teaching and learning in practice contexts, as well as providing an enjoyable and rewarding experience for research participants. This section is constructed on the premise that higher education teaching practice is best understood not just as a set of standards, but as a dynamic and inherently human practice (Patton & Sutton, 2017b). The findings of a phenomenological study that aimed to develop deep and rich understandings of how teaching strategies for professional practice are implemented in a university context are reported.

To date, despite the demonstrated effectiveness of professional education, little attention has been given to how it is implemented by university teachers (Letts, 2010). To address this imbalance the research reported here deliberately focused on university academics' teaching experiences and purposefully sought deeper and richer understandings of the lived experiences of university academics. This approach is especially important as teachers are people whose capability has been demonstrated as a significant factor influencing student learning outcomes (Hargreaves & Fullen, 2012).

As the aim of this research was to better understand teachers' lived experiences of teaching in a contemporary university context, a qualitative paradigm using phenomenology of practice was chosen to frame the research. Phenomenology of practice research addresses and serves professional practices with its specific value being its privileging of how human beings experience the world (van Manen, 2014). Consistent with research conducted in a qualitative paradigm, two data collection strategies were used in this research: semi-structured interviews and photo-elicitation. Photo-elicitation strategies were employed as the critical use of imagination and imagery in qualitative research provides a means by which matters important to people can be accessed and expressed (Patton, Higgs, & Smith, 2011). Visual information can also provide a wellspring for the development of new understandings about phenomena under investigation (Davidson, 2004). Participants were invited to take up to six photographs that represented their teaching experiences and then to discuss the photographs in a photo-elicitation interview. These interviews occurred via telephone, typically lasted up to one hour, were recorded, and the recordings transcribed verbatim. All data collected including researchers' observations, field notes, and interview transcripts were coded within a phenomenological tradition including holistic, selective, and detailed readings of and reflection on the texts to identify specifically evocative paragraphs and phrases (van Manen, 2014).

This research, through an exploration of the experiences of eight university teachers, illuminated the inherently human nature of university teaching and learning. Teaching was revealed to be dynamic, challenging, highly rewarding, and uniquely experienced with all of the participants exhibiting a passion for their teaching. Three key dimensions of teaching practice were identified: (1) Teaching as an embodied practice; (2) Responsibility and work of teaching and (3) Sustaining teaching practices.

The inherently human, relational, and embodied nature of teaching practice was highlighted in participants' descriptions of the emotional and physical dimensions of their teaching. This broad range of emotional and physical responses to teaching practice included excitement, happiness, anxiety, relief, frustration, annoyance, grumpiness, fatigue, concern, and sadness. The participants also described a need to regulate their relationships with students, specifically a need to 'get over' any student attachments.

The responsibility and work of teaching were evidenced in participants' disclosure of a strong sense of responsibility to 'do a good job' which often underpinned heavy workloads. The participants described a dual responsibility to provide students with positive learning experiences and to provide society with safe and competent professional practitioners. Of specific concern, given participants' strong sense of responsibility in relation to their teaching, was their description of limited support in the development of appropriate and effective learning and teaching strategies.

It was the inherently rewarding nature of teaching that largely enabled participants to sustain quality teaching practices over time despite the hard work and emotional investment involved. Rewarding teaching moments, such as when students understood a new concept, enabled participants to maintain their passion and energy for teaching. Creativity also emerged for some participants as an important part of teaching that invigorated teaching practices.

University teaching has been revealed as a dynamic, rewarding, and intensely personal experience that requires deliberate refreshment to remain sustainable (Patton & Sutton, 2017b). The use of photo-elicitation as a research strategy facilitated discussion of intensely personal dimensions of learning and teaching as participants used their photographs and opportunities to reflect (with the researcher in the photo-elicitation interviews) to peer beneath the skin of and critically examine their lived experiences of teaching.

6 Photo-Elicitation Strategies: Specific Challenges

Despite the value of visual research and education strategies to enrich research and learning and teaching pedagogies, its implementation raises many special challenges. Two key challenges are discussed in this section: (1) Ethical issues and (2) Publication issues due to the positioning of visual research outside of the research mainstream for many disciplines (those that privilege quantitative evidence-based practice). Ethical issues are of specific concern as researchers need to remain cognizant of the power of photographs to tap into deep emotions and feelings of participants, students, and themselves and respond appropriately. Issues of informed consent, anonymity, image ownership, permission, and copyright also require consideration.

6.1   *Ethical Issues*

While ethical considerations should be paramount in all research and teaching endeavors, visual strategies such as the use of photo-elicitation present unique ethical challenges for researchers and educators. These strategies raise specific concerns around issues of informed consent, inadvertent inclusion of other people, anonymity, permission, copyright (Flick, 2007), and the ability of photographs to tap deeply into the emotions of participants, researchers, students, and academics.

Consent is an especially complex issue in visual research (Close, 2007). When planning a visual research study careful consideration must be given to the issue of consent. Clear articulation of participant requirements, including, for example, the number of and any restrictions on photographs to be taken as well as time commitment for related interview(s) should be clearly stated in all information and consent forms. In the photo-elicitation component of my doctoral research, (undertaken in an acute hospital setting), the student participants were instructed not to take photographs of people because of the difficulty of gaining informed consent from a vulnerable population of people who were unwell without the possibility of coercion. It was anticipated that requesting the students not to include people in their photographs would not adversely affect the richness of the texts constructed since the student participants had the opportunity to discuss the influence of people on their learning during their interviews (see e.g. Hansen-Ketchum & Myrick, 2008; Radley & Taylor, 2003). I judged the success of this approach by taking note of how people were represented in students' photographs. The students' photographs regularly included images that represented people, their activities, and involvement, which led to rich discussions about the influence of people including clinical supervisors, nursing staff, other students, and patients on their clinical learning during the photo-elicitation interviews. Examples of these images included physiotherapy equipment, clinical supervisors' drinking bottles and shoes, empty hospital beds, staircases, coffee cups, bean bags, and tea rooms.

Visual research strategies provide immediate, tangible, and intimate ways of understanding participants' experiences (Patton, Higgs, & Smith, 2011).

A strength of visual research lies in the capacity of images to tap into wordless or tacit knowledge, the ambiguity between what we see and know, and what we are able to describe (Rhodes & Fitzgerald, 2006). Photographs can challenge participants more than verbal interviewing or focus groups because the literal character of the photograph intercepts with the participant's memory and returns attention to a familiar memory of reality (Collier, 1986). Photographs can, therefore, be charged with unexpected emotional images capable of triggering intense feelings and stimulating deep and meaningful dialogue between researchers and participants (Patton, Higgs, & Smith, 2011). While these emotions sparked by photographs may illuminate new ideas and ways of thinking, researchers are ethically bound to remain alert to participants' well-being during photo-elicitation interviews and respond appropriately should participants experience any distress.

6.2   Publication Constraints

The positioning of visual research strategies outside of the mainstream for many disciplines raises challenges for visual researchers around peer acceptance and publication of their work. Although visual research is claimed to have come to play an increasingly meaningful role in the exploration of professional practices the reality can be somewhat different. Researchers undertaking visual research methods can encounter resistance in the publication of their work. In my experience, while I initially encountered such resistance to the publication of my doctoral research in a physiotherapy professional journal, I persisted until I located another physiotherapy professional journal within which my research fitted, resulting in the publication of my research. Importantly this persistence meant that the findings of my doctoral research could be accessed by physiotherapists for whom the research was predominantly intended. I have found educational journals and conferences in general to be more welcoming of photo-elicitation research papers. I now advise researchers new to visual research strategies to consider their individual disciplines' propensity to accept and acknowledge creative research methods in order to be prepared for possible rejection. Researchers in these circumstances need to be not only innovative, creative, and rigorous in the development of research methodologies, but resilient and persistent in ensuring their research is published.

At the outset of the research, consideration of how images will be used once produced is also vital. For example, if images are to be used in subsequent publications such as books, journal articles and conference presentations, explicit, written permission must be gained from participants for use of the images in this way at the outset of the research. It must be remembered that once images have been publicly disseminated control over them is lost, highlighting the criticality of articulating publication intentions to participants at the beginning of the research (Patton, Higgs, & Smith, 2011). In my experience, the incorporation of participant-generated images greatly enriches conference presentations and book chapters imbuing them with a strong sense of authenticity. The inclusion of these images in conference presentations also greatly enhances audience engagement and stimulates robust dialogue around the phenomenon being explored. These benefits richly reward researcher efforts expended at the beginning of the research gaining appropriate participant consent.

7 Conclusion

Visual research and educational strategies are at a crossroads in that they can remain in a niche position or move into the mainstream. Visual strategies have the potential to greatly enrich qualitative research and strengthen student learning and their movement to the mainstream should be encouraged. The incorporation of visual strategies offers researchers and educators rich opportunities to develop innovative strategies to generate a new understanding of the human world. However, visual strategies should be only be employed when it is enlightening and appropriate to do so, and when the development of deeper and richer understandings of phenomena is facilitated. High-quality visual research and education practices must be underscored by an understanding of underpinning philosophical principles, a vision of the phenomena under investigation or being taught, and the ability to creatively develop and credibly enact ethical, trustworthy, and rigorous research and education strategies.

References

Banks, M. (2007). *Using visual data in qualitative research* (Vol. 5). Sage.

Bowden, J., & Green, P. (2010). The voice of the research in interpretive research: Rigour and research practices. In J. Higgs, N. Cherry, R. Macklin, & R. Ajjawi (Eds.), *Researching practice: A discourse on interpretive methodologies* (pp. 123–132). Sense.

Close, H. (2007). The use of photography as a qualitative research tool. *Nurse Researcher, 15*, 127–136.

Collier, J. (1986). *Visual anthropology: Photography as a research method.* University of New Mexico Press.

Davidson, J. (2004). 'I am fieldnote': Researching and teaching with visual data. *Interpretive Research Journal, 4*(2), 48–75.

Flick, U. (2007). *Designing qualitative research* (Vol. 1). Sage.

Frith, H., & Harcourt, D. (2007). Using photographs to capture women's experiences of chemotherapy: Reflecting on the method. *Qualitative Health Research, 17*(10), 1340–1350.

Gadamer, H.-G. (1989). *Truth and method* (J. Weinsheimer & D. Marshall, Trans., 2nd ed.). Sheed & Ward.

Gibran, K. (1994) *The prophet.* Bracken Books.

Grbich, C. (2010). Interpreting quality in interpretive research. In J. Higgs, N. Cherry, R. Macklin, & R. Ajjawi (Eds.), *Researching practice: A discourse on interpretive methodologies* (pp. 153–163). Sense.

Hansen-Ketchum, P., & Myrick, P. (2008). Photo methods for interpretive research in nursing: An ontological and epistemological perspective. *Nursing Philosophy, 9,* 205–213.

Hargreaves, A., & Fullen, M. (2012). *Professional capital transforming teaching in every school.* Routledge.

Kvale, S. (2007). *Doing interviews* (Vol. 2). Sage.

Letts, W. (2010). Exploring the pedagogical landscapes that are framing higher education. In J. Higgs, D. Fish, I. Goulter, S. Loftus, J. Reid, & F. Trede (Eds.), *Education for future practice* (pp. 123–133). Sense.

Paterson, M., & Higgs, J. (2005). Using hermeneutics as an interpretive research approach in professional practice. *The Interpretive Report, 10*(2), 339–357.

Patton, N. (2014). *Clinical learning spaces: Crucibles for the development of professional practice capabilities* (Unpublished doctoral dissertation). Charles Sturt University, Albury, Australia.

Patton, N., Higgs, J., & Smith, M. (2009). Imagining and imaging: creativity in qualitative research. In J. Higgs, D. Horsfall, & S. Grace (Eds.), *Writing qualitative research on practice* (pp. 183–193). Sense.

Patton, N., Higgs, J., & Smith, M. (2011). Envisioning visual research strategies. In J. Higgs, A. Titchen, D. Horsfall, & D. Bridges (Eds.), *Creative spaces for qualitative researching: Living research* (pp. 115–124). Sense.

Patton, N., & Sutton, K. (2017a, July). *Visual spaces for enhancing student learning.* Platform presentation HEA Conference, Manchester, UK.

Patton, N., & Sutton, K. (2017b). Leadership from within: Empowering curriculum transformation amongst higher education teaching staff. *Research and Development in Higher Education: Curriculum Transformation, 40,* 282–291.

Prosser, J. (2007). Visual methods and the visual culture of schools. *Visual Studies, 22*(1), 13–30.

Radley, A., & Taylor, D. (2003). Images of recovery: A photo-elicitation study on the hospital ward. *Interpretive Health Research, 13*(1), 77–99.

Rhodes, T., & Fitzgerald, J. (2006). Visual data in addictions research: Seeing comes before words? *Addiction Research and Theory, 14*(4), 349–363.

Rogoff, B. (1990). *Apprenticeship in thinking: Cognitive development in social context.* Oxford University Press.

Trump, J. L., & National Association of Secondary School Principals, Reston, VA. (1977). *A school for everyone. Design for a middle, junior, or senior high school that combines the old and the new.* Distributed by ERIC Clearinghouse. Retrieved from https://eric.ed.gov/?id=ED139109

van Manen, M. (2014). *Phenomenology of practice.* Left Coast Press.

Vygotsky, L. (1978). *Mind in society: The development of higher psychological processes.* Harvard University Press.

CHAPTER 3

Educating Reflective Practitioners through Video-Elicited Reflection

Minna Körkkö, Outi Kyrö-Ämmälä and Suvi Lakkala

Abstract

This study contributes to recent research on video usage by analysing the student teachers' and supervisors' experiences of conducting two video enhanced observation (VEO) trials that were carried out during practicum periods in the primary school teacher education programme of University of Lapland during the academic year 2016–2017. The results show that the VEO app worked well for student teachers' self-reflection and peer reflection. For some, watching themselves in a video was difficult. The supervisors reported that the video-based practice was more learner-centered than the traditional observation-based model. Technically, the use of the VEO app caused some challenges. Institutionally, some supervisors had difficulties in finding a new role as a promoter of student teachers' self-reflection. From a disciplinary angle, the results indicate that there is a need to invest in teacher educators' reflection skills and professional development. Moreover, the chapter introduces a research-based model for using VEO as a reflective tool in teacher education.

Keywords

primary school teacher education – reflective practice – reflection – video-elicited reflection – professional development – video application

1 Introduction

Teachers' abilities to reflect on their practice are considered important for professional development and are an essential part of most teacher education programs (Schön, 1983). Finnish teacher education follows a research-based approach which can be described by four characteristics (Krokfors et al., 2011). First, the structure of teacher education programs is based on a systematic analysis of education. Second, all teaching is guided by research. Third, students' reflective competence is enhanced in various ways when solving pedagogical problems. Fourth, students' formal research skills are developed during their studies. The aims are to educate pedagogically thinking, reflective teachers who have developed an analytical and critical approach to their work and provide student teachers with sufficient knowledge and skills to apply what they have learned and develop their teaching (Toom et al., 2010).

Despite all the efforts to guide reflective activities, only some progress in the quality of reflection seems to occur. Student teachers often still lack critical reflection skills at the end of their teacher education. Reflection levels appear to remain mostly superficial throughout students' education programs (Chitpin, 2006; Körkkö, Kyrö-Ämmälä, & Turunen, 2016). Thus, new ways of fostering reflection in teacher education are required.

With the technological advancements that have been made, the use of videos for teacher education and associated research has increased recently. Video usage has developed from microteaching (recording teachers' short lessons and analyzing them) to developing video analysis tools that extend teacher self-reflection and enable the viewing and sharing of videos as well as the documentation and examination of development over time (Rich & Hannafin, 2009). Previous studies have indicated that video is beneficial for reflecting on teaching because it improves one's ability to evaluate teaching and learn from experience (Miller, 2009; Rich & Hannafin, 2008; Stockero, Rupnow, & Pascoe, 2017).

This study contributes to recent research on video usage by analyzing the researchers' experiences of conducting two video enhanced observation (VEO) trials that were carried out during practicum periods in a primary school teacher education program (Körkkö, 2019; Körkkö, Morales Rios, & Kyrö-Ämmälä, 2019). Two groups of student teachers and their supervisors from the Faculty of Education, University of Lapland, used the mobile video app VEO in the advanced practicum during the 2016–2017 academic year. First, the main results of the video app trials are described. The research results contain both positive and negative experiences as well as practical obstacles that users faced while using the app. Next, these experiences are analyzed and discussed in light of technical, institutional, and disciplinary challenges that arose while conducting the research. Moreover, the chapter discusses further developmental suggestions and issues that should be considered when applying video-elicited reflection in teacher education.

The authors' contributions were divided. The first author collected and analyzed the data of the video trials. The second and third authors contributed to the analysis and theoretical conclusions.

2 Role of Video in Teacher Learning

In this chapter, student teachers are seen as active participants in the teacher education program, who construct their knowledge individually (Palincsar, 1998) and in interacting with others (Dillenbourg, 1999; Vygotsky, 1978) according to their personal background, theoretical teacher education studies, and practical experience (Kolb, 1984; Lave & Wenger, 1999). Supervisors and peer students facilitate student teachers' learning through feedback and discussions. Supervisors do not offer student teachers ready-made solutions, but encourage them to find their personal way of teaching.

Previous studies have indicated that video-elicited reflection has many advantages over traditional reflection tools. For instance, video evidence helps teachers notice aspects of their teaching that they do not remember, identify gaps between their beliefs about good teaching and their actual teaching, articulate tacit assumptions about teaching and learning, and change the focus of their reflection from themselves to student learning (Miller, 2009; Rich & Hannafin, 2008; Stockero et al., 2017).

However, as with all reflection, video-elicited reflection requires a guiding framework, such as reflection questions or a checklist, to enhance the quality of the reflection (Rich & Hannafin, 2008). Collaborative reflection is also essential in this context (Miller, 2009; Rich & Hannafin, 2008; Tripp & Rich, 2012). Sewall (2009) found that in the context of supervision, video-elicited reflection is more student-led and enables more analytical reflection than the traditional observation-based model. This is because the self-videotaped lesson enables student teachers to 'own' that artifact. However, a supervisor has an essential role in guiding a student teacher's self-reflection by asking for clarification and elaboration.

The results of previous studies have focused mainly on the advantages of video-elicited reflection and have assumed the effectiveness of video technology (Wang & Hartley, 2003). The barriers to using video refer to technical problems, student teachers' tendency to focus more on their appearance than deeper reflection, and the negative feelings that watching videos might evoke (see e.g. Coffey, 2014; Snoeyink, 2010). Moreover, as video shows only one side of the classroom, it presents a narrow view of classroom practice (Brophy, 2004). Previous studies have lacked a wider discussion of the disadvantages and obstacles concerning the use of video in teacher education. This chapter focuses on the technical, institutional, and disciplinary challenges that beset the research and, thus, sheds light on a topic that has received scant attention to date. Finally, the chapter offers an example of something that previous studies have not widely reported: applying and developing a video application in teacher education.

3   Context

The study concentrated on the primary school teacher education program at the University of Lapland, Rovaniemi, Finland. The program consists of theoretical studies, professional experience (practicum periods), and research methodological studies; these components are integrated throughout the duration of the program. Student teachers use reflective tools to guide their reflection: they use a pedagogical diary and reflective journal during the practicum periods, along with a pedagogical portfolio, which is used from the commencement of studies and completed after each period. Student teachers also perform reflective activities, such as reflective writing and seminars, where they discuss their practical experiences. During four practicum periods, student teachers are guided by class teachers from the teacher training school of the University of Lapland, and during one practicum period by class teachers from field schools. University supervisors participate in student teachers' guiding in three practicum periods. Annually written portfolios enable student teachers to follow changes that occur over time in their teaching, solve pedagogical problems, and develop their teaching (Chitpin, 2006; Stenberg, Rajala, & Hilppo, 2016). Although portfolios seem to be effective in changing one's teaching practice and constructing practical knowledge and professional identities, they usually include mere descriptions of student teachers' own practice and learning (Körkkö et al., 2016; Mansvelder-Longayroux, Beijaard, & Verloop, 2007). This led us to consider ways of developing reflective practice that would better enhance student teachers' analytical and critical reflection.

The video app VEO was launched in the program in 2016. VEO works on an iPad and allows users to time-stamp live video of lessons with tags that serve as lenses for observation. Tags allow for easily reviewing key moments instead of having to watch an entire video. Instances can be rated as positive, negative, or with a question mark and are used as a basis for collaborative reflection on practice. After the recording is complete, the videos are downloaded to the online VEO portal, where they are watched, commented on, and shared.

4   Research Design

The first author collected the data of the two VEO trials that occurred during the advanced practicum. Participants were student teachers and supervisors from the Faculty of Education. The first group participated in the study in the autumn term of 2016 and the second one in the spring term of 2017.

The advanced practicum is a five-week practicum aimed at developing student teachers' abilities to take overall responsibility for their pupils and classrooms and to adopt different pedagogical perspectives. This period is focused on professional identity and growth. Student teachers teach lessons alone and with a peer student. Both a class teacher from the teacher training school and a supervisor from the Faculty of Education guide the student teachers.

Before the use of the VEO app, the supervision of the advanced practicum centered on observing lessons in the classroom. The study of the first trial explored the student teachers' and supervisors' experiences of the VEO app, especially how the student teachers used it to support their professional development and how the app was applied in the supervision. The second study focused on the student teachers' and supervisors' experiences of the video-enhanced reflection procedure that they followed and its usefulness for self- and peer-reflection and supervision.

The participants and data collection methods in the two VEO trials are described in Table 3.1.

TABLE 3.1 Participants and data collection methods for VEO trials 2016–2017

Trial 1: Autumn 2016	Trial 2: Spring 2017
Participants: 12 student teachers (9 female, 3 male) and 9 supervisors (8 female, 1 male)	Participants: 10 student teachers (6 female, 4 male) and 9 supervisors (female)
Research methods: interviews (7 group interviews, 1 individual interview), reflective writing (1) and video diaries of student teachers (4)	Research methods: interviews (5 group interviews, 3 individual interviews), audio recordings of supervisory discussions (4)

For the first VEO trial, supervision was based on videos recorded by the student teachers using VEO. The supervisors did not attend the lessons. Instead, the student teachers shared their own videos with their supervisors in the VEO portal. Supervision included watching and commenting on videos and giving feedback in the VEO portal. It also included face-to-face or online meetings before, during, and after the practicum period. The student teachers' and supervisors' experiences were gathered through a semi-structured focus group or individual interviews, reflective writing, and video diaries.

The second VEO trial was based on the results of the previous trial. The data collection for the second trial consisted of a focus group or individual interviews and supervisory audio discussions recorded from those who permitted recording. The student teachers and supervisors were interviewed separately.

The data were analyzed following the principles of qualitative data- and theory-driven content analysis (NVivo) (Silverman, 2013). Since this chapter focuses on the use of the VEO app in practice, the results reported are based on the data obtained from interviews.

5 Results of Trial 1

The student teachers were guided to record and tag two lessons, or part of them, using the VEO app and ready-made tag sets, such as 'Communication,' 'Classroom atmosphere,' and 'Motivation and evaluation,' each including two sub-tags. Each student teacher had two teaching and two observation cycles during which the student teachers worked in pairs. The student teachers recorded each other's teaching in six videos with the VEO app. Afterward, the videos were uploaded to the VEO portal. The student teachers watched their videos and were able to add comments to or tag their videos. In two cases, there was only one student teacher in the class, and the class teacher recorded the videos.

5.1 *Advantages of Using the VEO App*

Mostly, the student teachers felt that they had succeeded in using the app, recording lessons, and sending them to their supervisors. One student teacher found that VEO was more practical than a traditional video camera. According to the student teachers, the VEO app worked best for self-reflection. They mentioned as benefits being able to see their own actions in the videos, observe themselves through an outsider's eyes, and learn something about themselves. The videos helped them notice details about their teaching and allowed them to see something they could not otherwise see (cf. Snoeyink, 2010). Two student teachers mentioned being surprised by the usefulness of the video recordings. When watching a recording, they realized that the lesson was not as bad as they had thought. The video recordings gave student teachers new insights, but did not necessarily cause them to change their behavior.

Six student teachers stated that the tag sets were beneficial because they helped them focus on certain issues and made observing the lessons easier. Tags supported giving feedback and, when watching one's own videos, tags made by a peer student could be compared with one's own thoughts. As Batlle and Miller (2017) found, tags work as an observation guide, and the observee can reflect on teaching and gain feedback through video tags. Therefore, tags work as lenses for self-reflection (cf. Tripp & Rich, 2012). The first VEO trial showed that tags can also benefit the observer and make examining teaching easier.

5.2   Disadvantages of Using the VEO App

Four student teachers found that they had not understood the role of the VEO app in their practicum period; therefore, they had considered recording as an extra job. Some student teachers did not see the video as a valuable tool for reflection and learning. As new users, it is possible that these student teachers would have required more time to become familiar with the video app and practice using its functions. There may have been a threshold to start using a new technological device, especially if some student teachers did not have experience with iPads.

The student teachers expressed difficulties with tagging videos while recording. The participants' views on tagging differed. Some student teachers found the tag sets restrictive. Two student teachers considered that tags narrowed classroom observation too much or created pre-conclusions for the supervisor and, therefore, ready-made tag sets should not be used. Similarly, Rich and Hannafin (2008) concluded that teachers can find using ready-made guiding frameworks difficult. Batlle and Miller (2017) recommended practicing tagging systems before using VEO. In this study, users were offered the option of practicing using the app beforehand, but because of technological problems, they had to begin using VEO for the first time at the beginning of their practicum period.

Three student teachers expressed difficulties in watching video recordings of themselves, which in some cases hindered learning through the video app. The results align with previous studies reporting that negative feelings can arise when watching videos of one's teaching (see e.g. Coffey, 2014; Snoeyink, 2010).

The student teachers' biggest critique focused on the implementation of supervision. The student teachers and supervisors, apart from one supervisor, were dissatisfied with the supervision. Supervisors with prior supervision experience in the advanced practicum said that they used almost double the time for supervision. The supervisors stated that they could not get the whole picture of the student teachers' classroom practices by only watching video clips and that poor screen and audio quality made watching difficult. Two other supervisors with prior experience experienced the main problem as the lack of interaction between the student teachers and their supervisors. In their opinion, the interaction became superficial when video was used.

The student teachers had similar thoughts, criticizing the supervisors' absence from the classroom. It seems that even though video can offer new insights into the classroom, it does not address all of the elements of teaching and can fail to capture, for instance, the emotional atmosphere in the classroom. Video reveals only one side of the classroom, which prevents seeing pupils' facial expressions (cf. Brophy, 2004). Moreover, the supervisors said that they could not watch videos only by focusing on tags. The student teachers varied in their recording and tagging skills, and sometimes the student teachers did not tag videos at all. One supervisor said that because she was unfamiliar with the lesson plan, she had no idea of the lesson content while watching the video, which made watching it difficult.

The supervisors stated that face-to-face or online meetings helped them better understand classroom situations when student teachers produced contextual knowledge of classroom situations. The supervisors' experiences highlight the role of contextual knowledge in making sense of classroom actions. In this study, the supervisors watched videos that offered limited content knowledge (usually only the video title, which indicated the subject of the recorded lesson). The results suggest two options: including the contextual information in reciprocal supervisory discussions or adding more contextual information to the video, especially to tags, would help supervisors better understand the content of lessons. Shepherd and Hannafin's (2008) results support our findings.

The student teachers and supervisors discussed the videos about three weeks after the videos had been recorded. This was because discussions occurred at the end of the practicum period. Sometimes, student teachers considered supervisors' feedback irrelevant because their teaching had developed in lessons held after the recording. Sometimes, a supervisory class teacher had given student teachers the same feedback right after the lesson. In supervisory discussions, the student teachers were forced to explain classroom events and their development to the supervisors. Consequently, the positive outcome of using videos was that the supervisory sessions became more student-led than before and presumably enhanced the students' reflection skills (cf. Sewall, 2009). Yet the data do not reveal the nature of student teachers' reflections during those discussions.

5.3   *Developmental Suggestions*

In the first VEO trial, the VEO app worked best in the student teachers' self-reflections. Thus, the student teachers used VEO as one source for their professional development. As reflection became a central concept of the study, we decided to focus on exploring reflection in the next VEO trial.

The biggest disadvantage of implementing supervision through VEO was that both the supervisors and student teachers were familiar with authentic observation and supervision. Despite the challenges, the participants recommended continuing and developing the use of the VEO app. The student teachers recognized individual video-based reflection and supervision as distinct parts of their learning process and did not suggest ways of integrating them, whereas the supervisors saw possibilities in connecting video-based reflection to supervision.

The first trial generated discussion about developing methods of supervision in the University of Lapland's teacher education program. The supervisors realized the importance of increasing student-centeredness and the student teachers' responsibility for their learning, which could be ensured by creating personal tag sets based on one's learning aims. The student teachers could record lessons by using these tag sets to select instances for further reflection with their peers and supervisors. The supervisors began to see video-elicited reflection as one part of the supervision process.

6 Results of Trial 2

Using an action-oriented teacher knowledge (ACCTEA) procedure (Leijen et al., 2015) as an example, the researchers established a procedure for supervision in the advanced practicum for the second trial in spring 2017. While the focus of the first trial was more on guiding student teachers through the VEO app, the second trial focus shifted to the process of student teachers' self-reflection and its facilitation. With help from their supervisors, student teachers created individual tag sets based on their learning aims. Two of each student teacher's lessons were recorded and tagged by a peer student using those tag sets. After recording, the student teachers discussed the videos together. They watched their own videos and selected instances for further reflection. Supervisory discussions were arranged at the end of the practicum period to occur either face-to-face or online so that both the student teachers and their supervisors were present to discuss the whole five-week period. The student teachers reflected on their experiences during the period and finished their reflections in their pedagogical portfolios and practicum reports after the period. In this procedure, the supervisors' role was to support the student teachers' self-reflection on their experiences to guide the students to notice integral aspects of teaching and learning and collaborate in their reflection with peer students and supervisors (Snoeyink, 2010; van den Bogert, van Bruggen, Kostons, & Jochems, 2014).

Student teachers and supervisors were guided to follow the reflection procedure, which included five stages: (1) creation of an individual tag set based on personal learning aims; (2) authentic lesson observation and feedback discussion (optional); (3) selection of a lesson to record and then the recording and watching of the video; (4) supervisory discussion; and (5) written reflection.

6.1   Advantages of the Reflection Procedure

The student teachers and supervisors were satisfied with the practicum period, the supervisory process, and the different phases of the reflection procedure. Eight supervisors were pleased because they had succeeded in creating a good relationship with their student teachers, which affected their discussions positively. Only one supervisor had faced difficulties in interacting with her student teachers. Two supervisors compared the VEO trial to the previous one and felt that the second trial had been more successful because the guidelines were clearer and the focus was limited to the student teachers' self-reflection and its promotion. One supervisor characterized the creation of tag sets and the possibility to observe lessons in the classroom as a good improvement.

Three student teachers stated that supervision was research-based. It had included a lot of discussion and connections between practical issues and theory, which the student teachers found important. These experiences indicate that some supervisors had aimed to promote the student teachers' reflection through questions and comments thus following the reflective approach in their supervision (cf. Franke & Dahlgren, 1996).

According to the supervisors, the structure of the reflection procedure worked well. One supervisor found video to be an integral part of supervision. Another supervisor mentioned student-centeredness as a good aspect of the procedure. The reflection procedure used during the practicum period seemed to energize the students and enable many kinds of interaction between the student teachers and their supervisors as well as among the student teachers.

The student teachers found the VEO app to be a useful tool for both individual and peer reflection. The videos heightened the student teachers' observations and offered new insights into teaching. In this way, the findings of the second trial are similar to the results of the previous VEO trial. They also corroborate previous results regarding video-elicited reflection, which reported that student teachers had gained new insights into their teaching through videos and noticed issues that they might not have noticed otherwise (see e.g. Coffey, 2014; Körkkö et al., 2019; Tripp & Rich, 2012).

6.2   Disadvantages of the Reflection Procedure

Student teachers reported that creating a tag set was the most difficult part of the reflection procedure, particularly creating a tag set that would fit in a certain lesson. Tag sets were too self-evident sometimes. Three student teachers suggested that it might be good to create a tag set a few weeks after the student teachers are already familiar with their classes and more aware of their personal developmental needs. In addition, three supervisors stated that creating a tag set is something that must be considered carefully and highlighted that the tags should be observable. Even though using the self-made lenses for observation may serve student teachers' learning, the participants' experiences indicate that it is important to attend carefully to the characteristics of those lenses (cf. Rich & Hannafin, 2008).

The interviews revealed that similar to the previous VEO trial, the number of reflections varied among the student teachers, some of whom were more active than others. Three student teachers said that their attitudes to video had been negative initially, but had improved during the practicum period once they had identified the benefits of video. Two student teachers almost forgot to record and use videos. Moreover, similar to the previous trial, four student teachers said that watching videos of their own teaching had triggered negative feelings. These findings corroborate the findings of the previous VEO trial, where some student teachers did not prioritize video use and where some student teachers struggled with watching videos of their own teaching (cf. Körkkö et al., 2019).

6.3 Developmental Suggestions

Student teachers suggested that during the first teaching cycle, they record lessons using a ready-made tag set based on the aims of the practicum period and watch their own video and use it to contemplate their personal learning aims for the entire practicum period. Based on these aims, they would then create a personal tag set, which they would use during the second teaching cycle. For the next trial, not included in this chapter, the procedure was modified according to the student teachers' feedback.

The orientation to recording had been difficult for some student teachers. This topic was discussed with the supervisors, who found it important to highlight the benefits of VEO to student teachers in future trials.

The second trial generated a wide discussion about supervision and ways of developing it. Four supervisors had no prior experience of supervising student teachers. The interviews revealed that the role of a supervisor was vague and unfamiliar for some supervisors and that methods of supervision varied. Three supervisors found it essential to develop a stronger theoretical basis for supervision and create theoretical tools to improve supervision quality. The supervisors' experiences related to the lack of formal training to become teacher educators (see e.g. Korthagen, 2001). Therefore, they can lack support in integrating theory and practice as well as the tools to promote this integration with student teachers.

7   Conclusions

When it comes to positive disciplinary conclusions concerning student teachers' competence for reflection, the VEO app was found to be beneficial for most student teachers' self- and peer-reflection. The videos allowed student teachers to see themselves through an outsider's eyes and notice things in their teaching that they had not noticed before. The results of the second trial show that the supervisors began to incorporate educational theories into discussions with the student teachers. In addition, the results confirm earlier findings of studies on video-elicited reflection (Körkkö, 2019; Rich & Hannafin, 2008; Stockero et al., 2017) by highlighting that it is most effective to connect individual and collaborative reflection in the process of guided reflection. Tags were useful in peer reflection as a feedback mode; this benefit is in line with previous research on the VEO app (see e.g. Batlle & Miller, 2017).

Besides advantages, our study also revealed obstacles that video use creates in teacher education. These are discussed in the following sections, classified into technical, institutional, and disciplinary challenges.

7.1   *Technical Challenges*

Even though video usage offered new insights into teaching, some essential elements, such as the emotional atmosphere in the classroom, were not part of the videos. Video recordings alone did not provide enough evidence for supervision, especially when technological problems, such as poor audio quality or a narrow screenshot, were presented (see also Brophy, 2004; Coffey, 2014; Rich & Hannafin, 2008). Therefore, we conclude based on our results that a supervisor cannot use videos as the exclusive basis for lesson observation but, rather, as a guiding tool for student teachers' self-reflection.

The results show that it was sometimes difficult for student teachers to use readymade tag sets or create a practical, beneficial tag set. Some tag sets worked poorly for their purposes (see also Rich & Hannafin, 2008). Our results indicate that student teachers would need stronger guidance to make an individual tag set that serves their unique professional aims.

The VEO app had some technical disadvantages as well as benefits when compared to other similar video analysis tools. Among VEO's strengths are that it is a mobile-based app and thus can be easily moved and transported anywhere.

Also beneficial is that the user can tag events and moments while recording. After completing the recording, it is easy to upload the video to the portal with one click; videos do not have to be transferred from a video camera to a computer. Other video analysis tools developed so far are not mobile-based but include many characteristics that enhance the possibilities for individual and collaborative reflection. For instance, the Video Analysis Support Tool (VAST) (Sherin & van Es, 2005) enables student teachers to select segments of their teaching and tag them, focusing on pupil thinking, teacher's role, and classroom discourse. Moreover, the tool includes a series of questions for student teachers to answer. They can write comments and share videos with other student teachers and supervisors who can watch and tag the same video segments. Many other video analysis tools, such as Video Analysis Tool (VAT) (Shepherd & Hannafin, 2009) and MediaNotes (Tripp & Rich, 2012), share similar properties.

The VEO app does not enable video editing and selecting segments for further analysis. Student teachers have to add notes to tags before uploading the videos to the online portal, where they cannot add further notes. Student teachers can tag their videos afterward in the portal, but they cannot add any comments to specific video segments. Moreover, the portal does not include an external reflection guide or reflective questions that would further deepen student teachers' reflection. These issues also limit the supervisors' ability to focus on specific learning instances from videos. Hopefully, along with software developments, the VEO app will develop to include some of these missing characteristics.

7.2 Institutional Challenges

In many previous studies, there seemed to be an expectation that all users would welcome new video technologies. However, both VEO trials showed that introducing a new reflection tool in teacher education can entail certain challenges. Resistance or reluctance to using the VEO app was seen especially during the first VEO trial. Those student teachers who saw the benefits of recording videos used the app more often than those who did not see any benefits. Presumably, the most active users also learned the most from videos. We also noticed that orientation to video-based reflective practice was most difficult for those supervisors who had many years of experience of guiding student teachers through the traditional observation-based model. Reasons for their reluctance might include inexperience with video-elicited reflection and familiarity with top-down supervision models based on feedback given by a supervisor. Emotional reactions, power relations, and contextual factors also affect users' attitudes (cf. Korthagen, 2001). Some student teachers and supervisors may have considered the app difficult to use especially if they had not used an iPad before.

The practical findings of this study indicate that the student teachers would need more training with the app and recording. This problem has been dealt with in our teacher education program by using the same app from the beginning of the teacher education studies in different ways. We believe that early familiarity with VEO will give users time to familiarize themselves with the app and may also enhance positive attitudes towards technical devices (cf. Fadde & Sullivan, 2013).

7.3   Disciplinary Challenges

After the first trial, the supervisor's role was focused on promoting the student teacher's self-reflection and followed a reflective approach (see e.g. Franke & Dahlgren, 1996). According to our results, using VEO as an integral part of supervision requires a learner-centered approach while the student teachers themselves analyze their own teaching. However, due to this, some supervisors considered their role vague. Indeed, there is a need to further discuss the role of a university supervisor in teacher education. The use of video shifts the focus of supervision from reviewing student teachers' actions to facilitating their self-reflection. Supervisors need support to adopt this new approach to supervision and adapt their existing teacher identity to a new role (cf. White, 2014). Therefore, we assert that it is important for teacher education to also invest in the teacher educators' reflection skills and professional development.

To strengthen the theoretical basis and increase the quality of supervision, a construct or framework for reflection in supervision is required. We recognize possible tensions between the roles of reviewing student teachers' practice and facilitating their self-reflection that supervisors might experience. Further, we see that different supervision models have advantages and disadvantages and that they can be used simultaneously when guiding student teachers in their practicum periods.

7.4   Research-Based Model for Using VEO as a Reflective Tool

Based on our results, Figure 3.1 illustrates how the VEO app is currently used as a promoter of reflective process in the University of Lapland's initial primary school teacher education program.

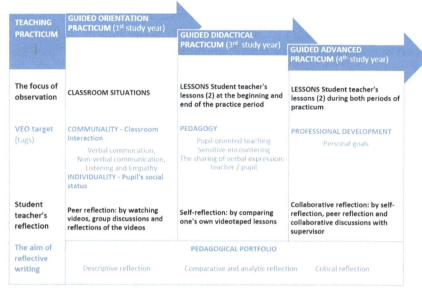

FIGURE 3.1   The reflective process in teacher education elicited by VEO

As Figure 3.1 demonstrates, student teachers use VEO in three practicum periods. Each period has a different focus on observation and VEO targets. The forms of reflective actions vary during teacher education. Finally, during their education, through reflective writing, the student teachers are expected to deepen their reflective skills and develop their own practical theory.

8   Discussion

The call from the International Study Association on Teachers and Teaching for critical reflections on research in teaching and learning led us to ponder our recent research from new perspectives. In our text, we described the process of developing our teacher education program through technical, institutional, disciplinary issues, and conclusions. The analysis process led us to gain deeper insight into the meaning of our recent studies concerning the use of the VEO video app as a reflective tool.

Technical challenges are the easiest ones to identify, but not the easiest ones to overcome. We found that videos recorded by VEO excluded essential aspects of teaching and learning and that the videos were often poor and with low audio quality. Therefore, we conclude that videos are most useful as a guiding tool for student teachers' self-reflection. Videos can be used for supervising student teachers' practice when accompanied by contextual information. We see the importance of considering technical restrictions when carrying out a video analysis. As researchers, we cannot affect the characteristics of video analysis tools, but we can use them in ways that minimize their possible limitations.

The institutional findings were identified before this writing process began. The results pointed out that users do not automatically accept new video technologies, especially when they have no previous experience of using them. Some student teachers and supervisors may have resisted the new technical application, but this modern tool also caused obstacles that they did not expect. Today, there are many devices and software that professionals find challenging to learn to use. We observed this in our research process. Therefore, when launching new equipment, it is imperative to give users time to embrace it.

When it comes to looking at the results through disciplinary eyes, we uncovered that some teacher educators may have felt insecure when trying new ways of supervising. From the point of discipline, it is important to understand the significance of teacher educators' in-service training. Without possibilities for professional growth in higher education professions, knowledge of new research and technical developments will not translate to new practices in higher education.

References

Batlle, J., & Miller, P. (2017). Video enhanced observation and teacher development: Teachers' beliefs as technology users. In *EDULEARN17 Proceedings, IATED* (pp. 2352–2361).

Brophy, J. (2004). *Using video in teacher education*. Elsevier.

Chitpin, S. (2006). The use of reflective journal keeping in a teacher education program: A Popperian analysis. *Reflective Practice, 7*(1), 73–86. doi:10.1080/14623940500489757

Dillenbourg, P. (Ed.). (1999). *Collaborative learning: Cognitive and computational approaches*. Pergamon, Elsevier Science.

Fadde, P., & Sullivan, P. (2013). Using interactive video to develop pre-service teachers' classroom awareness. *Contemporary Issues in Technology and Teacher Education, 13*(2), 156–174. Retrieved from https://www.learntechlib.org/primary/p/42133/

Franke, A., & Dahlgren, L. O. (1996). Conceptions of mentoring: An empirical study of conceptions of mentoring during the school-based teacher education. *Teaching and Teacher Education, 12*, 627–641. doi:10.1016/S0742-051X(96)00004-2

Kolb, D. A. (1984). *Experiential learning: Experience as the source of learning and development*. Prentice Hall.

Körkkö, M. (2019). Towards meaningful reflection and a holistic approach: Creating a reflection framework in teacher education. *Scandinavian Journal of Educational Research.* doi:10.1080/00313831.2019.1676306

Körkkö, M., Kyrö-Ämmälä, O., & Turunen, T. (2016). Professional development through reflection in teacher education. *Teaching and Teacher Education, 55,* 198–206. doi:10.1016/j.tate.2016.01.014

Körkkö, M., Morales Rios, S., & Kyrö-Ämmälä, O. (2019). Using a video as a tool for reflective practice. *Educational Research, 61*(1), 22–37. doi:10.1080/00131881.2018.1562954

Korthagen, F. A. J. (2001). Teacher education: A problematic enterprise. In F. A. J. Korthagen, J. Kessels, B. Koster, B. Lagerwerf, & T. Wubbels (Eds.), *Linking practice and theory: The pedagogy of realistic teacher education* (pp. 1–19). Lawrence Erlbaum Associates Publishers.

Krokfors, L., Kynäslahti, H., Stenberg, K., Toom, A., Maaranen, K., Jyrhämä, R., Byman, R., & Kansanen, P. (2011). Investigating Finnish teacher educators' views on research-based teacher education. *Teaching Education, 22*(1), 1–13. doi:10.1080/10476210.2010.542559

Lave, J., & Wenger, E. (1999). *Situated learning: Legitimate peripheral participation.* Cambridge University Press.

Leijen, Ä., Allas, R., Pedaste, M., Knezic, D., Marcos, J. M., Meijer, P., Husu, J., Krull, E., & Toom, A. (2015). How to support the development of teachers' practical knowledge: Comparing different conditions. *Procedia – Social and Behavioral Sciences, 191,* 1205–1212. doi:10.1016/j.sbspro.2015.04.455

Mansvelder-Longayroux, D., Beijaard, D., & Verloop, N. (2007). The portfolio as a tool for stimulating reflection by student teachers. *Teaching & Teacher Education, 23*(1), 47–62. doi:10.1016/j.tate.2006.04.033

Miller, M. J. (2009). Talking about our troubles: Using video-based dialogue to build preservice teachers' professional knowledge. *The Teacher Educator, 44*(3), 143–163. doi:10.1080/08878730902954167

Palincsar, A. S. (1998). Social constructivist perspectives on teaching and learning. *Annual Review of Psychology, 49*(1), 345–375. doi:10.1146/annurev.psych.49.1.345

Rich, P. J., & Hannafin, M. (2008). Capturing and assessing evidence of student teacher inquiry: A case study. *Teaching & Teacher Education, 24*(6), 1426–1440. doi:10.1016/j.tate.2007.11.016

Rich, P. J., & Hannafin, M. (2009). Video annotation tools: Technologies to scaffold, structure, and transform teacher reflection. *Journal of Teacher Education, 60*(1), 52–67. doi:10.1177/0022487108328486

Schön, D. A. (1983). *The reflective practitioner: How professionals think in action.* Temple Smith.

Sewall, M. (2009). Transforming supervision: Using video elicitation to support preservice teacher-directed reflective conversations. *Issues in Teacher Education, 18*(2), 11–30. Retrieved from http://eds.ucsd.edu/_files/edd/05sewall.pdf

Shepherd, C. E., & Hannafin, M. J. (2008). Examining preservice teacher inquiry through video-based, formative assessment e-portfolios. *Journal of Computing in Teacher Education, 25*(1), 31–37. doi:10.1080/10402454.2008.10784606

Shepherd, C. E., & Hannafin, M. (2009). Beyond recollection: Reexamining preservice teacher practices using structured evidence, analysis, and reflection. *Journal of Technology and Teacher Education, 17*(2), 229–251. doi:10.1080/10402454.2008.10784606

Sherin, M., & van Es, E. A. (2005). Using video to support teachers' ability to notice classroom interactions. *Journal of Technology and Teacher Education, 13*(3), 475–491.

Silverman, D. (2013). *Doing qualitative research* (4th ed.). Sage.

Snoeyink, R. (2010). Using video self-analysis to improve the "withitness" of student teachers. *Journal of Digital Learning in Teacher Education, 26*(3), 101–110. Retrieved from https://eric.ed.gov/?id=EJ881732

Stenberg, K., Rajala, A., & Hilppo, J. (2016). Fostering theory–practice reflection in teaching practicums. *Asia-Pacific Journal of Teacher Education, 44*(5), 470–485. doi:10.1080/1359866X.2015.1136406

Stockero, S. L., Rupnow, R. L., & Pascoe, A. E. (2017). Learning to notice important student mathematical thinking in complex classroom interactions. *Teaching & Teacher Education, 63*, 384–395. doi:10.1016/j.tate.2017.01.006

Toom, A., Kynäslahti, H., Krokfors, L., Jyrhämä, R., Byman, R., Stenberg, K., Maaranen, K., & Kansanen, P. (2010). Experiences of a research-based approach to teacher education: Suggestions for future policies. *European Journal of Education, 45*(2), 331–344. doi:10.1111/j.1465-3435.2010.01432.x

Tripp, T. R., & Rich, P. J. (2012). The influence of video analysis on the process of teacher change. *Teaching and Teacher Education: An International Journal of Research and Studies, 28*(5), 728–739. doi:10.1016/j.tate.2012.01.011

Van den Bogert, N., van Bruggen, J., Kostons, D., & Jochems, W. (2014). First steps into understanding teachers' visual perception of classroom events. *Teaching & Teacher Education, 37*, 208–216. doi:10.1016/j.tate.2013.09.001

Vygotsky, L. S. (1978). *Mind in society: The development of higher psychological processes.* Harvard University Press.

Wang, J., & Hartley, K. (2003). Video technology as a support for teacher education reform. *Journal of Technology and Teacher Education, 11*(1), 105–138.

White, E. (2014). Being a teacher and a teacher educator – Developing a new identity? *Professional Development in Education, 40*(3), 436–449. doi:10.1080/19415257.2013.782062

CHAPTER 4

Understanding Educational Leadership through Network Analysis: A Critical Reflection on Using Social Network Analysis in a Mixed Methods Study

Cherie Woolmer and Jee Su Suh

Abstract

Examining the informal conversational networks of postsecondary educational leaders can shed light on change process related to teaching and learning. Kezar (2014) argues that Social Network Analysis (SNA), a mathematical methodology that can quantify and 'map' networks of individuals and systems, can capture, analyze, and represent social processes involved in change. However, she notes how SNA has been underused in research on postsecondary education. Responding to this, we designed a mixed-methods, longitudinal study to examine the professional networks of faculty members taking part in a 2-year educational leadership fellowship at a research-intensive institution in Canada. Combining the visual ego network data provided by SNA sociograms with qualitative interviews, we sought to systematically explore the networks of individual Fellows. Centered on an illustrative case study, this chapter is an exploration of the rationale behind the study and the lessons gleaned from it. We discuss how it was informed by our respective research backgrounds and locations in the academy, further enriched within the context of a pedagogical partnership. We provide an overview of the practical and ethical challenges we faced and a frank discussion on the implications for praxis.

Keywords

Social Network Analysis (SNA) – mixed-methods – leadership – change – pedagogical partnerships

1   Introduction

Engaging with a new research methodology for the first time can feel both exciting and risky. As researchers, we are in the business of discovery and inquiry, fueled by our curiosity and a drive to understand the issues we are investigating. But what happens if we want to use a methodological approach that has not really been tried in our field before? What if the methods involved take us out of our 'traditional methods' comfort zone and require us to cross epistemological as well as methodological boundaries? What if the approach throws up interesting ethical and logistical challenges when adapting it to research on teaching and learning? These are some of the questions we explore in this chapter when reflecting on our use of Social Network Analysis (SNA) – a relatively underused methodology in research on teaching and learning – as part of a mixed-methods study to investigate the networks of individuals engaged in a two-year Leadership in Teaching and Learning (LTL) fellowship program at a Canadian university. We were motivated to develop a methodology that would enable us to understand the networks of educational leaders and saw great potential to combine SNA and interview methods as a way to develop rich and complex pictures of meaningful interactions between the fellow and their colleagues. Informed by prior evaluation of the fellowship program, we set out to systematically capture and analyze how networks and conversations about teaching and learning changed as a fellow progressed through their two-year appointment. Framed as a mixed-methods approach, we used SNA to quantify this data and create visual representations (sociograms) of fellows' networks which were used to inform follow up semi-structured interviews. Our experience, whilst laden with deep learning for us as researchers, was not what we anticipated. Here we provide a critical reflection on the challenges and successes of our study by providing a deep dive into the methodological challenges of using SNA as part of a mixed-methods study.
Specifically, we:
– present the rationale for taking a mixed-methods approach to investigate networks of educational leaders
– give an outline description of SNA, in recognition that there is relatively little published about this approach in teaching and learning research
– provide an illustrative example of data to demonstrate the possibilities and advantages of this approach
– discuss the implications for praxis arising from this approach

We hope to encourage readers to explore the opportunities and benefits that SNA (and the theoretical concepts underpinning it) offers to mixed-methods research on teaching and learning whilst highlighting some of the tensions we experienced in our study. Additionally, we hope that our personal reflections as researchers new to mixed methods and SNA highlight more fundamental issues related to epistemological and methodological boundary-spanning and the implications this has for research on teaching and learning.

2 Researcher Positionality

Our research experience has been informed by multiple intersecting positions and identities and these have shaped how we have conceived of and conducted our work together. We are both early in our research careers (as a Ph.D. student and postdoctoral fellow) and come from different disciplinary backgrounds (science and social science). We each identify as primarily quantitative (Suh) or qualitative researchers (Woolmer) and this was our first opportunity to conduct a mixed-methods study, bringing our perspectives from the fields of neuroscience, leadership, and education to inform the research. To add even further richness to our research experience, our approach had been grounded in the practice of pedagogical partnerships (Cook-Sather et al., 2014; Healey et al., 2014) whereby our work together has been co-developed and co-owned, recognizing the different expertise and knowledge we each bring as student and researcher whilst working outside of traditional research hierarchies. We share this insight at the start of our discussion as our positions and way of working fundamentally shaped our approach, experiences, and outcomes of the research. Not only were we engaging with and crossing different research paradigms, essential for mixed methods research teams, we were also engaging in a form of 'radical collegiality' where we were each learners in different ways, committed to working in a way that was driven by the underpinning values of respect, reciprocity, and shared responsibility (Cook-Sather et al., 2014).

3 Understanding Educational Leadership through Network Analysis

Within the field of research on teaching and learning, there is interest in understanding how and where conversations about teaching and learning occur, who they involve, and what they focus upon. Roxå and Mårtensson's (2009) influential study examined the meaningful conversations about teaching and learning in informal settings had by teaching staff, coining the term 'Significant Networks.' Their work has informed numerous studies that have taken and reinvestigated similar networks in other settings (for example, Elmberger et al., 2019; Marquis et al., 2018; Woolmer et al., 2017). A common feature in this body of literature is an interest in understanding connections with others and how the discussion that occurs between these connections informs, sustains, and enhances teaching and learning. They are further underpinned by concepts drawn from Social Network Theory which places importance on social interactions in networks as the primary locus for change in attitudes and behaviors of individuals. A relatively small number of studies have used SNA in varying degrees to investigate professional learning of new and experienced faculty (for example, Pataraia et al., 2015; van Waes et al., 2016), and there is an increasing body of literature that examines how to build capacity of faculty so that they become educational leaders and champions for teaching and learning amongst their peers (Fields et al., 2019; Quinlan, 2014).

Informed by the ideas of significant conversations, connections, and networks, as well as the gap in the existing literature to systematically describe the networks of developing educational leaders in teaching and learning, we saw value in using SNA to help investigate the networks of participants in a Leadership in Teaching and Learning Fellowship Program at a Canadian university. What follows is an introduction to SNA, including an overview of its theoretical foundations, a summary of key terminology used to describe features, and an analysis of networks using this approach. As SNA is inherently visual, we include diagrams/sociograms to illustrate the terminology we discuss. This is followed by an overview of how we used and adapted SNA and interviews, as part of a mixed-methods study, to investigate the networks of fellows and specifically their engagement in meaningful conversations about teaching and learning.

4 What Is Social Network Analysis?

Social network analysis is a quantitative and visual technique that is closely related to the mathematical concepts of graph theory. In simplest terms, *sociograms* (Figure 4.1) are used to represent and investigate the relationships, called *ties*, which exist among a bounded set of actors/objects, called *nodes*. Nodes commonly represent individual people, particularly in the social sciences, but can also be used to represent entire organizations and countries as discrete entities. Ties can represent relationships of all sorts, including and not limited to lines of formal or informal communication, resource exchange/trade, friendship, and other affective relationships, formal hierarchical ties, and working relationships. Given a set of nodes connected with ties, we can investigate several variables pertaining to the network. Starting from the most basic, network *degree* refers to the absolute number of nodes that are present and therefore is a straightforward measure of the size of the network. We can also obtain a measure of network *density* whereby we calculate the number of ties that exist relative to the total possible number of ties that can exist in the network. Density is a general measure of the interconnectedness of the nodes in the network, although on its own it cannot discriminate the presence of subgroups and isolated nodes.

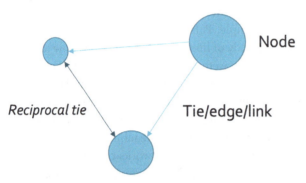

FIGURE 4.1   Basic sociogram representing 3 nodes (degree = 3) and 3 ties

There are additional measures that can be used to ascertain the finer-grained structural characteristics of the network. Measures of degree centrality can indicate which nodes are the most influential and important; in simplest terms, it can be measured by the absolute number of ties a given node has. Centrality can be further specified as being indegree or outdegree in terms of the direction of the ties flowing to (in) or from (out) the node. A more specific measure called *betweenness* of a node is defined by the number of shortest path lengths between any pair of nodes in the network that passes through it. For instance, a node with a high measure of betweenness centrality is in a good position to control a large portion of the information that flows through the network. Closely related to this concept is that of *structural holes*, which indicates a lack of cohesion and density within the overall network, where there are gaps between otherwise closely connected subgroups. The nodes that connect these disparate subgroups therefore have greater access and control over the content that flows through these subgroups that they themselves do not have access to directly; this concept has been referred to as *brokerage* or *gatekeeping*. In terms of the content of networks, we can calculate the extent of similarity among the nodes, called *homophily*. Conversely, *heterophily* is the extent to which nodes are different from each other, or in other words, indicates the extent of diversity of the network. For instance, we can define any variable by which to compare nodes in terms of similarity. One example might be socioeconomic status (high, middle, low), assessing whether a specific socioeconomic status is over-represented (homophilic) or whether all three are roughly well-represented among nodes (heterophilic). In an educational context, we can also define homo/heterophily by faculty membership (as demonstrated in Figure 4.2).

Lastly, we can define the network as either a *system* or an *ego* network. System, or socio-centric, networks are created by defining a set of nodes by some membership criteria and drawing the ties that exist between all nodes without defining any single focal node. Ego networks are defined by and constructed around a single node, the ego, and we describe as *alters* all the nodes that have ties to the ego. Our study focused on the networks of individuals and so looked to focus on ego networks. A caveat to constructing the ego network is that one should also collect information on how the alters are connected to one another, which can present additional methodological challenges in data collection, a point we return to later.

Ego networks, which were the focus of our study, have been used to investigate the optimal structure of a network of firms (Ahuja, 2000), the link between social capital and creative ideation (Bjork et al., 2011), innovative activity among a group of firms (Carnovale & Yeniyurt, 2015), and individual creativity (Soda et al., 2019) encompassing a range of disciplines including supply chain management and organizational research.

5 Application of Social Network Analysis in Research on Teaching and Learning

A small number of publications have already conceptualized the broad ideas that motivate the use of SNA in studying teaching and learning and change in higher education. To date, formal organizational theory has been heavily favored in studies of change, and Kezar (2014) argues that SNA can fill an important role in integrating context with managerial, political, and cognitive models of change and, noting specifically, its ability to systematically capture, analyze, and represent social processes. In terms of specific network characteristics that are important when investigating change, strong ties are necessary because they are defined by "frequent interaction, an extended history, and intimacy or mutual confiding between the parties" (Kezar, 2014, p. 98) that leverage the social support needed to implement significant change. Related to this idea is the central concept of trust, which helps bolster the strength of ties needed for creating the drive and initiative for change. On the other hand, weak ties are also necessary for the ego to gain access to innovative and out-of-the-box information and ideas that they may not have otherwise encountered

(Poole et al., 2019; Matthews et al., 2015). In this vein, networks that balance homophily and heterophily maintain the advantages of both and would be desirable when looking to enhance teaching and learning.

Expanding on the idea of informality, Roxå and Mårtensson (2009) laid out an oft-cited argument for how change in one's professional teaching and learning practice can be mediated and supported by informal interactions with a small number of conversational partners that make up one's 'small significant network.' These networks are highly contextual, individualistic, and dynamic and are characterized by trust, spontaneity, and exchange of ideas and experiences congruent with the idea of personal learning networks as described by Tobin (1998) and are frequently held in private settings. One can imagine that the nature of these conversations makes it a difficult concept to capture rigorously, given that they are "invisible, tacit and not easily explained out of context" (Thomson, 2015, p. 139). We believe that the systematic and visual approach utilized in SNA can help to define this context more clearly for each participant via customized sociograms. We further believe there is a distinct advantage of combining SNA with qualitative interviews so that a participant contributes to the interpretation of their individual networks by co-analyzing the sociograms that are developed.

Other researchers have used SNA to investigate issues of trust, innovation, and collegial interactions in faculty networks (Moolenaar & Sleegers, 2010; Pataraia et al., 2015; Thomson, 2015). Increasingly, researchers are interested in the idea that the impact and significance of informal conversations in teaching and learning are mediated in large part by the social cohesion brought about by strong ties, characterized by high levels of trust (Kezar, 2014; Penuel et al., 2012). Ego networks (connections within an individual's network) of faculty have been investigated by van Waes et al. (2015) in examining levels of teaching expertise and innovation. To our knowledge though, SNA has yet to be applied to investigate the characteristics of networks of emerging education leaders such as those engaged in the LTL fellowship program and the subjects of our study.

6   Applying SNA: A Case Study

6.1   *Context*

McMaster University is a medium-sized post-secondary institution in Southern Ontario, Canada. It is research-intensive and has a long tradition of problem-based pedagogies. The MacPherson Institute for Leadership, Innovation, Excellence in Teaching (referred herein as the MacPherson Institute), is the university's center for supporting and enhancing teaching and learning. The LTL fellowship program was launched in 2015 and was created to bring faculty from multiple disciplines together to work on projects that enhance student learning. Each year individuals are awarded a two-year fellowship and are invited to connect as a cohort during that time so they can build connections and enhance conversations about teaching and learning. In this way, the program seeks to develop a capacity of educational leaders from different disciplinary contexts who might otherwise not have the opportunity to connect.

Specifically, the program supports fellows to engage in an inquiry project where they research an issue or innovation relevant to their teaching context with students involved as partners and co-inquirers in the study. The fellows participate in several collegial activities with each other, supported by educational developers from the MacPherson Institute, including providing peer feedback on projects and participating in research methods workshops. This additional support and engagement provides cross-disciplinary spaces to connect, network, and discuss innovation. Throughout the lifecycle of the fellowship, it is intended for these individuals to become key contacts in their departments and beyond, creating distributed leadership networks. The LTL fellowship was designed to enable participants to not only innovate on an educational topic of their choice over a period of time, but to also network with one another and others within the institution who were similarly working to enhance teaching and learning. It was therefore hoped that the fellowship would facilitate contact with a range of different colleagues (educational developers, staff, faculty in other departments, as well as student partners who were co-researchers) to discuss teaching innovations, informed by research, in their local contexts. With this context in mind, we wanted to understand not only with whom the fellows discussed teaching and learning, but also the substance, frequency, and reciprocity of these conversations. This translated into research questions that investigated the frequency and reciprocity of three domains of conversations, namely: exchange/sharing of teaching resources, emotional support, and brainstorming/innovation.

6.2   *The Study*

The LTL program has been extensively evaluated and prior research was conducted in 2017 to capture and analyze a cohort of LTL fellows' networks through semi-structured interviews. Drawing upon social network theory and Roxå and Mårtensson's (2009) idea of significant networks, this study (Ross, 2018; Zeadin, 2017) was a preliminary investigation into the formation and development of LTL fellows' networks. Building upon useful insights from this study, we were keen to find a more systematic and visual means to capture fellows' networks and assess how they developed over time and differently between fellows whilst also acknowledging the value of rich narratives gathered in qualitative interviews in the 2017 study. As noted earlier, network data gathered using SNA can be visually represented in the form of sociograms enabling analysis of network density, ego centrality, and reciprocity between alters and the ego. However, this quantitative data does not provide insights into how the participant had interpreted the questions asked when data were collected nor does it capture information about the wider social and cultural context that a participant is situated within. To ensure we could engage with these complexities and capitalize on two data types (sociograms and interviews) we designed a longitudinal, mixed-methods study. Mixed-method studies provide opportunities for researchers to 'capitalize on the strengths of each quantitative and qualitative method [to build] stronger and more credible studies that can yield both complementary and corroborating evidence about the research problem of interest' (Plano Clark & Ivankova, 2016, p. 4).

In addition to collecting data in relation to (1) exchanging teaching resources, (2) emotional support, and (3) brainstorming and innovation, we asked fellows to record the frequency these conversation topics occurred in their networks and the primary direction of information flow. All these data generated an ego-network sociogram for each participant. We wanted to discuss and analyze the sociograms with the participant, giving the researcher and participant opportunities to check interpretations and use the sociogram data as a springboard into deeper conversations about connections in their network and the socio-cultural context in which they occurred.

6.3 Methods

Data collection for this mixed-method study included gathering network information from participants via an online survey which was used to construct sociograms corresponding to the three conversation areas mentioned above (exchanging teaching resources, emotional support, and innovation). Data were collected using the university's own survey tool, LimeSurvey. To ensure the anonymity of the third parties, as required by our institutional research ethics board, we asked participants to assign numbers to each person in their network (alter) and to generate a key that identified these individuals that only they would have access to. After participants identified the alters in their networks, they were then invited to answer seven questions for each one regarding items such as: frequency of overall contact, faculty membership, and rating of trust for each alter in the network on a scale out of 100. For each domain of conversation, we asked about how much time is taken up discussing issues in this domain relative to all conversations with the alter and the extent of reciprocity between themselves and the alter.

Specific to ego networks is the requirement to ask (ego) participants to list the connections among their alters, which can be accomplished by having the participant fill in the connections they are aware of in a x-by-x matrix of all possible ties, where x is the number of alters. This information is then tabulated and translated into the specific code required as input to a sociogram-generating software (i.e. Pajek). Describing and analyzing networks in this way enables us to accurately describe how (*network betweenness*), with whom (*network degree*) fellows connect, and how the composition of ties with new or different people over time can change (*network homophily and heterophily*). We produced four sociograms per participant: a 'base' sociogram, represented in Figure 4.2, displaying alters, ties, levels of trust between the ego and alters, and connectedness between alters. A further three sociograms were developed, focusing on participant responses regarding the amount of time spent and reciprocity in conversations related to resource sharing, innovation (Figure 4.3), and emotional support (Figure 4.4).

The second phase of data collection utilized the sociograms as a visual prompt for our participants during optional follow-up interviews. The interview offered the opportunity for the participant to update or correct any information contained in the sociograms as well as offer their interpretations and responses related to their context. This was an important aspect of our mixed-methods approach as we explored with participants certain patterns that might be interesting and revealing and allowed them to react to, reflect upon, and refine a visual representation of the professional network that they themselves indicated to be meaningful and significant in their teaching and leadership.

6.4 *Illustrative Results*

Due to the small sample size and the low response rate for our study, we do not attempt to offer a summary of results nor do we offer any summative claims about our approach here. Instead, to tangibly demonstrate our methods, we provide an illustrative example from our data of how combining a visual representation of a network relating to a specific conversation topic with the corresponding summary analysis of the accompanying interview can provide insight and understanding into how the participant understands and maneuvers in their network and responds to the sociograms. Importantly, our selection of data illustrates the value of combining different data types to reveal the complexity of network interactions. Figures 4.2, 4.3, and 4.4 are selected sociograms developed for Susan (participant pseudonym). She is indicated as the small white circle (the ego) in each figure. Figure 4.2 illustrates the base network for Susan. It shows the number of individuals (alters) in her network and the colors denote role. The size of the node for the alter indicates the level of trust with a larger circle denoting more trust with that alter than a smaller one. The further away the alter from the ego (Susan), the lower the frequency of contact. Even before we analyze data relating to conversation topics, we can glean many inferences about who Susan connects with, how often, and the relative level of trust she has with the alters in her network.

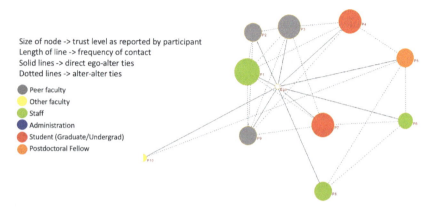

FIGURE 4.2   Base network

Figure 4.3 provides a representation of with whom Susan discusses innovation in teaching and learning. Given the leadership and innovation focus of the LTL program, we anticipated there to be numerous conversations relating to this topic. We can see that Susan has conversations on this topic with nearly all of the alters in her ego. Most of these are equally reciprocal, with two instances of her 'giving out' information and one instance of 'receiving' information about teaching innovation, as indicated by the direction of the arrow between Susan and her alters.

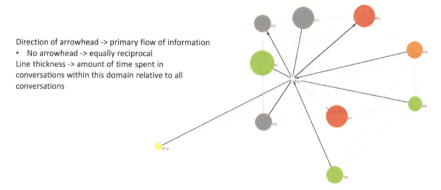

FIGURE 4.3   Conversations about innovation in teaching and learning

Another conversation domain we investigated was emotional support, i.e. how often does the participant provide or receive emotional support about teaching and learning from a given alter? Given the repeated theme of the importance of affective qualities and the expression of trust in many of the studies relating to faculty networks in higher education noted earlier, we anticipated that occurrences of emotional support, although perhaps not widespread throughout the network, would coincide with alters proportional to the levels of trust with those alters (more trust ~ more emotional support). In Figure 4.4, we can see this was only partially confirmed, with the participant depicted as having conversations relating to emotional support with only one alter, although with an alter with whom they expressed a significant degree of trust (size of node) and saw often (close distance). The interview data further reveals the participant's overall attitude towards emotional support in a professional context that sheds further light on the visual result.

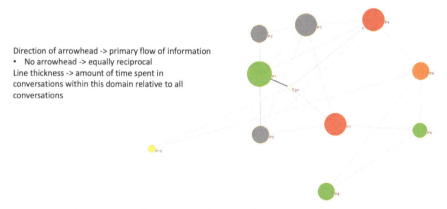

FIGURE 4.4   Conversations about emotional support for teaching and learning

All of the sociograms were shared with Susan before the interview. To orientate our discussion, we provided short, descriptive explanations of each sociogram for Susan before starting the interview. Our questions focused on inviting reflections on who was identified in the network, the nature of the conversations she had with different alters, and the importance of these in Susan's context. The interview highlighted numerous challenges with the anonymization process we had used, and time was needed for Susan to recall who she had listed as an alter for each node.

Importantly, the interview revealed the interconnectedness between the conversation domains we were investigating with Susan noting: "Sometimes the sharing of resources and innovation were conflated in my mind. I guess

I had a hard time teasing those two apart because teaching resources could also be innovations." Resources and spaces to brainstorm opportunities for enhancement and innovation were seen as conflated for Susan because of how she viewed her teaching practice.

Susan focused most of the interview time discussing how she had interpreted the concept of emotional support when answering the SNA survey, sharing that she had originally thought of it in terms of work-life balance, rather than support for teaching and learning. Her initial reaction to the sociogram shown in Figure 4.4 highlighted the importance of trust and non-judgment on this topic. For example, she shared, "I might talk to P1 a lot because I feel like there is a lot of trust and I feel like there is no judgment, but I think I just don't go to other people for emotional support." As we explored the idea of trust in conversations about challenging teaching scenarios, Susan reflected on the range of conversations she had recently had with her student partner (who was collaborating as part of the LTL program):

> I think probably I would talk to my student, yeah, in that broad category of emotional support. Like, we were talking about, for example, running a committee and I was confiding in her about some of the things that I was struggling with. So, I would probably include P7 but that wasn't the case when I filled this [survey] out two months ago.

This sample of illustrative data shows how SNA can provide compelling visual sociograms that can elicit further reflections and meaning-making about networks in interviews.

7 Discussion

We were at times excited and unnerved by the complexity of the challenge we set ourselves in this study. We had to contend with specific ethical and methodological challenges of using SNA in the context of a mixed-method study whilst at the same time navigating different research paradigms and operating in a partnership-informed model of co-inquiry. We discuss these points in turn, considering how the lessons we have learned might inform the practice of others interested in utilizing a network analysis framework in their research. We want to demonstrate that, despite the challenges we encountered, we believe there is great potential for researchers of teaching and learning to innovate and adapt SNA in numerous ways with advantages to be gained when combined with qualitative research methods.

8 Ethics of Using SNA

A key consideration when using SNA in this study was how we could balance mitigating the very real possible consequences of participant and third-party identification and other ethical issues while acquiring our data in a way that made it feasible and valuable for the participants to take part.

General ethical considerations involved in SNA research are discussed by Borgatti and Molina (2003), who outlined the following main issues of contention, the first of which occurred to us almost immediately: (1) anonymity of the participants cannot be guaranteed (a problem which, in our case, could possibly extend to the alters); (2) Research Ethics Boards (REB) do not have standard guidelines by which to judge network studies, given the relative novelty of the field in the social sciences and also in educational research; (3) there exists an ethically grey area concerning the reporting of alters by participants, considering they did not give explicit consent; finally, (4) there exists a larger overarching issue of how SNA research could be derailed if these ethical concerns, among others, are not handled to the satisfaction of participants and REBs.

For our study, the point regarding anonymity was especially salient, considering that we would be sampling from a small, public list of participants who were LTL fellows. We had hoped the anonymity of alters would be sufficiently protected if the ego (the LTL fellow) was anonymized appropriately. At the request of our REB, we were required to counter any risk of identification of alters as well as egos in networks. Indeed, we implemented the two main suggestions outlined in Borgatti and Molina's (2003) paper: to remove names and other identifying attributes, classifying nodes based only on general institutional relationships with the ego (e.g. same/different faculty, student, administration) and to provide value to participants by making available to them their personal sociograms in conjunction with an interview. However, we found these safeguards placed a disproportionate burden on the participant and caused confusion, as noted in Susan's interview above.

A confluence of factors likely contributed to the poor response rate we observed, not least of which was the very small number of individuals that were eligible to take part. However, we speculate that data collection procedures designed to offset ethical issues consequently increased the burden on the participant in terms of time and complexity of completing the survey, which we expand upon below.

8.1 Burden of Time for Participants

Following a low response rate, we speculated that the burden of time and effort for the participants, in exchange for maximizing anonymity, was likely overly excessive relative to the possible returns perceived by participants. One main factor is that only the participant had access to the self-generated key that identified the node to the individuals they listed in their network, thereby keeping their identities hidden even from the study investigators. This required the participant to make the extra effort to keep this list in a safe place and return to it for subsequent data collection and for interviews. For us to gain accurate measures of betweenness and density within the ego network, participants had to make their best guesses regarding the connections that existed between the alters they listed. This required them to fill out what is essentially an adjacency matrix containing 50 unique cells for a maximum of 10 alters. In a recent paper, Benbow and Lee (2019) asserted that 6 alters is the optimal number for balancing participant burden and obtaining sufficient information in order to capture significant social ties; Penuel et al. (2012) asked participants to list up to 5. Additionally, participants were asked to fill out the same (albeit short) survey as many times as the number of alters they listed. In sum, although each step might not require more than a few minutes each, the collective effort required was a significant hurdle to participation especially for faculty who are likely already pressed for time with their daily academic and teaching responsibilities. A perceived lack of value of a network-based study, specifically within the context of a relatively complex survey instrument, may also have contributed to poor response rates.

9 Learning the Language of SNA

Every research methodology is laden with its own specific concepts and language and SNA is no exception. While both of us were familiar with the outputs of SNA in published research, a significant amount of time was spent in the early stages of our work together learning the technical and practical aspects of 'using' SNA. This was an exciting, but time-consuming process for us. A significant issue we faced was a dearth in detailed methodological description and analysis in other published research. While SNA is founded in graph theory, it has been applied in multiple research settings such as urban geography, public health, and organizational development which is a testament to the utility of the methodology. We had to take this into account as we engaged in searches of existing literature, searching outside of educational research databases, and being open to reading studies that investigated ego-networks, but in non-educational contexts. Our keyword search terms included 'social network analysis,' 'social network theory,' and 'ego networks.' We found books such as Borgatti, Everett, and Johnson (2013); Daly (2010); and Kadushin (2012) were helpful in fully explaining concepts, such as alters, nodes, ties, as well as the forms of analyzes that can be conducted on ego-network sociograms but they themselves are often dense and somewhat inaccessible to those completely new to the methodology.

A turning point for our own development was the opportunity to connect with a more experienced SNA researcher who became a critical friend to our study. Dr. Hannah Chestnutt, from McGill University, had recently completed her doctoral study looking at the development of system networks of schools in Scotland (Chestnutt, 2017). Dr. Chestnutt's role was especially important as we navigated the ethical tensions in SNA research and when we tested our data collection tool. She was also able to discuss and recommend various software available for data collection.

Even with this input, we still had to do further work to articulate how SNA sociograms and interviews combined to inform our mixed-method research design.

10 Bringing a Partnership Lens to Mixed Methods Research

As stated earlier, our respective locations and roles in the academy as researchers have provided unique perspectives for our work together. We conceptualized this study as mixed methods research and, as a postdoctoral fellow with a background in social sciences and a PhD student from the quantitative life sciences, we approached the conceptualization of this work with differing perspectives, methodological biases, and analytical frameworks. Equally, we were working in a partnership model of co-inquiry, which was intentionally informed by a commitment to work outside of traditional power structures and hierarchies (Cook-Sather et al., 2014). In the writing of this chapter we have explored more fully some of the tacit assumptions we have made because of the multiple "personal, interpersonal, and social contexts" we inhabit and have had rich discussions about how they have shaped how we conceptualized, reviewed, designed and conducted mixed methods research (Plano Clark & Ivankova, 2016, p. 9). Indeed, one of the strengths of our collaboration related to how our differing backgrounds made significant complementary contributions. An example of such is illustrated in the way we each conceptualized, analyzed, and saw the value of ego-network sociograms. For example, one of the more novel aspects of our study was the use of visual representations of the sociograms as not only part of the study results, but to provide accurate and compelling data for participants to respond to in the interview. This was primarily motivated by a constructivist paradigm and a desire to explore the meaning and reality of the participant network with them. We found the interview to be useful for understanding the context in which a network exists as well as understanding how the participant had interpreted the phenomena we were measuring e.g., the idea of emotional support in the context of a professional support network.

Some of the main tenets of quantitative science are reproducibility, reliability, and validity. The goal in tool development is to be able to apply that same tool to a variety of different contexts and know that it is consistently mapping onto a given concept regardless of context. This challenge is particularly salient for measures such as trust and emotional support, as exemplified above. The quantitative elements of constructing the networks were essential for providing a rigorous and replicable framework for creating the sociograms, such that the self-reported information collected in the surveys could be represented in a systematic fashion for all participants and at multiple points across the longitudinal study. In developing a methodology that had not yet been applied in a similar study, we experienced some doubt as to whether or not we had properly translated the subjective survey responses into a systematic construction in the form of a sociogram. However, we eventually discovered that one of the main advantages of SNA, in addition to quantitative affordances, is precisely its ability to capture context. Rather than solely provoking tensions between quantitative and qualitative approaches, SNA is able to capture social phenomena (for us, understanding the networks of leaders in teaching and learning) to provide a richer interpretation of the data that is consistent with its fundamental purpose of conveying context via mathematical structure.

The synergy of our respective research backgrounds and frameworks is illustrative of the overarching principle of partnership that characterized our working relationship. In contrast to a more traditional supervisor-student dynamic, partnership proved to be well-suited and, at times, necessary for the challenges we would face in undertaking SNA research as novices to the methodology and to conducting mixed methods research. Indeed, both researchers approached the project with different underlying assumptions that were not readily perceivable at the outset, having to position ourselves as learners and teachers to one another in different ways and at different times of the project. It was only as we continued to communicate with openness and collegiality that these assumptions began to be unveiled. Effectively, we approached the same problem through different lenses, converging on unique solutions and ideas.

Operating outside of our comfort zones, in turn, facilitated effective partnership, as we both came to rely on and trust the other to take on unexpected challenges that were not in either person's wheelhouse. We both had to be equally willing and able to admit the gaps in our knowledge and where our own respective expertise fell short. In our view, maintaining a collegial atmosphere and exposure to a vastly different analytical mode from the other person were both crucial to ongoing innovation and successful problem-solving.

11 Conclusion

As with most exploratory endeavors, at the time of writing this chapter we were left with more questions than definitive answers, including, but not limited to, (1) whether SNA could be applied in any feasible way to small samples of participants, (2) how to manage ethical and administrative constraints of the process to ensure high participation rates, and (3) how to effectively retain the expertise developed in a transient research team. However, in addition to questions, we have emerged with numerous exciting insights on the possibilities available to be explored with this mixed-methods approach, acknowledging we are operating in a so-called 'Golden Age' of SNA (Borgatti & Molina, 2003) and on the process of knowledge creation and meaning-making in a partnership context.

To address questions 1 and 2 above, we would benefit from more opportunities to survey different and perhaps less-well defined populations of individuals to increase the chances of gathering more data and thereby refine our methods. With respect to the third question, we are in the process of developing a 'how-to' manual primarily on the technical aspects of SNA, such as surveying participants, exporting and translating these results to software code, and creating the sociograms necessary for the interview phase of a mixed-method study. This will provide a tangible document that could be referenced and improved upon by future researchers interested in applying this framework to other populations and research questions.

Having opportunities to reflect in-depth on methodological successes and challenges in research on teaching and learning is essential if we are to build capacity and expertise of new and emerging researchers in the field. This is especially true for research that adopts a multiple or mixed methods approach. Our experience has shown that attention to the research collaboration process is as important, if not foundational, to mixed methods research as we have occupied positions of learner, teacher, and scholar at multiple points as we have spanned epistemological as well as methodological boundaries. In writing this chapter, we realize our commitment to working in a partnership-focused way is likely a fundamental ingredient for any researchers who wish to conduct mixed methods research. Indeed, as Plano Clark and Ivanokova (2017) note:

Scholars with different philosophical and disciplinary contexts continue to engage with mixed methods research, they generate important controversies, issues, and debates that call for further discourse and dialogue among the many different perspectives and also for the need to understand how these perspectives shape the field of mixed methods research. (p. 8)

References

Ahuja, G. (2000). Collaboration networks, structural holes, and innovation: A longitudinal study. *Administrative Science Quarterly, 45*(3), 425–455. https://doi.org/10.2307/2667105

Benbow, R. J., & Lee, C. (2019). Teaching-focused social networks among college faculty: Exploring conditions for the development of social capital. *Higher Education, 78*(1), 67–89. https://doi.org/10.1007/s10734-018-0331-5

Björk, J., di Vincenzo, F., Magnusson, M., & Mascia, D. (2011). The impact of social capital on ideation. *Industry & Innovation, 18*(6), 631–647. https://doi.org/10.1080/13662716.2011.591976

Borgatti, S., & Molina, J. (2003). Ethical and strategic issues in organizational social network analysis. *The Journal of Applied Behavioral Science, 39*(3), 337–349. https://doi.org/10.1177/0021886303258111

Borgatti, S. P., Everett, M. G., & Johnson, J. C. (2013). *Analyzing social networks*. Sage.

Carnovale, S., & Yeniyurt, S. (2015). The role of ego network structure in facilitating ego network innovations. *Journal of Supply Chain Management, 51*(2), 22–46. https://doi.org/10.1111/jscm.12075

Chestnutt, H. R. (2017). *The potential of school partnerships to ameliorate educational inequity: A case study of two partnerships in Scotland* (PhD, University of Glasgow). Retrieved from https://eleanor.lib.gla.ac.uk/record=b3293061.s

Cook-Sather, A., Bovill, C., & Felten, P. (2014). *Engaging students as partners in learning and teaching: A guide for faculty*. John Wiley & Sons.

Daly, A. J. (2010). *Social network theory and educational change*. Harvard Education Press.

Elmberger, A., Björck, E., Liljedahl, M., Nieminen, J., & Bolander Laksov, K. (2019). Contradictions in clinical teachers' engagement in educational development: An activity theory analysis. *Advances in Health Sciences Education, 24*(1), 125–140. https://doi.org/10.1007/s10459-018-9853-y

Fields, J., Kenny, N. A., & Mueller, R. A. (2019). Conceptualizing educational leadership in an academic development program. *International Journal for Academic Development, 24*(3), 218–231. https://doi.org/10.1080/1360144X.2019.1570211

Healey, M., Flint, A., & Harrington, K. (2014). *Engagement through partnership: students as partners in learning and teaching in higher education*. Higher Education Academy.

Kadushin, C. (2012). *Understanding social networks: Theories, concepts, and findings*. Oxford University Press.

Kezar, A. (2014). Higher education change and social networks: A review of research. *Journal of Higher Education, 85*(1), 91–125.

Marquis, E., Cheng, B., Nair, M., Martino, A. S., & Roxå, T. (2018). Cues, emotions and experiences: How teaching assistants make decisions about teaching. *Journal of Further and Higher Education, 0*(0), 1–14. https://doi.org/10.1080/0309877X.2018.1499882

Matthews, K. E., Crampton, A., Hill, M., Johnson, E. D., Sharma, M. D., & Varsavsky, C. (2015). Social network perspectives reveal strength of academic developers as weak ties. *International Journal for Academic Development, 20*(3), 238–251. https://doi.org/10.1080/1360144X.2015.1065495

Moolenaar, N. M., & Sleegers, P. J. C. (2010). Social networks, trust, and innovation. How social relationships support trust and innovative climates in Dutch schools. In A. Daly (Ed.), *Social network theory and educational change* (pp. 97–114). Harvard University Press.

Pataraia, N., Margaryan, A., Falconer, I., & Littlejohn, A. (2015). How and what do academics learn through their personal networks. *Journal of Further and Higher Education, 39*(3), 336–357. https://doi.org/10.1080/0309877X.2013.831041

Penuel, W. R., Sun, M., Frank, K. A., & Gallagher, H. A. (2012). Using social network analysis to study how collegial interactions can augment teacher learning from external professional development. *American Journal of Education, 119*(1), 103–136. https://doi.org/10.1086/667756

Plano Clark, V. L., & Ivankova, N. V. (2016). *Methods research: A guide to the field*. Sage.

Poole, G., Iqbal, I., & Verwoord, R. (2019). Small significant networks as birds of a feather. *International Journal for Academic Development, 21*(1), 61–72. doi:10.1080/1360144X.2018.1492924

Quinlan, K. M. (2014). Leadership of teaching for student learning in higher education: What is needed? *Higher Education Research & Development, 33*(1), 32–45. doi:10.1080/07294360.2013.864609

Ross, W. (2018, February). *Teetering on the edge: A balancing act supporting faculty in the scholarship of teaching and learning* [Conference workshop]. Educational Developers Caucus, University of Victoria, Victoria, BC, Canada.

Roxå, T., & Mårtensson, K. (2009). Significant conversations and significant networks – Exploring the backstage of the teaching arena. *Studies in Higher Education, 34*(5), 547–559. https://doi.org/10.1080/03075070802597200

Soda, G., Stea, D., & Pedersen, T. (2019). Network structure, collaborative context, and individual creativity. *Journal of Management, 45*(4), 1739–1765. https://doi.org/10.1177/0149206317724509

Thomson, K. (2015). Informal conversations about teaching and their relationship to a formal development program: Learning opportunities for novice and mid-career academics. *International Journal for Academic Development, 20*(2), 137–149. https://doi.org/10.1080/1360144X.2015.1028066

Tobin, D. (1998). *Building your personal learning network*. Retrieved from http://tobincls.com/wp-content/uploads/2017/01/building-a-personal-learning-network.docx

van Waes, S., Bossche, P., Moolenaar, N., Maeyer, S., & Petegem, P. (2015). Know-who? Linking faculty's networks to stages of instructional development. *Higher Education, 70*(5), 807–826. https://doi.org/10.1007/s10734-015-9868-8

van Waes, S., Moolenaar, N. M., Daly, A. J., Heldens, H. H. P. F., Donche, V., Van Petegem, P., & Van den Bossche, P. (2016). The networked instructor: The quality of networks in different stages of professional development. *Teaching and Teacher Education, 59*, 295–308. https://doi.org/10.1016/j.tate.2016.05.022

Woolmer, C., Marquis, E., & Bovill, C. (2017, October). *Exploring the relationship between significant networks and faculty-student partnerships: Beyond partnership-as-initiative.* Conference Presentation, International Society for the Scholarship of Teaching and Learning Conference, University of Calgary, Calgary, AB, Canada.

Zeadin, M. (2017, October). *New Horizons: Exploring and effecting change through a non-traditional leadership fellowship program.* Paper presented at International Society for the Scholarship of Teaching and Learning Conference, University of Calgary, Calgary, AB, Canada.

PART 2

Critical Explorations through Affect, Voice, and Power Relationships

CHAPTER 5

Using Poetic Re-Presentation to Study Trust in Higher Education

Candace D. Bloomquist and Kim West

Abstract

In this chapter, we explore the use of poetic re-presentation to contemplate the role trust plays in fostering a positive learning environment within higher education. To introduce this chapter, we go backward before going forward. We begin with a brief story of why we chose to explore the topic of trust in higher education using the alternative qualitative method of poetic re-presentation. We demonstrate how poetic re-presentation has helped us frame our role more explicitly as researchers and has helped us more deeply listen to our participants' words and ideas. We tell the story of how poetry and poetic representation has shaped our study of trust within higher education. We then share a selection of poems with the reader that encapsulate fundamental concepts of trust gleaned from our use of poetic re-presentation. The chapter includes an analysis of poetic re-presentation as a method of inquiry for research in higher education. Finally, we conclude the chapter with a call to action for readers to critically reflect on the vital role trust plays in higher education and consider how poetic re-presentation can be used in their Scholarship of Teaching and Learning in higher education research.

Keywords

trust – poetic re-presentation – poetry – qualitative inquiry – higher education – graduate student teaching

1 Introduction

This chapter promotes discussion about poetic representation as a research method in higher education research. To introduce this chapter, we begin with a brief story of why we chose to explore the topic of trust in higher education using the alternative qualitative research method of poetic re-presentation. We discuss how poetic re-presentation helped us frame our role as researchers to be deep listeners, and how poetry shaped our journey as both teachers and researchers. In the next part of the chapter, we describe our application of poetic re-presentation. Poetic re-presentation is a strong qualitative methodology that lends itself well to the study of trust in higher education. In this section, we focus on presenting a picture of what poetic re-presentation looks like. We will use Glesne's (1997, 2005) work on poetic transcription as a model to describe and analyze the process behind the composition of research poems from our research project that asked, how is trust evident within higher education. In the final part of the chapter, we will analyze the challenges of using poetic re-presentation and the benefits of research poems to contribute important insights above and beyond conventional research. The chapter concludes with a call to action for teachers and researchers to consider using poetic re-presentation as a credible and high-quality method of inquiry.

2   Background

2.1   *Why Study Trust in Higher Education Using Poetic Re-Presentation*

To introduce this chapter, we thought it might be helpful to go backward before going forward, beginning with a brief story of why we have chosen to explore the topic of trust in higher education in the way we have, through poetry and using poetic re-presentation. Recalling many past conversations in which we reminded ourselves that trust is about relationships and needs to be looked at in a way that does not devalue or suppress our participants' subjective experiences, we realized it was time to critically reflect on how trust is studied has helped and sometimes hindered our abilities to explore this important higher education topic. We hope this chapter, can be used by you, dear reader, to facilitate dialogue about poetic re-presentation as an alternative research method for use in higher education research.

The complex circumstances that make up higher education today speak to the mutual responsibility to discover how students, teachers, and researchers can grow together with trust and honest dedication to learning in all its forms. Our rationale for this book chapter is to speak to interested readers and invite dialogue that is essential when creatively bringing elements of trust and poetry together. There are many approaches to exploring higher education, each useful under different circumstances. And sometimes, all we need are a few simple reminders and the encouragement to help us join the conversation. In the spirit of the great dialogical advocates Paulo Freire and bell hooks (Freire,

1970; hooks, 1994), we want to reignite the pedagogical practice of a genuine dialogue to critically reflect on how poetic re-presentation can be used in higher education research.

2.2 *Framing Our Role as Researchers*

O'Reilley (1998) speaks to 'deep listening' as a reflective practice that involves the recognition of a person's deeper self (Waxler & Hall, 2011). "One can, I think, listen someone into existence, encourage a stronger self to emerge or a new talent to flourish. Good teachers listen this way" (O'Reilley, 1998, p. 21). This is what our teachers and mentors have done for us, and it is what we hope to give back as teachers and researchers in our own work.

Throughout our journey, we have made choices about the story we are telling and how we are telling it. Our journey has involved us thinking critically and deeply during the research process: "Are we, as researchers, forced to reduce each and every topic to an object, while maintaining ourselves outside the drama, which we anyway are performing?" (Peperzak, 2013, p. 38). Who contributes the voice and who hears it? As an alternative research methodology, poetic re-presentation has helped us reframe our role as researchers, to deeply listen to our participants' voices, and make our discoveries, lessons, and writing available and conveyed in a way that speaks to students and teachers, writes for readers, borrows from and communicates with colleagues (Peperzak, 2013). We have been inspired by the ability of poetic re-presentation to contribute a diverse and complex richness of experience to the scholarly literature (Furman, 2006; Furman, Lietz, & Langer, 2006; Glesne, 1992, 2005; Richardson, 1992, 2002) and hope the following description might spark interest in others to see this alternative methodology for what it is: a creative form of inquiry with both weaknesses and strengths.

To deeply listen and to be honestly heard requires trust and courage on both sides of the research process. In poetic re-presentation, while the words from the transcripts create the basis for the research poems, it is the thoughts, feelings, pauses, tones, and even the speaking mannerisms of the participants that make the research poems what they are – this is the essence of what Richardson (1992, 2003) refers to as re-presentation. This means the poems are more than simple words or phrases from a research transcript. Instead, they are the re-presentations of the participants' deeper selves that emerge through O'Reilley's intensive practice of deep listening. In using poetic re-presentation, we invite participants to embrace the vulnerability that is needed to share their innermost feelings, thoughts, and experiences. As researchers, we have found ourselves embedded in deep listening and vulnerability, too, leaving tiny parts of ourselves in the presentation of our participants' experiences. Rousseau et al. (1998) define trust as the willingness to be vulnerable under conditions of risk and interdependence. With this research approach, we attempted to study trust by honoring trust.

2.3 *How Poetry Shapes Poetic Re-Presentation*

We admit, without reservation, that we are not poets. Indeed, we are not even literary scholars. But we are confident that poetry can help us 'pay a different kind of attention' and can act as reminders to help us get back on track or embark on a different journey (Tippett, 2016). Poetry has inspired ideas and learning, which is truly what is at the heart of education (Roberts, 1999). And as U.S. Poet Laureate Natasha Tretheway suggests

> Poetry is a thing that asks us to do that. It asks us always to learn something about ourselves through the intimate, unique experience of another, the voice speaking to us in a poem. And those voices are often people who are very different from us. (as cited in Tippett, 2016)

For researchers who clearly remember these principles, but fail to consistently act on them, poetic re-presentation can encourage them to use poetry as a 'play impulse' (Ciardi, 1959) and let their current reality slip a bit in order to expand knowledge and perceive something differently than before.

For us, as for Ciardi (1959), the practice of poetry is the act of playing against the norm. The question to put to poetry is not "What does it mean, but how does it mean?" (Ciardi, 1959, p. 996). Our practice of poetry is a way to create a pattern of expectation around the research enterprise and enter into both a metaphoric and sympathetic contract with readers. The metaphoric contract recognizes that thoughts are made of pictures, and the sympathetic contract recognizes that we depend on each other and need kindness not just for our survival but for our very being (Phillips & Taylor, 2009).

Poetry invites us to find a motion equal to emotion and feel the variations of a more human response. The everlasting charm of poetry's variety and richness, whatever the subject, can never be exhausted because there is never an end to the ways in which a writer can take a subject and take oneself in speaking of it (Ciardi, 1959). Our use of poetic re-presentation is not about creating poems that will win literary awards (we do not consider ourselves poets), it is about using poetry and poetic language to engage in a process of giving voice and truth. Our practice of poetry compels us and the reader toward playing with the sympathy and fellowship existing between the reader and the participant based on shared experiences or feelings. The research poems that result from the poetic re-presentation method do a different kind of work than the results of a coded or paraphrased result from a traditional qualitative study.

Though paraphrase may be useful in helping to explain a specific difficulty in the phrasing of a poem, it is unfailingly a destructive method of discussion if one permits the illusion that the paraphrase is more than a momentary crutch, or that it is in any sense the poem itself. No poem 'means' anything that any paraphrase is capable of saying. For, as noted by Ciardi (1959):

> The poem exists in time and it exists in balance and countermotion across a silence … That timing and that counterthrust are inseparable from the emotional force of the poem, and it is exactly that timing and counterthrust that paraphrase cannot reproduce. (p. 996)

3 Applying Poetic Re-Presentation

Poetic re-presentation is a creative methodology that attempts to let the reader understand the wholeness of 'lived experiences' (Richardson, 1992) through re-presented poems created from interview transcripts. To help you, dear reader, better understand the process behind poetic re-presentation we will use an example research poem from a study we conducted to answer the research question: how is trust evident within higher education? This research was completed under ethics approval from the University of Saskatchewan. The data presented in this chapter are part of a larger study that included semi-structured interviews conducted with participants from a variety of backgrounds. For the purposes of this chapter, we provide a snapshot of the use of poetic re-presentation using a graduate student participant's perspective on trust in higher education. To analyze the methodology used to generate the research poems, we will also provide our reflections on the process.

The research poem in this chapter and our larger study (West & Bloomquist, 2015) was created using a five-stage process. First, we coded the interview transcript for themes using a traditional approach. Second, we condensed and synthesized the words used in the transcript. Third, using participants' words, we shaped the words into makeshift poem-like compositions that were reflective of f- themes that were created (Glesne, 1997, 2005). Fourth, upon reviewing and re-reviewing the transcripts for reflections and themes, the poems were re-presented to reflect the 'essence' of the interview or the thoughts and feelings that were expressed during the interviews (Richardson, 2003; West & Bloomquist, 2015). Finally, we cross-checked the re-presented research poems between the co-authors and with the participant using a reflexive process of checking, reflection, and discussion.

3.1   Analysis of the Process Behind Poetic Re-Presentation

Our aim in using poetic re-presentation to study trust in higher education was to bring other speakers and ways of speaking into the Scholarship of Teaching and Learning. We want to draw attention to the collective impact that using poetic re-presentation as a unique qualitative methodology can have on academic innovation and excellence. Finally, we use poetic re-presentation as a means to bring participants' authentic voices and experiences to the forefront. This balanced perspective and shift in authority are essential in creating and building authentic and trusting relationships amongst researchers and participants (Eisner, 1997). The research poems re-present the lived experiences of the participants, how they see and feel trust, and the poems also provide an opportunity for others – including both researchers and readers – to examine their own lives and past experiences, to help create a dialogue about what trust means and why it is integral to learning and the culture of the university (Hirsch, 1999; Leggo, 2005). Although poetic re-presentation approximates poetry by using concentrated and condensed language from the participant, it is the researchers who shape and filter the language to re-present the perspective and experience of the participant. It is true there is no reliable way to recreate these research poem-like compositions, just as there is no reliable way to recreate an exact experience. Instead, our intention is to share these re-presented poems to communicate how trust is evident for our participants in their time and place within higher education.

3.2   What Does Poetic Re-presentation Look Like, a Study of a Graduate Student Teacher

The purpose of the next part of this chapter is to present a picture of what poetic re-presentation looks like from the vantage point of a higher education research project. The research poem-like compositions help us think about and answer the question, how is trust evident within higher education from the perspective of a graduate student teacher? Shannon (pseudonym) was a graduate student studying at a mid-sized public university. She was enthusiastic about her graduate studies and had sought out multiple opportunities to teach in the one-and-a-half years she had been enrolled in her graduate program. Her teaching experience was varied and included experience leading several tutorials as a teaching assistant, guest lecturing, and serving as a sessional lecturer with responsibility for the overall preparation and presentation of an academic course.

We began our interview with Shannon by asking her to describe what trust means to her. The interview then focused on three additional questions: (1) What tends to limit trust within the university? (2) What do you do to try to work around these limiting factors? And (3) When teaching, what actions/behaviors demonstrate your trust in yourself, your students, and the university? Following the guidance of Furman, Lietz, and Langer (2006), we identified recurring language in Shannon's transcript and distilled meaning from her words and phrases to arrive at three main themes on trust.

3.3 *Everyday Experiences*

Shannon's everyday experiences of trust as a university student were fundamentally based on the student-teacher relationship. These everyday experiences of trust as a university teacher were expressed through essential aspects of integrity. Shannon expressed that teachers and students share in the responsibility to co-create an environment like what Edmondson (1999) calls psychologically safe. In this environment, students can express their values even if they are not the same as the teacher's by "practicing your values rather than simply professing them" (Brown, 2017, p. 39). Shannon's everyday experiences were also influenced by how the university structure affects trust in her teaching and learning situations. A focus on structures gave Shannon the opportunity to explore the shared strategies, norms, and rules that make up the contextual dynamics that create the foundation of the institution of higher education where she went to school and worked. Shannon provided examples where structures that are too rigid do not allow individuals to work together to create a culture in which shared, mutually beneficial principles, such as trust, can contribute to the overall success of the institution. This theme of everyday experiences emphasizes the contextual dynamics of a situation that warrant acting in a way that acknowledges human dignity, kindness, mercy, and the inherent ambiguity of changing life circumstances, rather than sticking to rigid rules. As we explored this theme we saw similarities in other scholarly works on trust that suggest when information about the trustworthiness of the individual is available, we need to share in a willingness to practice the virtuous cycle of brave reciprocity, rather than the vicious cycle of distrust (Ostrom & Walker, 2003).

3.4 *Why Trust Matters*

A second theme that was generated from the interview with Shannon was trust matters because of the value of interpersonal trust between peers. As a graduate student teacher, Shannon was at the intersection of being a student and a teacher in higher education. At that time in her career, Shannon was seeing the profession from both sides. This unique but often forgotten perspective about teaching and learning speaks to the dissolution of a sense of simplicity that occurs after one has glimpsed life from another perspective. Trust deeply affects the quality and character of our relationships with others and shapes our perceptions of people, places, and things (Brookfield, 1995). Trust is a complex and multi-dimensional element that, on one side, may be practical and pragmatic, and on the other side, is personal, emotional, and even spiritual. Similar to poetry, the theme of why trust matters reminds us of our need to see situations from multiple perspectives and try to relate to another person's experience.

3.5 *Beliefs and Emotions*

The final theme that came from the interviews with Shannon was based on her beliefs and emotions related to trust that came from her life and educational experiences. Several interconnected words around beliefs and feelings emerged in her interview: faith, confidence, warmth, security, and comfort. Although each person will have a different interpretation of trust and what it means, Shannon's choice of the words *faith*, *belief*, and *confidence* merits special mention because these words are often associated with each other in formal definitions of the word trust. For example, the word faith is often used to describe the belief, trust, and confidence in a person, idea, or thing. To have faith or belief in a person generally implies trust in that person or confidence in the sincerity of their intentions and actions. When one trusts or puts their faith in someone or something, the result can be warm and comforting, and the result, as Shannon suggests, may be a sense of security or a safe environment. Also interwoven in the interview was another important belief – that of reciprocity – which for Shannon is like an embrace.

After generating the themes from Shannon's interviews we went through a process of reducing the transcript text to the main substance of Shannon's experience. A total of nine poems were created from the interview with Shannon. While some poems speak to situations in which trust is undermined because reciprocity between teachers and students is missing, others speak to the value of interpersonal trust. Overall, the themes these poems speak to, as mentioned already, are around the critical role that trust can play in influencing expectations and the emotional atmosphere of the learning environment. In the next part of this section, we present one of the research poems, *My Universe is Out of My Hands*, to demonstrate how we used poetic re-presentation to create the nine research poems.

The poem *My Universe is Out of My Hands* was created to help re-present Shannon's expressed experience around the theme of beliefs and emotions.

The following set of text reductions that led to a first draft research poem demonstrates how one researcher (CB) went through the stages of condensing and synthesizing the words used by the participant. Both researchers individually conducted two rounds of text reduction and then we came together to review and reflect on the essence of what we had each arrived at on our own. We exchanged first draft research poems and spent time individually reflecting on what the participant had said and what the other co-author had identified as the essence of the participant's experience being shared. From the first draft poems that each of us created, we narrowed down which poems best reflected the themes and the essence of the participant's experience. We found that individually we had both focused on the same interview transcript passages, but we had reduced the text in slightly different ways. We then held a meeting to reflect and discuss what each other had considered, make changes to the poems, and arrive at the final research poem. All poems were then shared with the participant to ensure they agreed that each poem re-presented their experiences verbally (in words) and emotionally or spiritually (in tone, speaking mannerisms, and impact).

3.6   *Original Transcript Passage*

Interviewer: You mentioned the real world when you talked about the teachers or departments curving the grades.

Shannon: Right, yeah so I mean, as a student if you know of teachers or departments or colleges that they curve the grades anyways at the end, I mean that says a lot to the student from the people up top that, well do what you want because, in the end, we are going to have a big say in what you come out of this class with. If a student goes through the typical progression of straight from high school to university, I mean I was 17 when I started university, so if I was told right away oh, well we are just going to curve your grades at the end. It kind of taints a little bit of your universe for you because things are sort of out of your hands. And it definitely undermines any trust that you would have in your prof, your department, the university, yourself maybe. Because I can work my butt off and not work my butt off and slack and either be punished or gain from it depending on which end of the spectrum you fall in with the grades.

Interviewer: Or even what the other people in your class do. It just depends on your cohort. So you are always being compared to your peers.

Shannon: Right, exactly. You are at the mercy of others really. It's really no longer in your hands. So I think that can really undermine, from the student's point of view the trust. But also it may be out of the teacher's hands too and it does come from the people up top who say you need to have that 70 average and if you don't we need to iron things out and make it fit to that bell curve.

First Round Reduction (CB). I was 17 when I started university, so if I was told right away oh, well we are just going to curve your grades at the end. It kind of taints a little bit of your universe for you because things are sort of out of your hands. And it definitely undermines any trust that you would have in your professor, your department, the university, yourself maybe. Because I can work my butt off and not work my buff off and slack and either be punished or gain from it depending on which end of the spectrum you fall in with the grades. You are at the mercy of others really.

Second Round Reduction (CB). I was 17 when I started university

If I was told right away, "we are just going to curve your grades at the end"
It would taint a little bit of my universe because things are out of my hands
It would definitely undermine any trust I would have in my professor, my department, the university, myself maybe
I could work my butt off or not work my buff off and slack
And either be punished or gain from it depending on which end of the spectrum I fall on
You are at the mercy of others

First Draft Poem Reviewed for Reflection of Essence. After exchanging drafts of poems we decided the first draft poem *Making the Bell Curve Fit* that KW had drafted best captured the essence of part of what Shannon was expressing about her beliefs about trust and the emotions related to those beliefs. We used this draft to find nuggets of distilled meaning to get at the substance of Shannon's experience.

Making the Bell Curve Fit
You are at the mercy of others really.
It's really no longer in your hands.

As a student
if you know of teachers
        or departments or colleges
that curve the grades anyways at the end,
it says a lot to the student from the people up top.

It says what you do want
>> because in the end
>> we are going to have a big say in what you come out of this
class with.

If a student goes through the typical progression
> straight from high school to university
> and are told right away
>> oh, well we are just going to curve your grades at the end
It kind of taints a little bit of your universe for you
because things are sort of
>>> out of your hands.
And it definitely undermines any trust
that you would have in your prof,
>> your department,
>> the university,
>> yourself maybe.

Because you could work your butt off
or not work your butt off and slack
and either be punished or gain from it
depending on which end of the spectrum
you fall in with the grades.

From the student's point of view
> that can really undermine trust.
But it may also be out of the teacher's hands too
If it does come from the people up top
who say you need to have that 70 average
and if you don't
we need to iron things out
>> and make it fit to the bell curve.

3.7 *Final Research Poem*

During our discussions and reflections on this poem, we decided to change the title and embrace the abruptness of Shannon's comment about being at the mercy of others and decided to move it to the end of the poem. During the meeting in which we cross-checked our first draft poems with each other, we discussed how each poem re-presented the context, words, ideas, and emotions that were being conveyed by our participant. For some poems, we needed to make adjustments to add more context that was gleaned from different parts of the transcript. For other poems, we needed to make adjustments to the order of different stanzas so that the emotion expressed during the interview could be conveyed using rhythmic and metrical arrangements that reinforce elements of the words' meanings. During our cross-check conversations, the titles and endings of the poems were where we spent a good deal of time. This allowed us to consider the bookends of the poems, i.e., the first impression a reader would get, and how the reader might embrace and be left with the last line.

> *My Universe is Out of My Hands*
> I was 17 when I started university
> If I was told right away,
> > "We are just going to curve your grades at the end."
> It would taint a little bit of my universe
> > > because then things are out of my hands.
>
> It would definitely undermine any trust I would have in my professor,
> > my department,
> > the university,
> > myself maybe.
> I could work my butt off,
> > or not work my butt off.
> And either be punished or gain from it,
> > depending on which end of the spectrum I fall on.
> You are at the mercy of others.

4 Challenges and Benefits to Using Poetic Re-Presentation

We were grateful when we published our first article in which we used poetic re-presentation in 2015 and quickly received positive feedback from readers. However, the journey to publishing our first article was not without its lessons and opportunities for growth. We received critical feedback on the methodology and struggled to find a reviewer who trusted our process. While this was disappointing, we were appreciative of the feedback we received. Because of this struggle, we had more time to consider (1) was this process authentic to who we are as researchers, (2) is poetic re-presentation the best methodology for our study of trust in higher education, and (3) how could we better communicate our methodology and rationale to our readers? The pause and the critical reflection made us more aware of the struggles of challenging norms about what should be studied and how it should be studied in higher education and helped us reckon with the critics, whether from the social sciences or the humanities.

4.1 *Challenges to Poetic Re-Presentation*

The interdisciplinary nature of poetic re-presentation required us to find ways to present our poetic re-presentation work that met the needs of social scientist reviewers who would say, "but there are no reliable ways to recreate this exact poem," as well as humanities reviewers who would say, "but the poems need to be better." The humanities reviewers would be sympathetic to our breaking away from the 'tyrannical conventions' of the social sciences, and then criticize a research poem for being "repetitive and comes across as though a grade 5 student wrote it." Similarly, a social scientist reviewer would acknowledge the transitional traits of moving from the oral interviews to transcript text, to themes, to the poems, but then get hung up on their desire for a result that is a value-free object, that uses a scientific method to reach a goal through proof or analytic reasons.

Our challenges to using an alternative qualitative research method to do something other than conventional social scientific research and bring a social-humanistic method to the Scholarship of Teaching and Learning in higher education landscape was an exercise in living in what Palmer (2011) describes as 'creative tension.' We enjoy this form of educational research because we get to bring the voice and emotionally expressed experience of our participants directly to the reader in an easily accessible and popular medium, i.e., the poetic structure. And, we would be denying reality if we glossed over the struggles that come with applying and finding recognition for this methodology.

The interdisciplinary nature of poetic re-presentation provides an opportunity to take two seemingly contradictory elements (social science and humanities), put them together, and create something completely new. As a display of interdisciplinary leadership (Bloomquist, Georges, Ford, & Moss Breen, 2018) poetic re-presentation recognizes that it takes courage to expose your thinking to others in the hopes that together we would be able to engage in an exchange of ideas that might end up with better ideas in the end. We acknowledge that the research poems are not prize-winning poems, "the fact that a good poem will never wholly submit to explanation is not its deficiency but its very life" (Ciardi, 1959, p. 779). We agree with Glesne (1997), when she said, poetic re-presentation "moves in the direction of poetry but is not necessarily poetry. What poetry is in itself, however, is hard to define" (p. 213). Additionally, we acknowledge that our role as researchers in this process is not value-free and objective;

instead, the co-central place of the researchers and participants in this process is what makes it an exercise in praxis (i.e., an action that is an end unto itself). Three other individuals in the roles of researchers and participant would not be able to replicate these exact results. However, "what matters is to raise the question in the most meaningful way possible" (Ciardi, 1959, p. 779) and poetic representation can help do that.

We were attracted to poetic re-presentation because it was creative, trustworthy, and would result in an artifact that could be read by as many people as possible. Choosing the right method to address our research question had a lot of great and difficult consequences for our research. As Jerome K. Jerome says, "I want a house that has gotten over all its troubles. I don't want to spend the rest of my life bringing up a young and inexperienced house." Like Jerome's inexperienced house, you, dear reader, may not want a research method that has yet to get over all its troubles, and then again, maybe you do. As we hold the inner and outer contradictions in creative tension (Palmer, 2011), we make no attempt to challenge existing methodologies. At the same time, we do believe that there is room for more.

4.2   *Benefits to Poetic Transcription*

As one of our reviewers said, "It may well be … that many academics just don't understand the value of this. But if that's the case, it is the authors' job to persuade us." Although, we were met with challenges to using poetic re-presentation, both the process and the results of poetic re-presentationcan contribute important insights above and beyond conventional research. The process of applying poetic transcription can be useful for anyone, we believe even those who do not believe they are or can be poets. As Ciardi (1959) describes, every poem is a mask the poet assumes. For poeticre-presentation, the poet is not just one person, but a team. Through our collective efforts the voice of someone who has not been heard, about a topic that still needs exploring, is shared.

Poetic re-presentation is also a useful method for higher education researchers and teachers today because of the research poems that are produced. Once the research poems are shared the reader has an opportunity to try on the mask through which the poet addressed the topic being studied. Because of the research poems, a reader can form a 'sympathetic contract' with the poet (i.e., participant), to feel and vicariously experience what the participant experienced (Ciardi, 1959). The research poem is unique from other forms of qualitative data representation because of the ability of poetry to be open to ways of seeing and saying (Eisner, 1997). For the study of trust in higher education, poetic re-presentation is particularly powerful. In today's increasingly interdependent world, professionals in a wide variety of social, economic, and political contexts must be able to work together effectively to address the complex problems of our time. These cooperative, interdisciplinary alliances require trust. There is much to be gained by exploring trust in higher education using poetic re-presentation because the process seeks to equalize the power between the researcher and the participants to bring forth a small 't' truth of description, re-presenting a perspective or experience of participants. Furthermore, the poems serve to bring the voice and emotionally expressed experience of participants forward in a way that others, by reading the poems, can try on and relate to each other through sympathetic experiences. Therefore, in the process of researching trust, trust can also be built.

The knowledge produced through engaging in poetic re-presentation we found was a worthwhile good for ourselves, participants, and the readers we heard from. As mentioned previously, we had multiple opportunities to engage in reflection about the process of poetic re-presentation, not just to ensure alignment between our research question and the method, but also to understand our position as researchers in society and how our position could, as happens with some other research methods, be used to perpetuate cycles of oppression. Our intentional use of poetic re-presentation as a method that acknowledges the expression and resolution of oppressive production, distribution, and use of power between participant and researcher was a key reason we have applied this method. For teachers and researchers in higher education who have a desire to hold creative tension, balance power, and practice interdisciplinary leadership, poetic re-presentation is a good option.

5 Conclusion

The chapter concludes with a call to action for teachers and researchers in higher education to consider using poetic re-presentation in their work. As we continue our exploration of trust in higher education, we would appreciate hearing from you. Feel free to send us your questions, comments, concerns, and queries. We believe trust creates strength and solidity. It stabilizes relationships and creates a hard foundation from which innovative leaps can be taken. This soft thing called trust is actually the hardest thing of all. When it's there, it allows you to take a risk, to leap higher and farther (Seidman, 2007).

The alternative qualitative methodology of poetic representation not only works to raise up the voices, in their own words, of participants who may not have been heard before, but it also shares their words through poems that provide an accessible object, a foundation from which dialogue could leap. As Nye states, "when you think, when you are in a very quiet place, when you are remembering, when you are savoring an image, when you are allowing your mind calmly to leap from one thought to another, that's a poem" (Tippett, 2016).

We, like other teachers and students, face the challenge of creating cultures of trust where we live and work every day. This means higher education truly needs to be a space for mentorship, open-mindedness, critical discourse, creativity, and debate in words and actions. We believe poetic re-presentation is a method that may not fit neatly into a single discipline, but can help higher education aspire to be a place where authenticity flourishes, respect is a cornerstone, safety is the foundation for exploration and unlimited possibilities, and trust is inculcated (Provitera-McGlynn, 2001). To create this, we need to foster what Brown (2017) describes as true 'belonging':

> The spiritual practice of believing in and belonging to yourself so deeply that you can share your most authentic self with the world ... True belonging doesn't require you to change who you are; it requires you to *be* who you are. (p. 40)

In this, the teacher has a degree of vulnerability and humility as well as the student, and the researcher. Palmer (1998), with Zajonc and Scribner in 2010, and again in 2011, has written about themes of distrust and the 'pain of disconnection' that are becoming more rampant in higher education. Clearly, there is a lot to lose if we choose the path of the status quo, but research methods like poetic re-presentation can cut across disciplinary silos and integrate processes with form to create a new, creative, worthwhile good. Many of us have been wounded in some form or another by being a little rebellious, and yet we keep rebelling despite the wounds. Part of mending is collectively sharing a responsibility to keep trying and keep practicing interdisciplinary leadership (Bloomquist et al., 2018).

Consider these words, dear reader, to be your invitation. They are not an ending, but rather a beginning. If we deny trust and creativity, to ourselves or others, then we deny the gifts we might potentially share with the world. The method and the poems we have shared can be an awakening if you let them be: to wake up to who you really are, to ask yourself what you truly need to trust yourself and others, to engage in a research method that not only allows for but encourages deep listening, reciprocal sharing, and creativity. And finally, to shape your vision of relationships and trust, however risky that may seem, into the dialogue and actions that will allow you to leap higher and farther than you have ever been before.

References

Bloomquist, C. D., Georges, L. C., Ford, D. J., & Moss Breen, J. (2018). Interdisciplinary leadership practices in graduate leadership education programs. *Journal of Leadership Studies, 12*(2), 60–63. doi:10.1002/jls.21579

Brookfield, S. D. (1995). *The skillful teacher: On technique, trust, and responsiveness in the classroom.* Jossey-Bass.

Brown, B. (2017). *Braving the wilderness: The quest for true belonging and the courage to stand alone.* Random House.

Ciardi, J. (1959). *How does a poem mean?* Houghton Mifflin.

Edmondson, A. (1999). Psychological safety and learning behavior in work teams. *Administrative Science Quarterly, 44*(2), 350–383. doi:10.2307/2666999

Eisner, E. W. (1997). The promise and perils of alternative forms of data representation. *Educational Researcher, 26*(6), 4–10. http://dx.doi.org/10.3102/0013189X026006004

Freire, P. (1970). *Pedagogy of the oppressed.* Herder and Herder.

Furman, R. (2006). Poetic forms and structures in qualitative health research. *Qualitative Health Research, 16*(4), 560–566. doi:10.1177/1049732306286819

Furman, R., Lietz, C., & Langer, C. L. (2006). The research poem in international social work: Innovations in qualitative methodology. *International Journal of Qualitative Methods, 5*(3), 24–34. doi:10.1177/160940690600500305

Glesne, C. (1997). That rare feeling: Re-presenting research through poetic transcription. *Qualitative Inquiry, 3*(2), 202–221. doi:10.1177/107780049700300204

Glesne, C. (2005). *Becoming qualitative researchers: An introduction.* Allyn & Bacon. http://dx.doi.org/10.1177/107780049700300204

Hirsch, E. D. (1999). *The schools we need and why we don't have them.* Anchor Books/Random House.

hooks, b. (1994). *Teaching to transgress: Education as the practice of freedom.* Routledge.

Leggo, C. (2005). The heart of pedagogy: On poetic knowing and living. *Teachers and Teaching, 11*(5), 439–455. doi:10.1080/13450600500238436

O'Reilley, M. R. (1998). *Radical presence: Teaching as contemplative practice.* Boynton/Cook.

Ostrom, E., & Walker, J. (Eds.). (2003). *Trust and reciprocity: Interdisciplinary lessons from experimental research.* Russell Sage Foundation.

Palmer, P. J. (1998). *The courage to teach: Exploring the inner landscape of a teacher's life.* Jossey-Bass.

Palmer, P. J. (2011). *Healing the heart of democracy: The courage to create a politics worthy of the human spirit.* Jossey-Bass.

Palmer, P. J., Zajonc, A., & Scribner, M. (2010). *The heart of higher education: A call to renewal.* Jossey-Bass.

Peperzak, A. T. (2013). *Trust: Who or what might support us?* Fordham University Press.

Phillips, A., & Taylor, B. (2009). *On kindness.* Pan Books Limited.

Provitera-McGlynn, A. (2001). *Successful beginnings for college teaching: Engaging your students from the first day.* Atwood Pub.

Richardson, L. (1992). The consequences of poetic representation. In C. Ellis & M. G. Flaherty (Eds.), *Investigating subjectivity: Research on lived experience* (pp. 125–137). Sage.

Richardson, L. (2003). Poetic representation of interviews. In J. F. Gubium & J. A. Holstein (Eds.), *Handbook of interview research: Context and method* (pp. 887–891). Sage.

Roberts, P. (1999). A dilemma for critical educators? *Journal of Moral Education, 28,* 19–30.

Rousseau, D. M., Sitkin, S. B., Burt, R. S., & Camerer, C. (1998). Not so different after all: A cross-discipline view of trust. *Academy of Management Review, 23*(3), 393–404. http://dx.doi.org/10.5465/AMR.1998.926617

Seidman, D. (2007). *How: Why how we do anything means everything.* John Wiley & Sons Inc.

Tippett, K. (Producer). (2016, July 28). Your life is a poem [Audio podcast]. Retrieved from https://onbeing.org/programs/naomi-shihab-nye-your-life-is-a-poem/

Waxler, R. P., & Hall, M. P. (2011). *Transforming literacy changing lives through reading and writing.* Emerald.

West, K., & Bloomquist, C. D. (2015). Poetic re-presentations on trust in higher education. *The Canadian Journal for the Scholarship of Teaching and Learning, 6,* 1–24.

CHAPTER 6

Narratives of Embodied Practice: Using Portraiture to Study Leadership

Jessica Raffoul, Beverley Hamilton and David Andrews

Abstract

Seeking to develop a theoretical framework to help guide leadership development in post-secondary institutions, we presented common characteristics, models, terms, and dimensions – identified in the literature – to educational leaders at a mid-sized Canadian university. While the research reflected leaders' experiences in one way or another, it did not resonate with the complexity of their experiences and practice – how they engage and react, even reversing themselves mid-stride in their effort to reach goals, influence people, and inspire change. Leaders' practices involve highly contextualized tacit knowledge (Janson & McQueen, 2007; Nonaka & Van Krogh, 2009), not easily unearthed using research methods such as questionnaires or structured interviews, or analysis of models and terms.

This chapter explores the use of a form of narrative research called portraiture (Lawrence-Lightfoot & Hoffman Davis, 1997) to explore the situational, relational, and uncertain nature of leadership, uncovering fundamental tensions leaders face. Through storytelling, analysis, and re-storying among a leader and two researchers, we identified a number of thresholds or bottlenecks, ultimately expressing these findings through interwoven first-person narrative and commentary situated within the broader literature, while detailing lessons learned, challenges, and limitations.

Keywords

educational leadership – narrative – portraiture – collaborative research – reflection – storytelling

1 Leadership as Embodied Practice

People told me that I was an educational leader and that I would be a good candidate for an external teaching award long before I knew, and accepted it, myself. At first, I struggled to see myself as a leader and was unable to adequately articulate how I was a leader using characteristics and definitions of leadership that are commonly cited in practice and in the literature. I also could not see how my particular experiences and approaches would be of interest or relevant to educational leaders. Moreover, when I realized that, in order to support future external teaching award applications that built upon the first, I would have to communicate my leadership style or approach through a leadership statement of some description, my struggles turned to paralysis. It was not until I was asked to describe situations that illustrated my leadership style and potential through personal narratives that I was finally able to begin to see myself as an educational leader and understand and convey what leadership was to me.[1]

In 2014, we undertook a study of embedded educational leadership initiatives campus-wide as part of a team of researchers from the University of Windsor (Wright, Hamilton, Raffoul, & Marval, 2014). Such initiatives have become increasingly common at Canadian universities (Boulos & Wright, 2011; Eansor, 2012; Hubball & Clarke, 2011), but research into the experiences and practices of these leaders in Canadian contexts remains limited (Morris & Fry, 2006). As part of this study, we organized a consultative forum for faculty and staff who had been identified as having led initiatives or projects to enhance teaching or student learning at the University. We hoped that they would help us to understand their motivations and practices as leaders, the challenges they face, and the kinds of professional development they would need to develop their leadership practice. We believed that integrating research on leadership practice with what our own campus leaders were experiencing would help us to establish a practical conceptual model that would drive program planning and leadership support.

This event proved extremely instructive in a number of ways, but especially with respect to the kinds of professional development that leaders felt would help them to understand and advance their practice. Leaders responded relatively unenthusiastically to workshops or other formal knowledge dissemination models as a means to develop skills and expertise. These did not seem, in their view, to resonate with the complexity of their practice, which they described repeatedly as a process of 'knowing who' or 'knowing when' or 'knowing where.' These recurring phrases provided compelling insights into how leaders perceived their leadership actions, but they did not tell us anything specific. Despite our best efforts, and the obvious knowledge of this group of experienced leaders, we had not yet found a way to distill their leadership practice into functional terms, let alone a conceptual model that might support the evolution of leaders.

A number of studies of educational leadership development suggest an alternative approach which focuses on sense-making, where leaders work with their own narratives of leadership, enabling them to become more open to the ambiguity and uncertainty of their actions in complex contexts like a post-secondary institution (Flinn, 2011; Flinn & Mowles, 2014). As leaders' practices involve highly contextualized tacit knowledge (Janson & McQueen, 2007), approaches that encourage them to articulate their own stories of leadership, rather than focusing on the exploration of fixed leader characteristics or models, can be more effective in supporting their ability to experiment with situationally appropriate practices (Yipp & Raelin, 2011). According to Polanyi (1966), tacit knowledge is gained through practice and experience. It is personal, practical, context-specific, and difficult to communicate. In fact, the individual may not even be aware of its existence (Kothari et al., 2012). McAdam, Mason, and McCrory (2007) note that tacit knowledge is "[k]nowledge-in-practice developed from direct experience and action; highly pragmatic and situation-specific; subconsciously understood and applied; difficult to articulate; [and] usually shared through interactive conversation and shared experience" (p. 2). As Polanyi (1966) puts it, "We can know more than we can tell" (p. 4).

Nonaka and Van Krogh (2009) explore the role of socially engaged action and reflection in externalizing tacit knowledge. This is an important practice, in part because it enables us to share knowledge among individuals. It is also important because of the degree to which tacit knowledge emerges from pattern recognition, unexamined beliefs, routines, values, and emotions, which can narrow the field of decision-making for leaders.

The University of Windsor study of leadership practice was successful in integrating research literature with the leaders' experiences insofar as it enabled us to better characterize the disconnect between the literature, which often focused on the characteristics of leaders divorced from their contexts, and leaders' experiences, which were completely embedded in their context and their understandings of them (Bolden, Petrov, & Gosling, 2008; Senge, 1990). This contextual awareness, often difficult to capture or share, informed entirely how the leaders 'knew when' to start, stop, hold back, lead, and follow. Like all of us, leaders operate through multiple social identities and networks.

Successful leaders navigate these networks and their attendant power dynamics and narratives skillfully and in real-time (Bolden et al., 2008; Roxå, 2008; Roxå & Mårtensson, 2013). Thus, while tacit knowledge was an important challenge to our goals, a better way to see and parse these dynamic and interacting contexts is also critical to unearthing leadership in ways that reflect leaders' actual experience. The individual, their leadership practice, and their context are not separable.

The forum and the subsequent research we undertook foregrounded gaps in the literature and in the methods being used to study this phenomenon. Our plan to facilitate leadership development through broad consultation and the application of traditional models of leadership resonated with the literature but not with leaders' lived experience, our own experiences of working one-on-one with leaders, or our understanding of the contexts that leaders were navigating. We were asking the wrong questions in the wrong contexts – possibly, with the wrong goals.

2   On Portraiture

> *Looking back, my inability to see myself as an educational leader and articulate my leadership style was grounded in the fact that I did not know the language of teaching and learning generally, and educational leadership specifically. I recognized this response as being consistent with what my students feel when they experience for the first time the Greek and Latin terms that form the structure of the language of anatomy. I confronted my lack of fluency by immersing myself in this new culture of teaching and learning and collaborating with experts in educational leadership who patiently worked with me through a process of sharing my stories during personal interviews and reflection. As I became more conversant with the language, I was better able to communicate in terms that I, and others, understood. But I continued to struggle with what it meant to be a leader, when described theoretically based on traditional characteristics of leadership, because I did not always see the relevance of this approach to my personal circumstances. And then I was asked to talk about leadership experiences that were significantly meaningful to me. Using this practice, it became easier for me to capture the essence of who I was as an educational leader. Being asked to tell stories about the things I have done, and what I thought about the things I did while I was in leadership roles, was the key I needed to unlock what leadership was to me in structural (what it is) and functional (how it works) terms.*

We were trying to understand leadership – a practice that is fundamentally relational and does not survive outside of the environment within which it is practiced. While parts of it – characteristics, strategies, principles – can be exported, the whole cannot. The decisions leaders make in their contexts are the result of many complex factors, not least of which is the interplay of identities and social dynamics in real-time. The person – the person communicating their leadership to us – is not the same as the person in a context with others. They may be operating from a different sense of identity (Bolden et al., 2008), and may not be conscious of this at all. As Schon (1983) notes, there is a significant difference between reflection on action and reflection in action. As we discussed above, leaders describe their practice as knowing when, reflecting what Van Manen (1994) describes as "improvisational readiness," knowing "exactly what is the appropriate thing to say, do, or not do," which depends on what the individual knows about the people involved, the situation, and their relationships (p. 157). In explaining such experiences, he argues, we tend to resort to narrative.

Narrative captures the dynamics of human experience. In telling stories, individuals, with their sometimes conflicting social roles across multiple contexts, tend to foreground some elements and deemphasize others. Stories do not represent 'life as lived,' but the teller's 're-presentations of those lives as told to us' at the moment of telling (Etherington, 2013). Narrative study systematically examines the human impulse to narrate experience, engaging in a deeper exploration of people's multi-layered stories over time and across contexts (Clandinin & Connelly, 2004).

While there are many methodologies intended for the gathering and analyzing of narratives, for a number of years, we have drawn on the work of Lawrence-Lightfoot and Hoffman Davis (1997) in working with educational leaders on their development. Portraiture captures the complexity of human experience:

> Portraitists seek to record and interpret the perspectives and experience of the people they are studying, documenting their voices and visions – their authority, knowledge and wisdom. The drawing of the portrait is placed in social and cultural context and shaped through dialogue between the portraitist and the subject, each one negotiating the discourse and shaping the evolving image. (Lawrence-Lightfoot & Hoffman Davis, 1997, p. xv)

Lawrence-Lightfoot and Hoffman Davis (1997) identify five essential features of portraiture: context, voice, relationship, emergent themes, and – setting it apart from most narrative approaches – the aesthetic whole. This narrative approach seeks to emphasize goodness while still recognizing that "goodness is inevitably laced with imperfection" as every "human endeavor possesses imperfection and weakness" (Lawrence-Lightfoot, 2016, p. 20). Through this approach, Lawrence-Lightfoot (2016) seeks to avoid what she describes as the pathologizing of experience in favor of documenting what is 'worthy and strong' and exploring what might make it possible to transport that goodness to other settings. Although it appears as though this method risks idealizing the teller's experience, the portraitist – who brings her own understanding and research-based knowledge to the portrait – is intended as a counterweight, intervening when necessary, and willing to listen for and weave in 'the deviant voice' (Lawrence-Lightfoot, n.d.). Portraiture reflected what we had learned about how individuals articulate their leadership practice. In particular, the approach's emphasis on goodness – the individual's efforts to realize aspirations and ideals despite their vulnerabilities – invited conversations and deep reflection. This method allowed the leader to explore his experience without having to adopt terminologies or frameworks of leadership that felt intimidating or alien. It also enabled them to gradually expand their awareness of the improvisational and contingent nature of leadership. Through their own stories, they could come to see the importance of identity and context.

As Lawrence-Lightfoot (n.d.) notes, portraitists typically approach this type of research with an extensive personal and theoretical understanding of the area of study. In our case, we had conducted environmental scans and literature reviews and worked extensively with educational leaders both as individuals and in groups. Through these experiences, we were able to develop what Lawrence-Lightfoot (n.d.) calls an 'anticipatory schema' – a starting point intended to be questioned and modified based on the 'realities of the setting' – premised on the notion that leaders experienced their practice as dynamic and evolving. We invited the leader in the current study to engage with this schema, encouraging reflection, analysis, and extensive critique, contesting with and clarifying this 'voice of preoccupation.' Though at first, this may seem to inhibit the story teller's voice, Lawrence-Lightfoot (n.d.) explains "the articulation of early presumptions … is likely to make [the portraitist's] lens more lucid, less encumbered by the shadows of bias. Making the anticipatory schema explicit allows for greater openness of mind."

For us, this became the preliminary ground for intense dialogue, storytelling, and reframing with an experienced educational leader as we formed the research team. In the initial stage, we took stock of where or whether our initial anticipatory schema resonated with the leader's experiences. It did not. In fact, the experience of reviewing it alienated and silenced him. After several such conversations, we approached him with a set of guiding questions to elicit his experiences with leadership as narratives, focused on positive experiences of growth and development. Through our engagement with his stories, our questions evolved: the direction of inquiry followed the thrust of the stories. Because the process requires stories to be reframed, reconsidered, and retold, the teller understands the stories differently and more fully, often through willing consideration of different lenses or factors. At the same time, the growing sense of complementarity of our partial understandings enabled the storyteller to interrogate research-based interpretations of leadership practice and to test those findings against the emerging story he was telling and its implications. Together, we began to intuit themes and narrative arcs that reflected some parts of the intellectual framework and to see other parts as less germane to the leader's experience. What resulted was an enlivened, aesthetic whole.

3 Challenges and Reflections on Practice

The narratives that I initially shared about my leadership roles and activities through the portraiture process were admittedly guarded. In addition to being very uncertain about the relevance of my stories in the broader context, I struggled with being able to trust those who were interviewing me. For the process to work well, participants need to respond authentically and share their true feelings. My initial inclination was to share how I truly felt, but I was concerned that what I was doing and the approaches I was taking as an educational leader would be judged as poor, and that my inadequacies and lack of training as a formal leader would be recognized by people who I very much respected and wanted to impress. It took me some time to be comfortable being myself and saying what was really on my mind, without worrying about how I sounded or how my opinions would be viewed. However, the most disruptive challenge I faced as a participant in the portraiture process was that I was extremely aware that it was taking me considerably longer than my colleagues to realize basic things about myself and about what leadership is, despite the repeated attempts to illustrate these things to me. I needed to process things at a much slower rate than they did, which created a visceral bottleneck in our collective experience, similar to what my anatomy students feel when trying to digest and interpret the extreme complexities and interconnectedness of the body's systems for the first time. Struggling with this troublesome knowledge slowed my progress of crossing certain thresholds that my colleagues had crossed long before I was ready.

When exploring the literature on the portraiture method, we were struck by, and at first uncertain about, the way in which the method as written focused so much on the positive to avoid pathologizing phenomena (Lawrence-Lightfoot, 2016). We have come to understand, though, that at least for us, a key challenge in the process was trust-building. As the story above attests, even among a research team who had worked together extensively, vulnerability around scrutiny seriously impeded progress. Although the goal was to portray the practice and inner world of a trusted and effective leader, unearthing complex practice is bound to expose the uncertainties, failures, and doubts that are interwoven in those stories of success and strength. Often, they are inextricable aspects of the experience. Without a focus on the positive, it is difficult to establish a relationship of trust. Without trust, the storyteller may self-select, omit uncomfortable details, or second guess the kinds of judgment that stories may elicit. Trust is fundamental to the creation of portraits that capture the essence of practice and experience, and to the storyteller's faith that his or her audience is truly 'listening for' rather than 'listening to' his or her stories. And change, as Covey (2006) puts it, moves at the speed of trust.

From our work with leaders, we knew that leadership is difficult to articulate and describe. Hence, eliciting and processing the experience involved was a major challenge. Members of the team began at very different places in their thinking and these differences created a situation where each member of the team at times worried about hampering the team's progress or the voice of others. Team member unease was also heightened by a sense that we were synthesizing knowledge and drawing conclusions at different rates. For example, the educational leader perceived that his contribution, based on his own experience, might be of limited value compared to the research-based knowledge others brought to the process. The researchers felt that their research-based knowledge, despite providing a fluency with the language of the field, lacked fundamental insights that limited its usefulness and resonance. For a time, this meant we were spinning our tires: the traction point was fully internalizing each other's belief that these understandings were complementary and neither competing nor linear. Each perspective offered important insights into individual narratives that were only part of the story and none of them represented a more 'advanced' understanding of the phenomenon. Most importantly, we learned that waiting is an action – often the most important one.

The intensely interactive nature of portraiture creates complex research relationships: Who is driving the story? Who decides what's salient? Who is the expert, and on what? Who and what should be in the portrait, and who determines what is not in the portrait? As English (2000) points out, these questions can be critical to the validity and meaning of the conclusions drawn in portraiture.

The researcher is as much a part of the story – distilling, sifting through certain details, urging elaboration on others – as the teller. Lawrence-Lightfoot (2005) is unapologetic about this interventionary approach:

> For the portraitist, then, there is a crucial dynamic between documenting and creating the narrative, between receiving and shaping, reflecting and imposing, mirroring and improvising. The effort to reach coherence must both flow organically from the data and from the interpretive witness of the portraitist. (p. 8)

A key factor that underlies this challenge is the messiness of power dynamics: while Lawrence-Lightfoot and Hoffman Davis (1997) emphasize the ethical responsibility of the researcher, the realities of that negotiation vary considerably from project to project. This was often an uncomfortable process, fraught with concern around the degree to which theories of leadership might be dictating the story or erasing it. In our case, the educational leader, who would be described as the 'subject' in Lawrence-Lightfoot's model, became a research partner – but his experience of this as an equal partnership only emerged gradually. More to the point, it would be possible for this equality to be more rhetorical than actual, particularly in cases where power, authority, or social capital differences are great. This was a process that we felt required practice and incremental evidence of good faith.

As our study evolved, the original goal, to make progress towards a conceptual model for supporting leaders' development, was called into question. What became clear was that the process of portraiture was actually a more practical applied approach to unearthing meaningful patterns of practice than the creation of a more abstract model derived from numerous leaders' stories. The process of storytelling and collective reflection in itself may generate more transferable wisdom than an abstract model. Sharing and unpacking stories, their themes, and meanings and contexts, made more explicit the leader's inner experience. These experiences offered insights into the essence of his leadership but reconfirmed the impossibility of distilling these insights into abstract guidelines. This obvious contradiction in our thinking was a fortunate casualty of the process.

As with all forms of narrative research, the generalizability of findings generated through portraiture has frequently been called into question (English, 2000). Lawrence-Lightfoot (2005) notes that "[t]he portraitist documents as a way of illuminating more universal patterns" (p. 12). To what extent were our portraits one person's experience, or capturing something more universal? How would we know? Although some of the team members had engaged with narrative methods before, working on a fully equal basis with the participant as a co-researcher foregrounded these questions for all of us. As Lawrence-Lightfoot (n.d.) explains:

> Goetz and LeCompte (1984) argue that when we speak about creating a believable story, we inevitably must consider the whole – not just the pieces ... but the assemblage .... In constructing the aesthetic whole, the portraitist seeks a portrayal that is believable, that makes sense, that causes that "click of recognition." We refer to this "yes, of course" (instead of a "yes, but") experience as resonance, and we see the standard as one of authenticity. The portraitist hopes to develop a rich portrayal that will have resonance (in different ways, from different perspectives) with three audiences: with the actors who will see themselves reflected in the story, with the readers who will see no reason to disbelieve it, and with the portraitist herself, whose deep knowledge of the setting and self-critical stance allow her to see the "truth value" in her work.

We found, first, that theory and stories operated as each other's feasibility filters: resonance was produced in the oscillation between theory and story, and each brought to light gaps and misconceptions in the other. But it subsequently became clear that our sense of the value and resonance of the stories was also informed by knowledge of the contexts in which they would be shared. Audience – readers or listeners with lived experience – function as an important litmus test for portrait resonance and credibility. Just as, at the outset, the team experienced imbalances in our perceptions of the relative value of their theoretical knowledge and lived experience, we were also divided at times by differences in our experiences of potential readers and audiences and what they would value. Some members of the team had worked with and presented (with mixed success) to educational leaders, leading to some clear understandings of what might resonate. Others did not bring that confidence to the work. Experiences of that resonance are important to the teller's confidence in the value of their stories. It is worth considering approaches that incorporate such sounding boards into the research process.

4   Structuring the Whole

> *Much like how the multitude of anatomical structures in the human body exist and fit together – under the skin, mostly without conscious knowledge, and in a way that ensures that people function as they need to in order to*

thrive and endure change in the world – leadership is a construct that you embody, that you cannot see nor describe until you break it down and learn about it in functional terms (how it works). While trying to understand the anatomy of leadership, like human anatomy, it can be overwhelming, confusing, and disruptive to learning, if you limit your inquiry and exploration of it to the individual structures or characteristics, of which each is comprised. Meaningful advances in learning, when studying anatomy, and when developing as a leader, usually occur following considerable effort, attention, struggle, and reflection on how the structures or characteristics functionally relate as a whole. This notion is consistent with what is experienced by students – as they revise for a cumulative examination after weeks of studying the body's systems in isolation – and by leaders as they go beyond describing who they are and what they do solely in terms of the characteristics, by which they may be defined. Through this transformative process, students and leaders become more aware of how the body functions, and leadership evolves, as complex and cohesive constructs, rather than numerous individual and unrelated parts or qualities.

Research that follows leaders' development emphasizes the importance of standing with them in the uncertainty as they make sense of their experiences (Flinn & Mowles, 2014; Yipp & Raelin, 2011). The educational leader in this study seemed to live in the threshold between established patterns and possibilities, constantly adapting and helping others to adapt to changing circumstances. Portraiture – with its configuration and reconfiguration of narratives – provided powerful tools for capturing the leader's efforts, helping him to become more conscious and reflective. In our case, this process enabled the leader to articulate and situate his practice. He became a teller of the stories of leadership, and in doing so, grew more comfortable with the identity created through those stories.

Though we have used elements of portraiture to support teachers as they have reflected on and articulated their teaching and leadership philosophies in the past, this study was our first effort to employ it more formally as a research method. The experience confirmed for us the value of narrative in capturing and illuminating embodied practice, but it is foreseeable that different leadership styles, disciplinary backgrounds, contexts, or roles may impact the outcomes and effectiveness of this method. Individual characteristics, knowledge base, and facility with leadership discourses or the Scholarship of Teaching and Learning, may impact how stories are told, what meaning is derived from them, and what is seen as salient or immaterial within them.

It would be beneficial to continue to explore the use of portraiture as a method of collaborative research for the Scholarship of Teaching and Learning in higher education since it is more commonly applied in K-12 contexts. Typically, scholars in higher education evolve informally, without the benefit of disciplinary training. They learn from doing and reflecting on the outcomes of their efforts. The leader involved in this study was an evolving scholar of teaching and learning, motivated to engage in the study, in part because of his interest in developing his own fluency and research acumen in the field. Consequently, the research team is conscious of the fact that other leaders, who have different backgrounds, understandings, and motivations related to teaching and learning, may respond differently to the process described herein. In addition, it should be acknowledged that the research relationship created within the team is distinct from other applications of portraiture currently described in the literature (Hackman, 2002; Lawrence-Lightfoot & Hoffman Davis, 1997; Quigley, Trauth-Nare, & Beeman-Cadwallader, 2015). While there are many criticisms of the validity and generalizability of portraiture, this method of inquiry is useful in capturing the essence of and meaning behind an individual's actions, specifically in situations where practice and context are interdependent, or where understanding and preserving agency is critical.

Given the richness of the insights gained in this study, we feel that there is certainly room for continued exploration of how portraiture, as a collaborative research method, can foster the development of educational leaders in higher education.

Note

1   The study outlined in this chapter involved a collaboration among two educational developers and an educational leader who teaches, among other things, introductory anatomy. Each section opens with an italicized passage written by the educational leader.

References

Bolden, R., Petrov, G., & Gosling, J. (2008). *Developing collective leadership in higher education, final report.* Leadership Foundation for Higher Education.

Boulos, P., & Wright, W. A. (2011, February). *Institutionally-funded teaching and learning research and development grant programs (impact for early career faculty).* Paper presented at Annual Conference of the Educational Developers Caucus, Sault Ste. Marie, ON, Canada.

Clandinin, D. J., & Connelly, F. M. (2004). *Narrative inquiry: Experience and story in qualitative research.* Jossey-Bass.

Covey, S. (2006). *The speed of trust.* Free Press.

Eansor, D. (2012). *Teaching chairs and teaching chair programs: A report to the Vice-Provost, teaching and learning.* University of Windsor.

English, F. W. (2000). A critical appraisal of Sara Lawrence-Lightfoot's portraiture as a method of educational research. *Educational Researcher, 29*(7), 21–26.

Etherington, K. (2013). *Narrative approaches to case studies.* Retrieved from https://www.keele.ac.uk/media/keeleuniversity/facnatsci/schpsych/documents/counselling/conference/5thannual/NarrativeApproachestoCaseStudies.pdf

Flinn, K. (2011). *Making sense of leadership development: Reflections on my role as a leader of leadership development* (Dissertation). University of Hertfordshire.

Flinn, K., & Mowles, C. (2014). *A complexity approach to leadership development: Developing practical judgment. Stimulus paper.* Leadership Foundation for Higher Education.

Hackman, D. G. (2002). Using portraiture in educational leadership research. *International Journal of Leadership in Education, 5*(1), 51–60.

Hubball, H., & Clarke, A. (2011). Scholarly approaches to peer-review of teaching: Emergent frameworks and outcomes in a research-intensive university. *Transformative Dialogues Journal, 4*(2), 1–32.

Janson, A., & McQueen, R. (2007). Capturing leadership tacit knowledge in conversations with leaders. *Leadership and Organizational Development Journal, 28*(7), 646–663.

Lawrence-Lightfoot, S. (2005). Reflections on portraiture: A dialogue between art and science. *Qualitative Inquiry, 11*(3), 3–15.

Lawrence-Lightfoot, S. (2016). Commentary. Portraiture methodology: Blending art and science. *Learning Landscapes, 9*(2), Spring, 19–27.

Lawrence-Lightfoot, S. (n.d.). *Portraiture.* Retrieved from http://www.saralawrencelightfoot.com/portraiture1.html

Lawrence-Lightfoot, S., & Hoffman Davis, J. (1997). *The art and science of portraiture.* Jossey-Bass.

Kothari, A., Rudman, D., Dobbins, M., Rouse, M., Sibbald, S., & Edwards, N. (2012). The use of tacit and explicit knowledge in public health: A qualitative study. *Implementation Science, 7*(20), 2–12.

McAdam, R., Mason, B., & McCrory, J. (2007). Exploring the dichotomies within the tacit knowledge literature: Towards a process of tacit knowing in organizations. *Journal of Knowledge Management, 11*(2), 43–59.

Morris, C., & Fry, H. (2006). Enhancing educational research and development activity through small grant schemes: A case study. *International Journal of Academic Development, 11*(1), 43–56.

Nonaka, I., & van Krogh, G. (2009). Tacit knowledge and knowledge conversion: Controversy and advancement in organizational knowledge theory. *Organization Science, 20*(3), 635–652.

Polanyi, M. (1966). *The tacit dimension*. Doubleday and Co.

Quigley, C., Trauth-Nare, A., & Beeman-Cadwallader, N. (2015). The viability of portraiture for science education research: Learning from portraits of two science classrooms. *International Journal of Qualitative Studies in Education, 28*(1), 21–49.

Roxå, T. (2008, November). *How does one change a university? A socio-cultural approach for improved teaching*. Paper presented at Invited Scholars Seminar, University of British Columbia, Vancouver. http://ctlt.ubc.ca/files/2010/08/Torgny-Roxa-PowerPoint-Presentation-11-28-08.pdf

Roxå, T., & Mårtensson, K. (2013). *Significant networks for educational development*. Retrieved at http://www.konferenslund.se/pp/CEQ_Roxa_Martensson.pdf

Schon, D. A. (1983). *The reflective practitioner: How professionals think in action*. Basic Books.

Senge, P. M. (1990). *The fifth discipline: The art and practice of the learning organization*. Doubleday Business.

Van Manen, M. (1994). Pedagogy, virtue, and narrative identity in teaching. *Curriculum Inquiry, 4*(2), 136–170.

Wright, A., Hamilton, B., Raffoul, J., & Marval, P. (2014). *Embedded educational leadership initiatives at the University of Windsor: A Ministry of Training, Colleges, and Universities productivity and innovation fund initiative (July 2014)*. University of Windsor.

Yip, J., & Raelin, J. A. (2011). Threshold concepts and modalities for teaching leadership practice. *Management Learning, 43*(3), 333–354.

CHAPTER 7

Complexity, Negotiations, and Processes: A Longitudinal Qualitative, Narrative Approach to Young People's Transition to and from University

Henriette Tolstrup Holmegaard

Abstract

The chapter argues how longitudinal, qualitative methods respond to the criticism of the qualitative interview as being unable to capture the complexity of life. The method enhances our knowledge of the *complexity, negotiations,* and *processes* played out over time and enables researchers to avoid the reduction of the participant or the cultural context of the interview. The chapter introduces the origin of longitudinal interviews in general and the application in science education research in particular. Longitudinal methods can be allied to various theoretical positions. The chapter provides an example by analyzing the knowledge interests pursued by a narrative longitudinal approach. The chapter further shares practical advice on how to plan and carry out the interviews, and how to approach the relationship of the interviewer and the participant developed over time. Finally, limitations of the method are discussed. The narrative longitudinal approach presumes a participant being able to accumulate narratives, and thus prevents narratives of vulnerability, feeling disadvantaged, or being introverted. Therefore, the chapter provides tools, which can be combined with the narrative longitudinal interview, in order to support and facilitate the interview dialogue. The chapter ends with a discussion of the knowledge accessed through a longitudinal, narrative lens.

Keywords

longitudinal studies – negotiations – transitions – narrative – higher education – qualitative method – interviews

1 Introduction

Christine lives in a rural area of Denmark and dreams of becoming a civil engineer. Although she actually prefers mathematics, she abandoned plans to study mathematics at university as she read somewhere that it would lead to a teaching job, which did not appeal to Christine. Engineering studies, on the other hand, interest her and there are many job possibilities as she explains to me when I meet her for the first interview just before she finishes upper secondary school:

> I had considered applying to the University of Copenhagen to study mathematics and design. That would have qualified me to teach at upper secondary school level. The more I think about it, the more I'm convinced that I would end up strangling the children before I ever taught them anything (laughs). Now that I think about it, I don't think I'd make a very good teacher (...). I don't think that I could stand being a teacher. (Christine, attending upper secondary school, April 2010)

Shortly after the summer holidays, I exchanged a series of text messages with Christine. I ask her how things are going and what she is doing. Her answer surprises me: "I've started studying at the teacher training college. I have *always* wanted to be a teacher" (text message from Christine, September 2010).

The quotations are interesting for several reasons. If I had only interviewed Christine about the choices she was considering shortly before she graduated, the first quoted passage would be interesting in terms of understanding the meaning attributed to the teaching profession, and why it is difficult to attract new students. The second quotation could be indicative of young people who choose to study for a teaching degree, and their interests and aspirations. But the analysis is complicated by the fact that the statements were made by the same person who contradicts herself within a very short period of time. In this chapter, I intend to examine what we have to learn from longitudinal studies in spite of such complexities. I will show the strengths of using a longitudinal methodology in studies of young people, but also discuss some of the associated challenges when observing young people over a prolonged period of their life. I will continuously return to the example of Christine.

I will draw on my experience from two research projects. In one, I studied the choices of young people and their transition to long-cycle, advanced science study programs. I am also currently involved in a research project dealing with the transition from selected science master's programs to a professional career. Within both studies, I followed a group of young people with whom I conducted recurring narrative interviews over a three-year period. I followed four of the young people all the way from the end of upper secondary school, through their university studies, and out onto the labor market. Excerpts from these studies will be used as examples in this chapter.

The purpose of the chapter is to analyze the specific knowledge available by applying a longitudinal approach and how this methodology is crucial for the researcher's perspective and analysis. Not only will I discuss the knowledge configured by the researcher when following young people over a period of time, but I will also simply share the possibilities and limitations embedded in the method. In doing so, I will emphasize key considerations that require special attention that the researcher should keep in mind when engaging in longitudinal studies especially in research in teaching and learning.

2   Longitudinal Studies

Studies conducted over a period of time and involving repeated interactions with the same subject are called longitudinal studies. Longitudinal studies do not necessarily study people; they can also study groups, institutions, organizations, or even societal trends over time. The longitudinal aspect primarily describes a temporal dimension, but it is also characterized by the same object of research being repeatedly involved in the study. This is also why the term 'waves' is used to describe the collection of empirical data since it represents the number of times data is collected. Longitudinal studies are probably characterized more by their differences than their similarities, however, and the methodological approach can be framed in a variety of ways in different academic fields. Therefore, the longitudinal aspect is more of a design or methodological approach than an actual method.

2.1   *Origin and Use*

Some of the first longitudinal studies were introduced by the work of developmental psychologists who charted what was called 'the whole child' in the 1930s. This involved the collation of various data about the child including diet, behavior, health, education, and conditions for growth, but they also examined the interplay of these factors and the child's development over time (Sontag, 1971). Back then, the longitudinal aspect involved carrying out specific measurements of the same variable at different points of impact in the child's life and doing so in a manner that rendered data comparisons possible. Since then, an abundance of longitudinal studies, primarily quantitative, has emerged. For instance, large-scale quantitative longitudinal studies are widely used in the health sciences where researchers are interested in monitoring the course of an illness, heredity, and illness treatment over time in various contexts. In a

Danish context, the research project 'Kost, kræft og helbred' (Diet, cancer, and health) is an example of a longitudinal cohort study that has been collecting data on dietary habits, lifestyles, and biological material from selected families across generations since 1993.

The longitudinal approach cannot always be unequivocally categorized into either a quantitative or qualitative school of thought, and it is often incorporated into other methodological designs. Examples of these include case studies, observations, or ethnographic studies (Hermanowicz, 2013). Most studies continue, however, to draw on quantitative or qualitative knowledge interests in which the quantitative approach is interested in isolating and measuring selected variables over time and the qualitative approach, which I will explain in more detail later on, is interested in monitoring processes, negotiations, and development.

Qualitative longitudinal studies are not nearly as widespread as quantitative studies. This is mostly because qualitative studies are enormously time-consuming. The interest in qualitative longitudinal studies is traceable to urban sociology in the Chicago school. This is where the interest in understanding the temporal dimension in studies of social life began, inspired by the work of Mead, among others, and the school of researchers developed methods that incorporated a temporal dimension into anthropological field studies, interviews, and observations of subjects. These studies were characterized by their retrospective and prospective elements where research subjects were urged to share perspectives on their past, present, and future. Although this is not what we would define today as a longitudinal study, it is still highlighted as the time when researchers began to take interest in the longitudinal aspects of qualitative research (Hermanowicz, 2013).

2.2 *Longitudinal Approaches in Educational Research*

Within Education, qualitative longitudinal research is sparse; however, I will point your attention to four scholars that do apply longitudinal approaches in their research in education and conduct research of very high quality. First, Reiss provides us with an example of a five-year in-depth qualitative classroom study of science teaching (Reiss, 2000). The study is based on many hours of observations as well as interviews with teachers, pupils, and parents. In addition to the many details and perspectives portrayed in the analysis, it is a unique example of making qualitative research transparent. In a paper Reiss reflects on the challenges in ending the study after having built relations with the participants in many years, specifically with the teachers:

> One group of teachers were deeply hurt by the book. I trace this mainly to my failure to consider adequately their fears of the consequences of the

book's publication and possibly to my failure to consider with them the psychological significance of my withdrawing from the school after five years of regular study. (Reiss, 2005, p. 123)

Another longitudinal contribution to education is proposed by Barton and colleagues. Barton works with social justice by applying critical ethnography to understand the lives of among other urban minority youth, immigrants, and homeless children and their meeting with formal schooling in general and science in particular (Barton, 1998, 2001; Carreón, Drake, & Barton, 2005). Her research is done by following and engaging actively with the participants through many hours and sometimes by building relationships and trust throughout a period of years. The longitudinal research developed by Barton has offered a unique contribution to understand the interaction of culture and power science education:

> We need to continue to develop rich portraits of a variety of experiences from the lives of inner-city children and parents if we are to genuinely construct science for all. (Barton & Yang, 2000, p. 886)

Carlone and colleagues have done several longitudinal studies where she has followed a group of students, both with interviews and classroom observations, at various educational levels (Carlone, Scott, & Lowder, 2014). In a study of successful women of color and their transition through university, she shows how success is negotiated and experienced in many different, sometimes unpleasant, and challenging ways that cause the participants to compromise and submit themselves to higher education (Carlone & Johnson, 2007).

Finally, Louise Archer and her colleagues have applied mixed methods longitudinal approaches to follow children's science aspirations and choices from years 10 to 18. The study combines surveys over time with interviews with students and their parents. The study presents unique data as it follows the participants through a long and significant period of their lives. The study is an excellent example of how following students' choices over time allows for insight into how choices intersect with social background, gender and ethnicity (Archer et al., 2010, 2012a, 2012b; Archer, DeWitt, Osborne et al., 2013; Archer, DeWitt, & Willis, 2013, 2014; Archer, Osborne et al., 2013).

3 Longitudinal Interviews

As I will unfold in this chapter, a longitudinal design is logistically challenging, and it can also be difficult to deal with analytically. Therefore, one may ask, why go through all the trouble? When is it relevant to apply a longitudinal qualitative approach to study young people's lives? In qualitative research, reflecting on and being transparent in relation to one's own practice are essential to the methodological approach. This involves both the researcher's own position in the field, but also the perspective with which the researcher approaches the field (Alvesson & Sköldberg, 2008). Therefore, I will examine the perspective that is available to a researcher who takes a longitudinal methodological approach.

3.1 Longitudinal Interviews Respond to Criticism of the Research Interview

A research interview provides a snapshot view of what the world looks like to the interview subject here and now. Depending on the knowledge interests, the researcher can zoom in on the interview subject's language, attributions of meaning, experiences, perceptions, resources, defense mechanisms, and other aspects. No matter the approach, most will agree that this provides insight into knowledge accumulated in a unique context at a unique point in time. This is precisely one of the points of criticism which anthropologists and sociologists have long been leveling at the research interview: it is disconnected from the subject's life and customary behavior, and it results in an isolated understanding of the complexity of the life being lived (Becker & Geer, 1957). The interview is often conducted in a closed room far from the rest of the subject's life, which can make the interview seem stilted, staged, and artificial. One way to capture the complexity is, like anthropologists, to attempt to understand the individual's participation in a cultural context by the researcher participating in it himself/herself. There are also interview methods that take account of this criticism, however, and these interviews are conducted either by bringing the subject's life into the interview, e.g. by asking the subject to take pictures of his/her life and focus the interview on them (Staunæs, 2003) or by extracting the interview from the twosome relationship and putting it into an everyday situation for the subject. This is the case, for instance, when an ethnographic interview is conducted while the researcher and the interview subject are engaged in a practical task together (Spradley, 2016).

Another way to respond to the criticism is seeking to understand through repeated interviews the transitions taking place over time and making room for the complexity of the life being lived. In this instance, narrative longitudinal interviews are useful. It is worth emphasizing, however, that narrative longitudinal interviews do not provide access to a truer or more correct version of the subjects' lives than other methodological approaches. Instead, they make room for narratives that are being negotiated, are disconnected, and part of an ongoing process being played out over time.

3.2 *Complexity, Negotiations, and Processes*

By employing a qualitative longitudinal method, the researcher is able to understand the *negotiations* in the young peoples' narratives, and, in my research, it is been important for my view of choice as an ongoing process that is being shaped, retold, and changed over time. Let's take an example of trying to understand what took place between the first interview of Christine and the subsequent text message received from her cited in the example above.

The interesting aspect is that Christine does not describe ruptures or dramatic changes in her choice-narrative. In a subsequent interview, Christine explains that, since the first interview, she had moved in with her partner somewhere outside of Copenhagen. During the summer holiday, they had enjoyed the summer as a small new family in their new home. This suddenly lengthened the distance to the engineering university, and Christine started considering whether the long commute could ultimately measure up to her interest. By contrast, the teacher training college was just around the corner and embodied many possibilities, and she could also study mathematics there. This choice, which seemed dynamic and inconstant on the face of it, did not seem very inconstant at all from Christine's point of view. Both of her parents work as teachers and this has been a recurring aspect of Christine's life, which she related to herself. When Christine says, "I have *always wanted to be a teacher*," it is not necessarily because she is lying, but because she detects and singles out other parts of her past and incorporates them into her own narrative. The adverb 'always' is used in quite a number of choice narratives in my empirical research as a marker that emphasizes the authenticity, the stability, and the correctness of the choice. The choice narrative, as recounted here and now, thus contains a temporal dimension that extends both forward – when the young person is considering the choice's meaning for his/her future life, e.g. career opportunities, but also goes back into the past in the narrative about the authenticity of the choice. This temporal dimension is significant for understanding young people's educational choices and, in my research, this understanding was made possible by a longitudinal qualitative design.

4 Narrative Psychology

Narrative psychology covers a wide variety of theoretical approaches and my agenda in this chapter is not to explain it here, which is why I present my own position in brief only. As previously mentioned, longitudinal designs belong to a methodology that is crucial for how it is implemented in practice. The point of my brief introduction of narrative psychology is therefore to provide an example of what a longitudinal study can look like and to present the field I access through this type of interview, and the significance of it for the knowledge I produce.

Narrative theories and methodology arose in opposition to established research in the 1970s. The 'narrative turn' as it is called, focuses on a subject-centered approach within the arts and social sciences (Andrews, Squire, & Tamboukou, 2008). The interest in narrative research was initiated by the French philosopher Ricoeur and his ideas on narrative identities and the temporal dimension (Ricoeur, 1976, 1990). His work has inspired narrative theories across a wide range of fields such as comparative literature, rhetoric, anthropology, philosophy, and psychology.

The basic idea of narrative psychology is that we understand our life as a simple, interconnected, and progressive narrative. This means that the way we create narratives continuously interconnects our past, present, and future, where we narrate our life forward as if we possess a coherent, cumulative self, which builds our new experiences and perceptions on top of the old ones. This is determinative for the degree of flexibility and dynamism we can infuse into the narratives we fabricate, and it also imposes demands on our negotiating skills in a constantly changing world. The point is that identities are constantly shifting – one's identity is an ongoing process being negotiated both into the future and into the past, and we are constantly being challenged to retell who we are as new experiences and events meet our narrative. At the same time, we position ourselves as if we possess a stable, unchangeable self which we must believe in. "There is no such thing psychologically as 'life itself.' At the very least, it is a selective achievement of memory recall; beyond that, recounting one's life is an interpretive feat" (Bruner, 2004, p. 693).

The way in which young people interpret their surroundings is interesting to researchers who subscribe to a narrative approach, which studies how young people structure the complexity of the life being lived for causality and coherence:

> Narrative is a meaning structure that organizes events and human actions into a whole, thereby attributing significance to individual actions and events according to their effect on the whole. Thus, narratives are to be differentiated from chronicles, which simply lists events according to their place on a time line. Narrative provides a symbolised account of actions that includes a temporal dimension. (Polkinghorne, 1988, p. 18)

The temporal dimension cited by Polkinghorne in the phrase quoted above is important for understanding the object of one's research, to which a researcher gains access through a longitudinal narrative design. I would like to dwell on this before returning to the more practical aspects of the method.

4.1   Temporal Dimension and Identity

Imagine that you are driving a car. When the car turns a corner, new perspectives and landscapes come into view through the front window. Not only that, the view through the rear-view mirror suddenly looks different as well. The same is true of narratives such as the example of Christine, which illustrated how the act of moving in with her partner suddenly afforded different perspectives on the future. As well, these perspectives also prompted her to renegotiate the past and the dream of becoming a teacher, which suddenly came into view in the rear-view mirror after having been in the dark in the previous interview. In other words, new resources and events were made available to Christine which provided her new matrices through which to see her past: "events in our lives may provide us with resources to understand ourselves differently, leading to changes in our biography" (Roth & Tobin, 2007, p. 1).

Whereas the past is often described as a chronological, cumulative narrative, the future is portrayed as "a terrain that is empty, open and subject to colonization" (Adam & Groves, 2007, p. 200). I am inspired by the thoughts underlying possible future selves, which are the selves one expects to become in the near and distant future (Markus & Nurius, 1986). In narrative psychology, the future is not freely open to interpretation, however. The narratives fabricated by young people are rooted in a specific social and cultural context (Polkinghorne, 1988) and they are restricted by psycho-historical formations in the form of our previous narratives (Holland, Lachicotte, Skinner, & Cain, 1998), but also our surroundings' understanding of who we are, and the resources available to us (Smith & Sparkes, 2008).

I will give an example of how narratives are culturally rooted through an empirical example. As previously mentioned, my current research studies the transition from selected master study programs within science and engineering and into a career. I follow a group of students from the time they write their thesis and three years forward. At the first meeting with the students, I asked them to draw the future version of themselves three years later. The figures below were made by PhD students studying biochemistry and molecular biomedicine respectively. The two study programs are very close to one another and share several courses of study. The vast majority of students in both programs aspire to a PhD position, but in very different ways.

FIGURE 7.1   Drawing by biochemistry student of future self in 3 years

Figure 7.1 depicts a PhD student in biochemistry. As is evident, it illustrates a quite frustrated PhD student who dreams of chocolate and the Nobel Prize but who has difficulty with laboratory work. Figure 7.2 depicts a cheerful PhD student. This figure depicts a baby and family life in balance, instruction in cells, which she is responsible for, and the experiment she is currently doing. In many ways, the two figures aptly portray the studies in which they are situated. In biochemistry, students generally had a vague idea of the type of career that awaited them upon completion of their studies. Several recount how they experience being met with astonishment and having to explain if they did not share the PhD dream with their fellow students. Students who consider working in the manufacturing industry explain that they must keep this aspiration to themselves as it is not something anyone talks about, neither in the classroom nor with fellow students. However, the PhD pathway is not talked about very much either; in fact, several students describe how future plans play an insignificant role in their studies. On the other hand, student life is about interests, and a number of students respond to questions about the future by explaining their thesis. The situation is quite the opposite in molecular biomedicine. In this study program, students talk about everything from the working environment, laboratory facilities in the private versus the public sector, career options, working hours, possibilities of cooperation projects, etc. By contrast with biochemistry, students in the molecular biomedicine program were very articulate about their future selves albeit only within research as the students here found themselves being positioned as not being ambitious or clever enough if striving for at career outside research.

FIGURE 7.2   Drawing by biomedicine student of future self in 3 years

The example shows two things. The first is that the culture in which the narrative about the future is fabricated is decisive for the extent to which the students' possible future selves are developed. But the second is how the possible future selves simultaneously interact with the students' current strategies in their studies. In molecular biomedicine, this meant that the elective courses, study jobs, and qualification profiles were carefully thought out – and that the electives, thesis topic, and supervisor were all part of a bigger plan. In biochemistry, the study strategy was interest-driven, and a few of the students considering a career outside of research experienced this narrative as being difficult to discuss in the study environment since research was emphasized as space where one is free to pursue one's interests. The point is that the study program not only enables specific narratives and future selves, but also that these narratives and future selves play into study strategies here and now. Therefore, past, present, and future are continuously interwoven and interacting.

An angle that I have yet to develop in my research, but which is interesting nonetheless, is how specific groups of students' narratives and their possible, future selves interact with their gender, ethnicity, and social background. I can recommend Archer and her colleagues' work involving *science capital* as an example of this dimension. Even if Archer does not draw on narrative psychology, the interest is identical (Archer, DeWitt, Osborne et al., 2013; Archer et al., 2014).

5 Longitudinal Interviews and Positionality

As the research interview became more widespread during the 1980s, the idea was that the interview, by contrast with quantitative and experimental approaches, etc., could involve the subjects by 'giving them a voice.' According to Kvale (2006), the underlying agenda was to create a space of trust:

> Creating trust through a personal relationship here serves as a means to efficiently obtain a disclosure of the interview subjects' world. The interviewer may, with a charming, gentle, and client-centered manner, create a close personal encounter where the subjects unveil their private worlds. (p. 482)

But as Kvale (2006) points out further on, the interview is in many ways an artificially fabricated space, convoluted by power relationships that render actual dialogue impossible. In many ways, the interview resembles a therapeutic space and it can be criticized for drawing on a confession discourse where 'opening up' or 'getting things off your chest' are identified as meaningful (Foucault, 1997). Despite the criticism, the interview is still a widely used qualitative research method, perhaps because it is logistically easy to use. There are many other arguments in favor of using interviews as a method, however. In my research, interviews make it possible to study the subjects' meaning systems and their narratives, for instance. Anyone who has ever conducted an interview knows that it is a difficult task and that there are several factors which mean that it does not become easier to interview the same subject multiple times. No matter if an interview is longitudinal, an interview as a research method requires a wide range of reflections – before, during, and after the interview. However, I will only touch on the elements here that are specifically relevant to longitudinal qualitative studies. In this section, I will focus on reflections on the role of the interviewer and the liberty of action of the interview subject.

5.1 *Position of the Interviewer and Relationships Over Time*

In a longitudinal interview, reflections on the interviewer's position take on an added dimension, namely the relationship that develops over time. In this section, I will share reflections on and specific examples of how the relationship that develops over time in a longitudinal interview is significant to the interview situation.

Previously, I have been inspired by the description of the 'naive' interviewer, where the interviewer assumes an unknowing role and conversely positions the participant as the expert in his/her own life (Søndergaard, 1996). In this situation, it is the interview participant who explains and reflects, and the interviewer asks investigative, inquisitive, and follow-up questions. This maintains distance between the participant and interviewer, as the research object is composed of the participant's attributions of meaning and formation of meaning. This requires the interviewer to stay in the background, as compared to more structured interviewing approaches, for instance.

This approach can become challenged in a longitudinal interview. After multiple interviews and in some instances, spending many hours with the same interview participant – where they shared experiences, concerns, challenges, and, in some cases, problems from their own life – I experienced that this distance and these positions were more difficult to maintain. It could seem callous to ask participants to share their life with me if I did not give anything in return. In some cases, I experienced that I had to be more present with myself. This meant that I had to become more aware of the significance of my position in the interview situation and ensure that my analytical perspective examined my own position both during and after the interview. When did I laugh/grin? Did I interrupt? When did the narrative flow by itself? When did I have to prompt the participant with questions? And when did I leave the interviewer's role and engage in everyday conversation, and what impact did this have? The position of the interviewer is therefore important in terms of investigating how narratives are supported, excluded, and ignored during the interview situation. The relationship built up through longitudinal interviews is both a strength and a weakness. It is a strength by virtue of the safety and confidentiality which frame the interview and enable aspects of the narrative that are significant for understanding the subject's life. As was the case for some of the participants in my study, who experienced illness or alcohol-related problems in their close family, the relationship could allow access to ongoing experiences of the challenges they are encountering in their life. This is exemplified by Emily who explained her thoughts on dropping out of her studies before actually formally leaving her studies:

It seemed to me that I felt stupid and I felt the same way in the other subjects, and I felt like all the other students could figure everything out. I didn't seem to be motivated to study, and it just got too boring and I didn't feel that I could keep my self-confidence or self-respect when I had the feeling of being stupid every day. (Emily)

Through prolonged contact, the relationship provided a unique opportunity to gain access to the student's negotiations of dropping out of their study program, a negotiation which several explained was difficult to share with their fellow students and study supervisors until they felt certain about their decision. This means that most studies of dropping out run into a brick wall when they contact former students. First of all, it is difficult to schedule appointments with students who have dropped out and, secondly, the researcher gains access to retrospect accounts of the narrative. The ongoing contact with the interview subjects provides an opportunity to establish a relationship that allows access to experiences and perceptions that can be difficult to share with an interviewer who one meets for a single hour of one's life.

Another strength of the relationship that is built up at recurring interviews was how the participants sent text messages and e-mails between the interviews to tell me about their experiences. This ended up being a significant secondary empirical analysis that I had not planned for when the study began.

One of the weaknesses of the relationship, however, is that the intimacy establishes an implicit understanding of sorts that restricts the interviewer's possibility of asking questions about all the implicitly understood aspects. This is because the interviewer develops blind spots, but also because it becomes more difficult to ask questions from without if the participant is talking from within. This constitutes the same type of challenges outlined by Adriansen and Madsen (2009) when they reflect on what it is like to interview colleagues in geography when they themselves are geographers. As a result, the interview becomes an ongoing balance between asking exploratory, open questions, and, at the same time, refraining from positioning oneself as unsympathetic to the participant's narrative.

5.2 *Position of the Interview Participant*

Having reflected on the interviewer's position in longitudinal interviews, I will now discuss the positions available to the interview participant through the interview, the positions they are offered, and the implicit interview participants which the method calls for.

During my first wave of interviews in studying the transition from upper secondary school to university, I had an experience that would be significant for the remaining interviews in the study. It was my encounter with Daniel. Daniel was an upper secondary (technology/science) school student who was quite interested in mathematics and IT and he was enormously difficult to interview. He responded in monosyllables, and the less he said, the more prominent I became in the room. The interview was a disaster. Daniel did not accept the underlying assumptions of the interview, that he was the one sharing his narratives, and it was clear from the transcript of the interview that I took over the narratives in an attempt to get Daniel to at least say something. Since the interview with Daniel – and through my encounter with science study programs – I have met other students like him: young people who have little to say about themselves or their surroundings. This prompted me to ponder which type of interview subject the methodology calls for and consider how the interview situation itself can alienate young people unfamiliar with practical reflection, disadvantaged young people, introverted young people, or perhaps just timid young people. At the same time, I discovered that my favorite informants were those who filled out the space, interrupted themselves with animated narratives, and enthusiastically responded to my questions.

After the encounter with Daniel, I decided to try out other formats during the interview, i.e. to use different approaches for different types of young people. One example is that at the end of the interview with students in their first year of university studies, I would ask them to depict their motivation as it had developed over time.

I gave the student some time to think it over and draw while I reviewed my interview notes. The drawing that worked best was the graph because it became an object which both of us could look at. At the same time, it turned out that I was surprised by the graph, even if we had already talked about motivation during the interview, as I believed that I had a distinct idea of how they perceived it. The graph gave rise to questions about why the level of motivation had declined, what had made it increase, and what could have supported it. All of these questions shifted the focus from the relationship with the interview participant to the graph. Another activity was to ask upper-secondary students to reflect on the question: "In your opinion, what has had the greatest impact on your choice?" I also used other activities, such as brainstorming, drawing a circular diagram about the participant's task in a work week, and drawing himself/herself in the future. This way, I was able to insert some pauses for thought during the interview which could shift focus away from the interview participant.

6   Planning the Longitudinal Interview

Lastly, I will stop to take a look at some of the more practical points deserving attention that are important to include in methodological considerations. This specifically involves some of the considerations that are important *before* the interview, but also reflections on the interview setting in general. This is just a sample of the reflections one can make. More inspiration on narrative interviews can be found in these methodology books: (Andrews, Squire, & Tamboukou, 2013; Butler-Kisber, 2010; Clandinin & Connelly, 2000; Hollway & Jefferson, 2000).

6.1   *The Temporal Dimension and Retrospective Questions*

My narrative-interview guide was structured into themes as an open, semi-structured interview guide (Kvale & Brinkmann, 2009). Although working on the interview guide is relevant, my reflections in this chapter solely center on factors that are of specific interest in relation to the longitudinal interview, i.e. retrospective questions.

Previously in the chapter, I indicated how past, present, and future are constantly shifting and how the retrospective view of the past purports to be stable, even if it is continuously being negotiated. With this in mind, it was important for me to refrain from referring to previous interviews in subsequent interviews. My initial question in the interview was: 'What has happened since the last interview?', and in this context, it needed to be the interview participant who brought the past into the interview, not me. I considered that questions such as 'Last time, you described your deep interest in mathematics. How is that going?' would have retained the interview participant in my version of their past, instead of their own, and it was notably their narrative that I was interested in. Let me give an example of how this empirically manifests itself if previous interviews are not brought into the subsequent interviews. Simon has started studying at the Technical University of Denmark and he is mostly interested in the aspects of the program dealing with management. Immediately after he began his studies, he explains:

> I dream of opening my own business. I look forward to getting involved in management. How to manage technicians/builders when something has to be built? I'm also interested in the more human aspects. People don't think civil engineers work with people, but in my view, they just take a different approach than doctors or psychologists. They incorporate management techniques. (Simon)

A few months later, Simon explained that he has met some teachers and his tutor (a professor) who did not share his enthusiasm for management. He recounts their conversation.

> Don't focus too much on management. It's overly arrogant to enter the labour market as a fledgling civil engineer and say, "I want to be a manager here. In other words, I'm not that good at mathematics, I'm not that good at the technical aspects, but I want to be your manager" – it simply won't fly (...) So instead, study a technical subject, he says (...) So the conclusion I drew from that was that I think I want to pursue a path called energy, and then management at the same time. Of course, I can't take the entire energy course and the entire management course, but hopefully, I can get it all to work out somehow, and in my view, energy is a relevant path to pursue because it has some of the challenges facing the world right now. (Simon)

I interviewed Simon again during his second year of study. I return several times to the question of why he chose to study energy technology. The interesting aspect is that there was no trace of management in his narrative, even if I specifically ask about his choice of – and interest in – energy technology in a variety of ways during the interview. Instead, when asked when he started to think about energy technology he explains:

> (Breathes out) Well, so it ... Actually, I've probably been heading in that direction for many, many years, I think ... Er ... When I was a little kid, I thought engines were cool, you know? And engines are also an energy conversion machine, of course. I once thought that nuclear power was really super cool, and that's also in the energy sector, too. In fact, I planted the seed of this flower many years ago. (Simon)

The quoted passages show how Simon managed to relate to energy as a field and how it is significant not only to his interests and aspirations but also to his understanding of himself, as someone who is at home in this line of study. The methodological decision to refrain from bringing snatches of previous interviews into the interview room makes it possible to allow other narratives to play out. This would turn out to be an important decision. By not fixating on the participant's past, I gained access to knowledge that I would not otherwise have retrieved. First of all, it enabled me to understand the choice narrative as changeable, and something continuously being performed and negotiated over time, in interaction with the subjects' experiences, perceptions, and events (H. Holmegaard, 2015). Secondly, I discovered that 'always' was used as a marker for authenticity, instead of actually meaning 'at all times' – as the example of Christine showed (Holmegaard, Ulriksen, & Madsen, 2012). Thirdly, it enabled me to understand the choice as a negotiating process that also continued into the higher education study program which the young people ended up choosing, as in the example of Simon (Holmegaard, Madsen, & Ulriksen, 2014). In this case, I learned how repeating, changing, and rejecting choices were constant elements of the narrative, and how thoughts such as 'Is this study program right for me after all?' were an unavoidable part of dealing with the new study program. Thus, the methodological choice has been crucial for the knowledge and conclusions I have produced. It has also led to discussions with colleagues who through questionnaire surveys, for example, find out that those who study science have *always* been interested in it, or that those who drop out of a study program simply do not fit in.

6.2   Considerations about the Interview Setting

The last section of this chapter will examine some of the issues dealing with the general circumstances of longitudinal interviews. I have chosen to gather them under the heading 'interview setting' as they refer to the setting constructed by the researcher.

In addition to logistics and the long waiting time from the beginning of the study to the formation of the analysis, an objection to using longitudinal interviews is whether it is even remotely a viable method in a changing world and in particular dealing with young people. One might ask: How is it possible to design meaningful longitudinal studies of a phase of life in which many factors can rapidly change? There are two significant points worth noting here. First of all, it is enormously difficult to retain young people in a study when they are rushing headlong through life, moving across long distances to study for instance. My participants attended folk high school, traveled to Peru, contracted illness, had their hearts broken, and much more. Even so, I was astonished by the goodwill and receptiveness I encountered. The interview participants themselves chose where they wanted to be interviewed. I have conducted interviews in dormitory rooms, libraries, cafés, and educational institutions – and very few of my participants backed out of the study, which can be a challenge and a vulnerability of longitudinal studies. Secondly, the longitudinal study examines specific points in time. In a changeable phase of life, this is challenging, not just for longitudinal studies, but for qualitative research in general. The researcher must plan the waves of interviews to the best of his/her ability, to avoid too much time passing and to ensure that the study is still possible to carry out. It is not only the interview participant who changes, however. The researcher and the researcher's perspective and interests change as well. By re-interviewing the interview participant, it becomes possible for the researcher to use insights from previous waves to ask, challenge, and invite in ways that differ from the initial meeting.

Another challenge that arises when interviewing a group of young people repeatedly about their choices and transitions is the extent to which the interview situation can resemble a counseling space. The space for reflection created in the interview can support reflections that the young person would not otherwise have made, and this is reinforced in a longitudinal study. An example of this can be found with Johannsen (2012) who studied the drop-out rate among a class of physics students. He ended up wondering why no one in the group he was monitoring had dropped out of the study program (Johannsen, 2012). But it is also a matter of how easy it is for an interviewer to find himself/herself in situations resembling that of a student counselor. An example from my own data is an interview participant who is in the process of making a choice based on incorrect information about the admissions system. In the interview situation itself, I refrained from correcting the student – fearful that it would have unfortunate consequences for my data if I suddenly abandoned my investigative and exploratory role in favor of seeming to have all the answers. When I returned home, however, I regretted having given higher priority to my data than the young person's life and choices. Accordingly, I ended up writing to her afterward saying that I was uncertain about what she had said about the admissions system and that it was probably a good idea for her to look into it.

Interviews are difficult and no interview is perfect. In this chapter, I have examined the specific knowledge made available by a longitudinal approach and how a methodological approach is crucial to the researcher's perspective and analysis. I hope that the chapter can serve as a source of inspiration for researchers, students, and developers to apply the use of longitudinal qualitative methods themselves.

7 Discussion: What Can Be Accessed through a Longitudinal, Narrative Lens?

In this chapter, I have presented how longitudinal, qualitative methods can enhance our knowledge of the lives of the research participants. I focused on the knowledge and the field to which a researcher gains access through the method, and by means of empirical points from my own longitudinal narrative studies. I have reflected on this field and the positions constructed by a researcher when monitoring young people over time.

Even though longitudinal qualitative methods have been around for a long time, they are still not widely used in research. This is probably because they are both time-consuming and logistically challenging. However, there are good reasons for using longitudinal methods, particularly narrative longitudinal methods. The method notably responds to the criticism of the qualitative interview as a reduced and isolated perception of the complexity of the life being lived. The narrative, longitudinal method offers notably a view into *the complexity, negotiations,* and *processes* as they play out over time. In my own research, this method has enabled me to approach choices as ongoing negotiations of the narratives, which are adjusted, reshaped, and recounted whenever the choice is challenged by new experiences and perceptions. Keenly focusing on negotiations makes it impossible to reduce either the student or the educational context to something static.

Longitudinal methods are always part of a theoretical framework. In the chapter, I show how narrative psychology contributes to an interesting platform from where the temporal dimension and identities become significant focal points. Methodologically speaking, the theoretical perception was significant for how knowledge from previous interviews was used in subsequent interviews. Whereas the interviewer can use insights from the previous waves of interviews to ask, challenge, and invite in other ways, the interviewer refrained from bringing her own versions of the past and previous interviews into the actual interview setting. This was crucial for the knowledge produced during the interviews. It enabled the interviewer to comprehend the choice narrative as a negotiating process, a process that did not only take place at the upper secondary school, but continued into the higher education study program which the young people ended up choosing. Thus, the repetition, change, and rejection of choices was a constant focal point of the narrative. At the same time, the theoretical background provided a critical platform from which to understand how 'always' was used as a marker to indicate authenticity, rather than literally meaning 'at all times.'

In the chapter, I discuss the positions available to the interview participant and the researcher in the longitudinal interview, and I share my reflections about the interview setting. Recurring interviews undeniably creates a closer relationship between the interviewer and interview participant. One of the benefits of this was that it provided a unique sense of intimacy that framed the interview and enabled certain aspects of the narrative that can be difficult to access for the researcher but which are significant for understanding the subject's life. A drawback was how the relationship also meant an unavoidable establishment of an implicit understanding with the participant which created blind spots in the interview situation and made it more difficult to ask follow up questions about all the things that were implicit/taken for granted. This posed challenges in that the interview subject positioned the interviewer within his/her personal sphere, whereas the interviewer tried to ask questions from outside this sphere.

In terms of the space into which the interview subject was invited, it also prompts reflections which the interviewer should consider. The implicit interview participant in narrative interviews is expected to elaborate and accumulate narratives. This does not suit all participants, such as those who feel vulnerable, disadvantaged, or introverted. Therefore, the chapter provides various tools that can be combined with the interview and which can shift the focus away from the dialogue and the expectations of the young subject.

Through the chapter, I have shown how qualitative longitudinal studies over time open up for a more nuanced perception of participants' lives. As is true of all qualitative methods, this requires the researcher to be transparent about and to reflect on the methodological practice. In the best of all worlds, the method can advantageously be combined with methods that study young people in their everyday lives. This is rarely logistically possible, however. As shown, the method can easily stand on its own two feet and contribute to new realizations in youth research. I hope this chapter can be a source of inspiration for new complex knowledge in science education.

Acknowledgments

This chapter is based on a chapter in a Danish publication: Ed. Pless, Sørensen (2018), Ungeperspektiver, Aalborg Universitetsforlag. Consent has been provided by the editors to publish in English.

The project about the students' transitions is funded by the Novo Nordisk Foundation. The project about the transition from upper secondary school to university was part of an international project named IRIS (Interests and Recruitment in Science and Engineering), funded by the Seventh Framework Programme of the European Union. The Danish part of the project was carried out in cooperation with Lene Møller Madsen and Lars Ulriksen.

References

Adam, B., & Groves, C. (2007). *Future matters: Action, knowledge, ethics.* Brill.

Adriansen, H. K., & Madsen, L. M. (2009). Studying the making of geographical knowledge: The implications of insider interviews. *Norsk Geografisk Tidsskrift–Norwegian Journal of Geography, 63*(3), 145–153.

Alvesson, M., & Sköldberg, K. (2008). *Tolkning och reflektion: vetenskapsfilosofi och kvalitativ metod.* Studentlitteratur.

Andrews, M., Squire, C., & Tamboukou, M. (2008). *Doing narrative research.* Sage.

Andrews, M., Squire, C., & Tamboukou, M. (2013). *Doing narrative research.* Sage.

Archer, L., DeWitt, J., Osborne, J., Dillon, J., Willis, B., & Wong, B. (2010). 'Doing' science versus 'being' a scientist: Examining 10/11 year old schoolchildren's constructions of science through the lens of identity. *Science Education, 94*(4), 617–639. doi:10.002/sce.20399

Archer, L., DeWitt, J., Osborne, J., Dillon, J., Willis, B., & Wong, B. (2012a). "Balancing acts": Elementary school girls' negotiations of femininity, achievement, and science. *Science Education, 96*(6), 967–989. doi:10.1002/sce.21031

Archer, L., DeWitt, J., Osborne, J., Dillon, J., Willis, B., & Wong, B. (2012b). Science aspirations, capital, and family habitus: How families shape children's engagement and identification with science. *American Educational Research Journal, 49*(5), 881–908.

Archer, L., DeWitt, J., Osborne, J., Dillon, J., Willis, B., & Wong, B. (2013). 'Not girly, not sexy, not glamorous': Primary school girls' and parents' constructions of science aspirations. *Pedagogy, Culture & Society, 21*(1), 171–194. doi:10.1080/14681366.2012.748676

Archer, L., DeWitt, J., & Willis, B. (2014). Adolescent boys' science aspirations: Masculinity, capital, and power. *Journal of Research in Science Teaching, 51*(1), 1–30. doi:10.1002/tea.21122

Archer, L., Osborne, J., DeWitt, J., Dillon, J., Wong, B., & Willis, B. (2013). *ASPIRES: Young people's science and career aspirations, age 10–14.* King's College London.

Barton, A. C. (1998). Teaching science with homeless children: Pedagogy, representation, and identity. *Journal of Research in Science Teaching, 35*(4), 379–394.

Barton, A. C. (2001). Science education in urban settings: Seeking new ways of praxis through critical ethnography. *Journal of Research in Science Teaching, 38*(8), 899–917.

Barton, A. C., & Yang, K. (2000). The culture of power and science education: Learning from Miguel. *Journal of Research in Science Teaching, 37*(8), 871–889. doi:10.1002/1098-2736(200010)37:8<871::AID-TEA7>3.0.CO;2-9

Becker, H., & Geer, B. (1957). Participant observation and interviewing: A comparison. *Human Organization, 16*(3), 28–32.

Bruner, J. (2004). Life as narrative. *Social Research, 71*(3), 691–710.

Butler-Kisber, L. (2010). *Qualitative inquiry: Thematic, narrative and arts-informed perspectives.* Sage.

Carlone, H. B., & Johnson, A. (2007). Understanding the science experiences of successful women of color: Science identity as an analytic lens. *Journal of Research in Science Teaching, 44*(8), 1187–1218.

Carlone, H. B., Scott, C. M., & Lowder, C. (2014). Becoming (less) scientific: A longitudinal study of students' identity work from elementary to middle school science. *Journal of Research in Science Teaching, 51*(7), 836–869.

Carreón, G. P., Drake, C., & Barton, A. C. (2005). The importance of presence: Immigrant parents' school engagement experiences. *American Educational Research Journal, 42*(3), 465–498.

Clandinin, D. J., & Connelly, F. M. (2000). *Narrative inquiry: Experience and story in qualitative research.* Jossey-Bass.

Foucault, M. (1997). *Ethics, subjectivity and truth: Essential works of Foucault 1954–1984* (Vol. 1). The New Press.

Hermanowicz, J. C. (2013). The longitudinal qualitative interview. *Qualitative Sociology, 36*(2), 189–208.

Holland, D., Lachicotte, J. W., Skinner, D., & Cain, C. (1998). *Identity and agency in cultural worlds.* Harvard University Press.

Hollway, W., & Jefferson, T. (2000). *Doing qualitative research differently: Free association, narrative and the interview method.* Sage.

Holmegaard, H. (2015). Performing a choice-narrative: A qualitative study of the patterns in STEM students' higher education choices. *International Journal of Science Education, 37*(9), 1454–1477.

Holmegaard, H. T., Madsen, L. M., & Ulriksen, L. (2014). A journey of negotiation and belonging: understanding students' transitions to science and engineering in higher education. *Cultural Studies of Science Education, 9*(3), 755–786. doi:10.1007/s11422-013-9542-3

Holmegaard, H. T., Ulriksen, L. M., & Madsen, L. M. (2012). The process of choosing what to study: A longitudinal study of upper secondary students' identity work when choosing higher education. *Scandinavian Journal of Educational Research, 58*(1), 21–40. doi:10.1080/00313831.2012.696212

Johannsen, B. F. (2012). *Attrition and retention in university physics: A longitudinal qualitative study of the interaction between first year students and the study of physics.* Department of Science Education, Faculty of Science, University of Copenhagen.

Kvale, S. (2006). Dominance through interviews and dialogues. *Qualitative Inquiry, 12*(3), 480–500.

Kvale, S., & Brinkmann, S. (2009). *Interview: introduktion til et håndværk.* Hans Reitzel.

Markus, H., & Nurius, P. (1986). Possible selves. *American psychologist, 41*(9), 954–969.

Polkinghorne, D. E. (1988). *Narrative knowing and the human sciences.* State University of New York Press.

Reiss, M. J. (2000). *Understanding science lessons: Five years of science teaching.* Open University Press.

Reiss, M. J. (2005). Managing endings in a longitudinal study: Respect for persons. *Research in Science Education, 35*(1), 123–135. doi:10.1007/s11165-004-3436-z

Ricoeur, P. (1976). *Interpretation theory: Discourse and the surplus of meaning.* TCU Press.

Ricoeur, P. (1990). *Time and narrative.* The University of Chicago Press.

Roth, W.-M., & Tobin, K. (Eds.). (2007). *Science, learning, identity: Sociocultural and cultural-historical perspectives* (New Directions in Mathematics and Science Education, Vol. 7). Sense Publishers.

Smith, B., & Sparkes, A. C. (2008). Contrasting perspectives on narrating selves and identities: An invitation to dialogue. *Qualitative Research in Psychology, 8*(5), 5–35.

Søndergaard, D. M. (1996). *Tegnet på kroppen. Køn: Koder og konstruktion blandt unge voksne i Akademia.* Museum Tusculanum Press.

Sontag, L. W. (1971). The history of longitudinal research: Implications for the future. *Child Development, 42*(4), 987–1002.

Spradley, J. P. (2016). *The ethnographic interview.* Waveland Press.

Staunæs, D. (2003). *Etnicitet, køn og skoleliv: en ph.d.-afhandling.* Institut for Kommunikation, Journalistik og Datalogi, Roskilde Universitetscenter.

PART 3

Clinical Explorations through Dialogue, Collaboration, and Ethics

∴

CHAPTER 8

Participatory Action Research: Navigating Nuances

Nicola Simmons

Abstract

Action research has a long history for curriculum review and K-12 work but is less often used in higher education and even less in the Scholarship of Teaching and Learning, where it finds a close methodological match. Participatory action research involves a balanced relationship with research participants, wherein they become co-inquirers. In this chapter, I provide a literature summary of participatory action research as a methodological approach and then outline one such research partnership. Drawing on Kemmis and McTaggert's four moments of action research, I focus on the roles of the researcher and participant and how they navigated and negotiated the nuances of the research process, including tips for submitting to the Research Ethics Board. Lessons learned include consideration of the additional time commitment for the participant, along with role and research ownership negotiation. The chapter is intended as both a guidebook and a cautionary note to others engaging in such research partnerships.

Keywords

participatory action research – researcher roles – scholarship of teaching and learning – research ethics

1 Introduction

Action research is relatively well known in K-12 schools as "a tool of curriculum development consisting of continuous feedback that targets specific problems in a particular school setting" (Ferraro, 2000, p. 2). It has seen wide use internationally (see work by Australian colleagues Carr & Kemmis, 1986; Kemmis & McTaggert, 1982), but has been underused in the Canadian postsecondary education community, particularly regarding the Scholarship of Teaching and Learning (SoTL), for which I argue it is ideally suited.

Action research requires a journey through Schön's (1983) model of reflective practice of cycles of act-observe-reflect-plan, which match the cycles of experiential learning and action research. All three have their roots in work by Lewin done in 1946 (Carr & Kemmis, 1986; Kemmis & McTaggert, 1982; Kolb, 1984). Within the research approach of continuous improvement of plan, act, observe, and reflect, the researcher seeks to address an issue and improve the outcome. It is a generative research approach; that is, it is theory-building rather than theory-testing, and the researcher must be open to new directions that arise as the research progresses. Ultimately, it is intended to lead to an improvement in practice. In this way, it is representative of the way scholars of teaching and learning undertake inquiry into their teaching and learning and is a very good methodological framework for this work.

Participatory action research adds a layer of potential complication wherein a practitioner (educator) partners with a researcher to investigate a specific teaching and learning issue. As Elliot (1991) noted, "this kind of joint reflection about the relationship in particular circumstances between processes and products is a central characteristic of what Schön has called reflective practice and others, including myself, have termed action research" (p. 50). This facilitated reflective practice can make for rich dialogue between the partners and can also complicate the research process as agendas must be clearly negotiated and sometimes the intention of one partner is at odds with the interests of another. In the literature, these partnerships tend to be discussed in positive, even glowing, terms. Too often the research papers are written as if everything went smoothly; we tend to politely hide or smooth over challenges and errors. While that may be strategic in permitting the focus to remain on the research findings, it means that others have little opportunity to learn from our mistakes.

In this chapter, I tease apart the roles of researcher and participant in one participatory action research study and turn the spotlight on lessons learned – highlighting several things that went smoothly – our face to face meetings to negotiate roles and responsibilities at several stages in the project and our way of presenting our roles to the Research Ethics Board such that approval of the project was immediate. I also explore some lessons learned about potential challenges: the selection of a participant, the additional workload for the participant, negotiating roles, and determining ownership. I hope this chapter will serve both as a guide and caution to others, especially those undertaking Scholarship of Teaching and Learning (SoTL) work, as they navigate the nuances of the research relationship.

2 Action Research

Action research, according to Leedy and Ormrod (2001), is a "type of applied research that focuses on finding a solution to a local problem in a local setting" (p. 114). Action research is intended to lead to praxis or improvement in practice. Carr and Kemmis (1986) detail three purposes of action research:

> Firstly, the improvement of a practice; secondly, the improvement of the understanding of a practice by its practitioners; and thirdly, the improvement of the situation in which the practice takes place. The aim of involvement stands shoulder to shoulder with the aim of improvement. (p. 165)

These purposes align strongly with the intentions of the Scholarship of Teaching and Learning (SoTL) in which postsecondary educators seek to improve teaching and learning in their own courses, to understand the context and issues more deeply, and hopefully, to positively affect the context towards future improvements.

As Hutchings, Huber, and Ciccone (2011) define it, the Scholarship of Teaching and Learning is:

> Best understood as an approach that marries scholarly inquiry to any of the intellectual tasks that comprise the work of teaching – designing a course, facilitating classroom activities, trying out new pedagogical ideas, advising, writing student learning outcomes, evaluating programs (Shulman, 1998). When activities like these are undertaken with serious questions about student learning in mind, one enters the territory of the scholarship of teaching and learning. (p. 7)

Or, as Poole and Simmons (2013) summarize, "the overall intention of SoTL is thus to improve student learning and enhance educational quality" (p. 118).

The aims of action research also link it closely to transformative learning. Grundy (1988) notes three different modes of action research: technical, practical, and emancipatory. Technical action research seeks to improve the teaching strategies; practical action research includes the idea of improvement incorporating the participant's knowledge gain (possibly through collaboration); emancipatory implies action research that can improve more than the single situation at hand. Action research can thus facilitate stronger connections between theory and practice.

Action research is generative: That is to say, specific directions to pursue in subsequent phases are uncovered as the research progresses. The study must be viewed through a lens of theory-building rather than one of theory-testing. Royer (2002) articulates the unique approach of this type of research: "Unlike traditional hypothesis-based research, the research question emerges as action research progresses" (p. 235). Themes of significance emerge through data analysis; while some of these themes are expected to derive from the study purpose, others emerge from the data. The original research question may be revised several times as the study progresses.

3 Collaborative/Participatory Action Research

Collaborative or participatory action research, in which participants/ researchers collaborate through cycles of plan-act-observe-reflect, provides both participant and researcher with a sounding board for reflection as well as a second opinion on that reflection, such that they become critical friends (Carr & Kemmis, 1986).

> Outside facilitators form cooperative relationships with practitioners, helping them to articulate their own concerns, plan strategic action for change, monitor the problems and effects of changes, and reflect on the value and consequences of the changes actually achieved. (Carr & Kemmis, 1986, p. 203)

Kompf (1993) writes of the possibility that collaborative reflection may uncover deeper meaning in the reflection since "this type of research interaction involves higher levels of meaningful exchange" (p. 519). Participation in a collaborative action research project can also provide the faculty member participants with a support system and can facilitate moving towards an improvement in practice. "In action research, participation is a requirement; it generates greater commitment and increases the likelihood of action" (Royer, 2002, p. 234).

Thus, the opportunity for collaboration between the researcher and the participant can bring strength and breadth to the research process. Interpretations made from the data can be examined by both and plans for further practice can benefit from collaborative brainstorming, bringing together divergent perspectives and acknowledges the fundamental truths in each (Creswell, 1998; Guba & Lincoln, 1988).

The symbiotic relationship between researcher and practitioner can also be useful for reducing the blindfold of perceptual filters, which Noffke (1995) has cited as one of the drawbacks of practitioner action research: "Action research may help practitioners 'to know' that their practice is successful. Yet ... it may only reveal those parts of education that they are positioned to see" (p. 7). Collaboration in the research process seeks to diminish this natural limitation by providing a continual process of review and feedback between researcher and participant. Research by outsiders runs, by its very nature, the risk of being divorced from the reality of the participants' perspectives; collaborative action research involves participants in determining the outcomes.

There is a further important aspect of action research, which is the empowerment of those involved as participants. Empowerment can be viewed in terms of improvement in conditions for those who may have been marginalized; it can also be viewed in terms of knowledge gain. As Grundy and Kemmis (1981) summarized, "There are two essential aims of all action research activity: to improve and to involve" (p. 84).

Bringing a slightly different perspective, Whitford et al. (1997) discuss two themes of action research. "One theme concerns the relationship between reflection and action. A second theme emphasizes collaboration as a means of linking reflection and action." (p. 151). This linkage represents the learning that is possible through action research, or what I term learning-in-action. That learning is possible for both the researcher and participants, who become a team seeking to address a teaching and learning issue.

"Action research ... therefore precipitates collaborative involvement in the research process, in which the research process is extended towards including all those involved in, or affected by, the action" (Carr & Kemmis, 1986, p. 199). Students, teaching assistants, colleagues, faculty developers, and administrators can all play roles as collaborative partners and therefore contribute to the communicative learning process. Action research thus "creates a forum for group self-regulation which transforms communities of self-interest into learning communities" (Kemmis, 1980). Sammon (2003) sees action research as providing a supportive framework for change implementation. "Faculty, students, and administrators may find action research useful in their attempts to gain support and minimize resistance by engaging significant people in defining, planning and implementing changes" (p. 4). In this way, the collaboration amongst teaching professionals parallels the principles of collaboration amongst students.

In summary, what collaboration brings to the research process is "a co-enquirer who could address complexities of teaching alongside the mentee within a spirit of open enquiry" (Stofflett, 1998, p. 3). Clear negotiation of roles before beginning the process can assist in strengthening the relationship and avoiding difficulties. Carr and Kemmis (1986) position the researcher as a facilitator whose "role is Socratic: to provide a sounding-board against which practitioners may try out ideas and learn more about the reasons for their own action, as well as learning more about the process of self-reflection" (p. 203).

4 Action Research Case Study: Online Learning Communities in a Science Course

To illustrate the process of action research, I will outline an example in which a researcher partnered with a faculty member on a joint project. I (the researcher) was interested in examining the cycles of reflective practice of one practitioner (the participant faculty member) as she moved through an academic term while undertaking a new teaching initiative: implementing online learning communities as an additional component in a large face-to-face science course. The study grew out of my awareness of two key points from reading the literature and from discussions with practitioners I was working with at the time. First, some faculty members are motivated to create online learning communities, seeing them as a way of providing constructivist learning opportunities that will engage students, particularly within a large class setting. Second, there may be little in the way of support for faculty to implement these new teaching initiatives and they may have little awareness of where to begin.

Kemmis and McTaggert's (1982) "four moments of action research" of "plan, act, observe, and reflect" (p. 7) gave rise to the study process:

1. Plan. Researcher and participant created a strategic plan for implementation that empowered participant to be more effective (p. 8).
2. Act. Participant implemented the plan, allowing flexibility and openness to change (p. 9).
3. Observe. Participant observed and documented the effects of the action on her practice. Observations related to planned categories but were responsive and open-minded (p. 9).
4. Reflect. Researcher and participant reflected on their insights through the cycle.

"Through discourse, reflection leads to the reconstruction of the meaning of the social situation and provides the basis for the revised plan" (Kemmis & McTaggert, 1982, p. 9).

In addition to the four stages in the cycle, Kemmis and McTaggert (1982) recommend an initial meeting, which they refer to as the "reconnaissance stage," to clarify goals and process or "to define the field of action" (p. 21). This term has meaningful application to each of the subsequent cycle planning meetings, as the roots of the word 'reconnaissance' are both getting to know again, and rebirth (Dubois, Keen, & Shuey, 1975, pp. 189, 226). In this way, action can be taken, observations noted, reflections made, and the idea reborn into a new plan.

At an initial meeting, therefore, we established and clarified our shared goals for the process and created an initial action plan for implementation. During this meeting, we reviewed the indicator list I had researched and compiled for creating successful online learning communities. I created some initial questions for this meeting (see Appendix A for these and other guiding questions). I also asked the participant to be mindful of the indicators of successful learning communities and to continuously reflect on the path towards achieving these indicators throughout the study term, but that these lists should not be viewed as comprehensive and that the generative nature of the study should yield additional indicators to be included in subsequent cycles. During this meeting, we also clarified the research process and respective researcher and participant roles and reviewed the ethics details. We further created a schedule for the rest of our meetings to follow the student posting dates as outlined in her syllabus. See Table 8.1 for the detailed plan.

Through the rest of the term, we met as noted in Table 8.1; these meetings were used as the *reflect* and *plan* stages of each cycle. While we started with an informal question list (Appendix A), we remained open to pursuing other paths as they arose. At each meeting, we reviewed the plan, act, and observe stages of the cycle and the participant's progress against the study indicators. Our notes and reflections from previous meetings became the data summaries that I reviewed for emerging themes and categories. In addition, I had asked the participant to keep a journal of insights about any aspect of the process, and in particular, "experiences in ... carrying out action research" (Stevenson et al., 1995, p. 61), which in this case was her progress towards implementing online learning communities and factors that affected that path. I also kept a research log and reflective journal to track issues, challenges, and insights that arose during the process. Specifically, I noted questions arising from the raw data for inclusion in subsequent meetings.

In our final meeting, we discussed the degree to which the goals and indicators were met, to review the process of reflective practice and collaboration as applied to implementing online learning communities, and to discuss the participant's overall learning. I developed a set of questions from Lock and Munby (2000) to guide this interview (see Appendix A) and added questions that arose from previous data collection and analysis.

Table 8.1 sets out the chronology of the process following the plan, act, observe, and reflect cycle. The time-lapse between the last reflection cycle and the date for the final interview was intended to accommodate end-of-term review and exams and to allow the participant time to include these activities in reflecting on the overall process.

TABLE 8.1   Timelines for action research cycles

Cycle	Date	Cycle stage	Notes
Pre	Sept 15	Pre	First meeting. Negotiated process. Discussed indicators.
1	Sept 15	Plan	Plan for first cycle.
	Sept 15–Oct 1	Act	Participant implements first stage of plan.
	Sept 15–Oct 1	Observe	Participant makes journal entries re: effects of plan.
	Oct 1	Reflect	Meeting to discuss observations, effects of plan.
2	Oct 1	Plan	Review data, revise goals per observations and insights.
	Oct 2–Oct 21	Act	Participant implements second stage of plan.
	Oct 2–Oct 21	Observe	Participant makes journal entries re: effects of plan.
	Oct 22	Reflect	Meeting to discuss observations, effects of plan.
3	Oct 22	Plan	Review data, revise goals.
	Oct 23–Nov 3	Act	Participant implements third stage of plan.
	Oct 23–Nov 3	Observe	Participant makes journal entries re: effects of plan.
	Nov 4	Reflect	Meeting to discuss observations, effects of plan.
4	Nov 4	Plan	Review data, revise goals.
	Nov 5–Nov 18	Act	Participant implements fourth stage of plan.
	Nov 5–Nov 18	Observe	Participant makes journal entries re: effects of plan.
	Nov 19	Reflect	Meeting to discuss observations, effects of plan.
5	Nov 19	Plan	Review data, revise goals.
	Nov 20–Dec 2	Act	Participant implements fifth stage of plan.
	Nov 20–Dec 2	Observe	Participant makes journal entries re: effects of plan.
	Dec 3	Reflect	Meeting to discuss observations, effects of plan.
Post	Jan 17	Post	Deconstruction interview to review process and insights.

One of the strengths of using action research was that the study's key findings arose directly from the iterative process. By meeting with the participant several times over the academic term, it was possible to see that the participant's growth through the process fit with Mezirow's (1991) model of transformative learning. This learning occurred in three areas. First, she demonstrated instrumental learning as she planned and improved her development of online learning communities. She became aware of constraints on that process such as workload and lack of institutional supports or time to use those that did exist. Her learning in this regard helped her to identify aspects of her own management of the constraints that might be a hindrance. Second, she demonstrated communicative learning that occurred as a result of her interactions with others, including students, teaching assistants, and the researcher. She saw her own needs for feedback and interaction more clearly as they were highlighted by her communications with other process partners. Third, she demonstrated emancipatory learning in her learning about herself. She revisited and questioned the suitability of her process goals, developed personal confidence in implementing new strategies, and came to value the benefits she derived from the collaborative aspect of the research process.

5   Negotiating Roles and Responsibilities

In the example study, the participant's role was to reflect critically on the progress towards the goal of creating online learning communities. The researcher's role was to support and participate in that critical reflection by providing a sounding board, by asking provocative questions, and by guiding the participant through the stages of action research. The researcher provided data analysis for review with the participant and guided discussion interviews around emerging themes and their implication for planning further action phases. As the study progressed, it was intended that the locus of control and responsibility for the collaborative meetings would move towards the participant, such that the participant took a greater role in guiding the reflective process and the planning stage (Mitchell, 1995, p. 248); see Table 8.2 for specifics of this process.

The role of the researcher in action research is one of a 'critical friend' who provides a sounding board for the research process. The concept originated with Carr and Kemmis (1986), who describe a critical friend as someone who helps "'insiders to act more wisely, prudently and critically in the process of transforming education" (p. 161). In the words of Costa and Kallick (1993), a critical friend is "a trusted person who asks provocative questions, provides data to be examined through another lens, and offers critique of a person's work as a friend" (p. 50). Costa and Kallick (1993) summarize the responsibilities of critical friend and participant during the research cycles. Initially, the participant describes an area of practice and asks for feedback. The critical friend asks questions for clarification. The participant then sets the direction for feedback, and the critical friend provides feedback about significant points of the area of practice. The critical friend then asks further questions and critiques the work, and both critical friend and participant reflect and write about the meeting.

> The success of the work of such 'critical friends' is to be measured in the extent to which they can help those involved in the educational process to improve their own educational practices, their own understandings, and the situations and institutions in which they work. (Carr & Kemmis, 1986, p. 161)

This positions the researcher as an integral part of the collaborative research process, but with a clearly defined role:

> Qualitative researchers believe that the researcher's ability to interpret and make sense of what he or she sees is critical for an understanding of any social phenomenon. In this sense, the researcher is an instrument in much the same way that a sociogram, rating scale, or intelligence test is an instrument. (Leedy & Ormrod, 2001, p. 147)

It is the responsibility of the researcher to view that role with respect and to allow the participant's story to be the one that is heard in the data.

6 Smoothing the Ethics Approval Process

Obtaining research ethics permission can be a further potential challenge to planning timelines, but I argue it is one that is easily addressed by careful clarity. I knew that the 'lens within a lens' process, where the participant was researching her teaching process while I was researching her might be difficult for others to understand and I was quite keen to make sure ethics approval was not delayed by any lack of clarity in my REB proposal. While the REB form asks only for a "brief, sequential description of the methodology to be used in this study (approximately one page)," I felt more detail of the distinct roles and responsibilities of the researcher and participant would be useful to understanding the methodological process. Given that these roles shifted with each stage of the action research cycle, I decided to provide a chart so the REB committee could more clearly understand what was involved. I also provided an overview preamble of what was intended through the partnership process: the study methodology will follow several cycles of collaborative action research as outlined by Kemmis and McTaggert (1982), who present a four-stage model of ongoing cycles of Plan, Act, Observe, and Reflect. The participant has responsibility for the act and observes stages, while the researcher, in the role of active facilitator, works collaboratively with the participant in the reflection stage, as well as facilitates initial planning stages. As the study progresses, the locus of control for the plan and reflection stages will shift towards the participant.

The chart as presented in Table 8.2 was provided with the research submission to clarify our roles.

TABLE 8.2 Overview of principal investigator and participant roles

Research stage	Details	Participant role	Researcher role
1. Initial Meeting	– Establish and clarify goals and process	– Participate in discussion around indicators and goals – Inform researcher of desired changes	– Provide indicator lists as starting point for discussion – Audiotape (and subsequently transcribe) meeting – Begin and maintain a research log to track issues, challenges, and insights that arise during study process
2. Plan	– Create initial plan for implementing online learning communities.	– Form an initial plan for implementation of online learning communities	– Facilitate discussion around goal implementation – Provide literature as requested by participant – Maintain research log
3. Act	– Implementation of initial plan	– Implement the plan	– Available if needed as a sounding board – Group and analyze data from previous meeting and prepare summary of themes to inform discussion at next reflection/planning meeting – Maintain research log

(*cont.*)

TABLE 8.2   Overview of principal investigator and participant roles (*cont.*)

Research stage	Details	Participant role	Researcher role
4. Observe	– Observations of implemented plan	– Record observations in a written journal	– Available if needed as a sounding board – Subsequently group and analyze journal entries for subsequent reflection and planning meeting – Maintain research log
5. Reflection	– Reflect on process as implemented and observed	– Participate in discussion regarding observation of implementation – Discuss compelling as well as progress along stages of reflective practice – Review and purge data analysis	– Facilitate discussion regarding themes that have emerged from journal and previous meeting transcript analysis – Audiotape (and subsequently transcribe) meeting – Subsequently group and analyze transcript for recurring and compelling themes – Maintain research log
Repeat 2–5	– As above (2–5)	– As above (2–5); locus of control for reflection and planning meetings shifts towards participant as study progresses	– As above (2–5); facilitates a shift of locus of control to participant as study progresses.

(*cont.*)

TABLE 8.2 Overview of principal investigator and participant roles (cont.)

Research stage	Details	Participant role	Researcher role
Final interview	– Reflect on overall study process and success at achieving indicators	– Participate in discussion around degree to which goals and indicators have been met, and review the process of collaboration and reflective practice	– Facilitate discussion as needed – Audiotape (and subsequently transcribe) meeting – Subsequently analyze transcript for recurring and compelling themes – Maintain research log
Document review	– Review and purge documents and study report	– Review and purge documents and study report	– Make amendments as indicated by participant

I also note that having this document was extremely useful in the role negotiation process and the participant's input was invaluable.

7   Challenges of Collaborative Action Research

As with any methodology choice, researchers and participants must make their own careful decisions about what is involved in this style of research. "Reform initiatives have pressed teachers toward collaboration and collegiality with a fervor that far outstrips our present understanding of the conditions, character, and consequences of such relationships" (Little & McLaughlin, 1993, p. 2). While we each expressed our strong satisfaction with our research partnership (and have presented on the study since), we were and continue to be aware of some inherent challenges that invited careful consideration. These potential challenges include how participants are chosen, the additional workload for the participant, negotiating roles, and determining ownership.

7.1   Select Participant(s)

The question of action research process ownership is tied to the importance of voluntary participation in the collaborative endeavor and is critical to its success. Forced collaboration, in which participants are required to work together with little thought given to a suitable match of beliefs or goals is unlikely to lead to success, regardless of the amount of role negotiation. At the same time, practitioners who may benefit from collaborative opportunities for professional development may not come forward to participate. Altrichter (1993) points out this potential weakness in the model: "Its insistence on voluntary participation and its attraction to innovative, professional teachers repels, at the same time, less innovative, less professional teachers. Thus, action research is in constant danger of elitism" (p. 53).

In addition, there can be a limitation inherent in using only one participant. As Mitchell (1995) notes, "because action research projects tend to be conducted in unique settings, the results cannot be generalized, nor can they be replicated" (p. 60). Practitioners must decide for themselves, after reading the description of the study context, whether the results pertain to their own setting. Having said that, we learn from others' stories, so rich accounts of an educator's learning about their own teaching can and will be informative to others. It becomes important, therefore, in writing up any study, to include enough detail of the context that others can see the ways in which the findings may be relevant to their own situation.

7.2   Consider Workload

The demands of a busy academic life may make simply participating in the research challenging. Grundy and Kemmis (1981) write of this concern:

> It should be noted in this context that participation in action research adds further demands to the work of busy practitioners, and that techniques need to be made accessible to practitioners so that action research can be carried out with the least possible disturbance to practice itself. (p. 94)

With any added project comes additional workload for the practitioner, which will likely be added to an already overfull schedule. Not only may reflection time and meetings be difficult to fit into the available time, but they may also take longer than anticipated. For example, in our study, six cycles of practice had been planned, but that was adjusted to five to accommodate a delayed start in getting students online and into group discussions as well as to adjust to the ongoing student discussion deadlines. In addition, while the participant had been keen to keep a reflective journal, it became one task too many, and rather than the rich narrative she had been hoping for, it became a folder to house her myriad post-it notes of thoughts on the fly. The researcher and participant must both be careful to view these variances as minor adjustments to the study process required by the circumstances rather than any kind of failure of the study process, or worse, their relationship.

7.3 Negotiate Roles

Clear negotiation of roles and goals will be critical to the success of the collaborative venture, but not everyone is an effective negotiating partner. Some may have difficulty expressing or even understanding personal aims, while others may feel powerless against an older, more experienced, or simply more forceful partner. In addition, goals may (and perhaps should) change throughout the process; this change may not always be immediately apparent to or even welcomed by the collaborators. As Mitchell (2001) points out, "from both a psychological and sociological perspective, it is probably safe to assume that the original purpose of a study or the initial collaborative planning will seldom, if ever, suffice" (p. 32). Roles and goals must be revisited throughout the process, and all collaborative partners must be attentive to their changing nature.

7.4 Determining Ownership

A central concern with collaborative action research is the possibility that the work will be owned by the researcher rather than by the participants. "When 'facilitators work with teachers and others in establishing teacher-research projects, they often create circumstances under which project control is not in teachers' hands" (Carr & Kemmis, 1986, p. 202). This is not in keeping with the spirit of action research, which seeks to involve the participant in the research and progressively to hand control over. This is also essential to any Scholarship of Teaching and Learning work, as one intended outcome is to position the faculty member as researcher in their own classroom.

"Lewin documented the effects of group decision in facilitating and sustaining changes … and emphasized the value of involving participants in every phase of the action research process" (Carr & Kemmis, 1986, p. 163). This shared responsibility is key to the process of collaborative constructivism. Kompf (1993) writes that "co-determination of processes and procedures emphasize the collaborative spirit between research and study participants. Imposition of meaning on research protocols becomes a shared responsibility between co-scientists" (p. 519). As Smits (1988) reminds researchers,

Questions of how the research is to be done, what is to be done and who is to do it perhaps need to be preceded with opening such questions for discussion, uncovering various meanings and interpretations people hold about the process, their positions, expectations and so forth (p. 19).

Whitford et al. (1997) present room painting as a metaphor for the usual roles of practitioner and consultant researcher. While practitioners are often in the situation of acting without planning that action or reflecting upon it afterward, "researchers must spend their lives saying, 'ready … ready … ready' … it's sort of like thinking about what color to paint a room but never getting to paint it" (p. 165). To extend their metaphor, in contrast, practitioners might spend significant time throwing paint on a canvas and hoping the effect will be pleasing. The goal in collaborative research is to strengthen the connections between the two – but that does not mean it will always be as smooth as we were lucky enough to experience!

Another potential challenge (which we happily did not face) is that the participant, having determined improvements to practice, may be reluctant to implement them. This can happen, as Lock and Munby (2000) found, because the recommended improvements are at odds with the participant's philosophy about teaching; it can also happen because the workload and other stresses of the term do not always make space for making instructional improvements.

8   Summary

Careful consideration of each of these areas: selecting a participant, making plans to deal with the extra workload for the participant, negotiating roles, and determining ownership of the study findings can result in a successful action research or Scholarship of Teaching and Learning partnership, as shown in Figure 8.1.

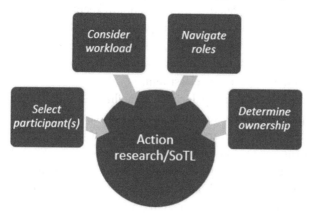

FIGURE 8.1   Navigating potential challenges to participatory action research/SoTL

9   Moving Forward

In this chapter, I have described action research and collaborative (or participatory) action research, and detailed the steps involved in negotiating a successful participatory action research or jointly owned Scholarship of Teaching and Learning study. I point out that the detailed account of roles that smoothed the research ethics process also provided a prompt to careful discussion with the participant of what each of our roles would comprise and how the ownership for the study process would shift from me, the researcher, to the participant faculty member over the duration of our work. I also point to the four areas that threatened our success but that we managed to navigate: careful selection of a participant, acknowledging and working around the extra workload for the participant, negotiating roles with great clarity, and determining ownership of the research process and findings.

Areas for potential future research arise. For example, we found our collaborative research partnership transformed both participant and researcher. The participant in this study was predominantly a social reflective practitioner rather than one who preferred reflection in isolation. The same was true for the researcher. Further research could examine whether this preference is linked to other contributory factors. In addition, it would be interesting to study ways in which action researchers are professionally and personally transformed through their involvement in the collaborative research process. Further research might suggest a model in which practitioners become involved as a critical friend in someone else's work in order to experience transformative learning.

Mitchell and Sackney (2000) wrote of Ferdinand Magellan's circumnavigation of the world and the significant change in perceptions that resulted from the realization of the loss of 24 hours during the trip. No longer could scholars believe the sun revolved around the earth; a new model was indicated of the earth and planets revolving around the sun. This historical event provides an inherent metaphor for the benefits of collaborative action research and SoTL. What strikes me most profoundly is that the moment was dependent on two separate groups of people: those who left to make the journey and those who had stayed behind. It was only through discussion with those who did not complete the circumnavigation that the knowledge of the loss of the 24 hours became apparent. Without the second group, no one would have noticed the date change nor realized its implications. This is the strength of collaborative research efforts: Different individuals or groups bring their unique skills such that some can provide the experience and others can act as sounding boards and point out the discoveries.

References

Altrichter, H. (1993). The concept of quality in action research: Giving practitioners a voice in educational research. In M. Schratz (Ed.), *Qualitative voices in educational research* (pp. 40–55). The Falmer Press.

Battaglia, C. (1995). Confused on a higher level about more important things. In S. Noffke & R. Stevenson (Eds.), *Educational action research: Becoming practically critical* (pp. 74–91). Teachers College Press.

Carr, W., & Kemmis, S. (1986). *Becoming critical: Education, knowledge and action research*. The Falmer Press.

Costa, A. L., & Kallick, B. (1993). Through the lens of a critical friend. *Educational Leadership, 51*(2), 49–51.

Creswell, J. W. (1998). *Qualitative inquiry and research design: Choosing among five traditions*. Sage Publications.

Dubois, M., Keen, D. J., & Shuey, B. (1975). *Larousse's French-English/English-French dictionary*. Simon & Schuster of Canada Ltd.

Elliot, J. (1991). *Action research for educational change*. Open University Press.

Ferraro, J. (2000). *Reflective practice and professional development*. Eric Clearinghouse on Teaching and Teacher Education.

Grundy, S. (1988). Three modes of action research. In S. Kemmis (Ed.), *The action research reader* (3rd ed., pp. 353–364). Deakin University Press.

Grundy, S., & Kemmis, S. (1981). Educational action research in Australia: The state of the art (an overview). In S. Kemmis (Ed.), *The action research reader* (3rd ed., pp. 83–97). Deakin University Press.

Hutchings, P., Huber, M., & Ciccone, A. (2011). *The Scholarship of Teaching and Learning reconsidered*. Jossey-Bass.

Kemmis, S. (1980). *Action research in retrospect and prospect*. Paper presented to the annual meeting of the Australian Association for Research in Education (Sydney, Australia, November 6–9, 1960). Retrieved from https://files.eric.ed.gov/fulltext/ED200560.pdf

Kemmis, S., & McTaggert, R. (1982). *The action research planner* (2nd ed.). Deakin University Press.

Kolb, D. (1984). Experiential learning: *Experience as the source of learning and development*. Prentice Hall.

Kompf, M. (1993). Ethical considerations in teacher disclosure: Construing persons and methods. *Teaching and Teacher Education, 9*(5–6), 519–528.

Leedy, P. D., & Ormrod, J. E. (2001). *Practical research: Planning and design*. Merrill Prentice Hall.

Lincoln, Y. S., & Guba, E. G. (1985). *Naturalistic inquiry*. Sage.

Little, J., & McLaughlin, M. (1993). Introduction: Perspectives on cultures and contexts of teaching. In J. Little & M. McLaughlin (Eds.), *Teachers' work: Individuals, colleagues and contexts* (pp. 1–8). Teachers College Press.

Lock, C., & Munby, H. (2000). Changing assessment practices in the classroom: A study of one teacher's challenge. *The Alberta Journal of Educational Research, 46*(3), 267–279.

Mezirow, J. (1991). *Transformative dimensions of adult learning.* Jossey-Bass.

Mitchell, C. (1995). *Teachers learning together: Organizational learning in an elementary school* (Unpublished doctoral dissertation). University of Saskatchewan, Saskatoon, Canada.

Mitchell, C. (2001). Negotiating agendas in collaborative research. In M. Richards, A. Elliot, V. Woloshyn, & C. Mitchell (Eds.), *Collaboration uncovered: The forgotten, the assumed, and the unexamined in collaborative education* (pp. 31–46). Bergin & Garvey.

Mitchell, C., & Coltrinari, H. (2001). Journal writing for teachers and students. In T. Barer-Stein & M. Kompf (Eds.), *The craft of teaching adults* (pp. 21–38). Irwin.

Noffke, S. (1995). Action research and democratic schooling: Problematics and potentials. In S. Noffke & R. Stevenson (Eds.), *Educational action research: Becoming practically critical* (pp. 1–10). Teachers College Press.

Poole, G., & Simmons, N. (2013). The contributions of the scholarship of teaching and learning to quality enhancement in Canada. In G. Gordon & R. Land (Eds.), *Quality enhancement in higher education: International perspectives* (pp. 118–128). Routledge.

Royer, R. (2002). Supporting technology integration through action research. [Electronic version]. *The Clearing House, 75*(5), 233–237.

Sammon, S. (2003). *Good idea, but no results? Action research as a method for implementing change and addressing resistance* [Abstract]. Proceedings of the Society of Teaching and Learning in Higher Education, Canada.

Schön, D. (1983). *The reflective practitioner.* Basic Books.

Smits, H. (1988). The question of collaboration. In T. Carson & J. C. Couture (Eds.), *Collaborative action research: Experiences and reflections. No. 18. Improvement for Instruction Series.* The Alberta Teacher's Association.

Stevenson, R., Noffke, S., Flores, E., & Granger, S. (1995). Teaching action research: A case study. In S. Noffke & R. Stevenson (Eds.), *Educational action research: Becoming practically critical* (pp. 60–73). Teachers College Press.

Stofflett, R. T. (1998). Putting constructivist teaching into practice in undergraduate introductory science. *Electronic Journal of Science Education, 3*(2), 1–12.

Whitford, B. L., Schlechty, P. C., & Shelor, L. G. (1997). Sustaining action research through collaboration: Inquiries for invention. *Peabody Journal of Education, 64*(3), 151–169.

Appendix A: Questions to Guide Interviews

Questions to Guide the Initial Meeting (developed from sample selection criteria, and Kemmis & McTaggert, 1982)
1. What factors have contributed to your readiness to create online learning communities?
2. How would you describe your philosophy around creating online learning communities?
3. What challenges do you anticipate?
4. What goals do you visualize?
5. What questions do you have?

Questions to Guide Reflection (Reconnaissance) Meetings (Battaglia, 1995, p. 86)
1. What patterns or principles have emerged for you as a result of this process?
2. What does this affirm for you?
3. What has this meeting caused you to think about?
4. What are you taking away from this meeting?
5. Where will you go from here?
6. What role would you like me to play?

In addition, the questions guiding the reflective journal entries below also served to guide the discussion as well as questions suggested by the participant.
Questions to Guide the Final Interview (developed from Lock & Munby, 2000)
1. What was the effect of contextual influences on this process?
2. How did your philosophical approach affect the outcomes you sought to implement?
3. What effects did the collaborative process have on your success at achieving goals?
4. Additional questions such as emerge from the action research cycles will be added.

Questions to Guide Journal Entries (Battaglia, 1995, p. 84; Mitchell & Coltrinari, 2001, pp. 25–31)
   Narrative or descriptive reflection
1. What parts of the plan have I implemented? What worked well and what didn't? Why did it work well?
2. What was the student response? What strategies did I use that positively affected their learning?

Metacognitive, analytic, evaluative, and reconstructive reflection

1. What is my philosophy of teaching in online environments and where did it come from? How is it different from or related to my philosophy of face-to-face teaching? How comfortable am I with moving towards being a 'guide on the side' versus a 'sage on the stage'? Why did I choose the plan that I did?
2. How do I perceive my role in facilitating online learning communities? What connections have I noticed between my perception, my plan and implementation?
3. How does my institutional culture support or hinder my planning and implementation? What institutional factors affected my process toward creating online learning communities?
4. How aware was I of students' reactions to my plan? In what way did that awareness affect my implementation, observation, reflection, and subsequent plans?
5. What problems have been resolved, and what problems have not? Are there new problems?
6. How have I responded when things didn't proceed according to my plan? What effect does my reaction have on my subsequent observe, reflect, plan, and act stages?
7. How comfortable am I being honest with myself about my teaching practice? How open am I to plans for change? How open am I to being questioned about my teaching practices?
8. When does the process seem easy, and when does it seem difficult?
9. If I had to do it again, what would I do differently? What changes do I think might be necessary in my plans and responses? What worked and what did not, and how do I distinguish the two?
10. What differences do I see between anticipated outcomes and realized outcomes? To what do I attribute this?

CHAPTER 9

Making Learning Visible: Research Methods to Uncover Learning Processes

Klodiana Kolomitro, Corinne Laverty and Elizabeth A. Lee

Abstract

This chapter addresses qualitative methods that enable educators to examine the learning processes of individuals. The cognitive skills enacted during moments of interpretation, understanding, and thinking are not immediately observable to teachers, although we assume they are taking place. Is it possible to slow down and capture these invisible thought processes by documenting them verbally or visually as they occur? We describe methods used to make learning visible, specifically using think-alouds, where verbalization reveals mental thought processing, and mind mapping, where thinking is recorded visually. The first case describes the use of think-alouds with second-year anatomy students to uncover problem-solving approaches in a multiple-choice test with the goal of designing higher-order thinking questions. The second case draws on mind maps, collaborative dialogue, and video documentation with graduate students to better enable the in-depth elaboration of research topics. The research methods in these two studies helped participants to break down and articulate active thinking steps. The resulting analysis can better enable educators to understand the learning that individuals apply to complex tasks which contributes to how we teach learning tasks and the multi-faceted steps they comprise.

Keywords

think-aloud – visible learning – multiple-choice questions – anatomy – mind-mapping – thinking processes – visualization – verbalization – cognitive skills

1   Using Think-Alouds to Explore Problem-Solving Procedures for Anatomy Students

This case study presents the use of think-alouds as a powerful qualitative method to unravel student thought processes as they complete multiple-choice assessments in anatomy. Multiple-choice assessments in the anatomical sciences are often perceived to be targeting recall of facts and regurgitation of trivial details. Moving away from this assumption requires the design of purposeful multiple-choice questions that focus on higher-order cognitive functions as opposed to rote memorization. In order to develop such questions, we needed to first understand the strategies that students use in solving multiple-choice questions. Our goal was to uncover patterns in the reasoning process that students used when solving multiple-choice questions. Our study required participants to verbalize their thought processes when solving six multiple-choice questions covering five key areas of anatomy. The multiple-choice questions targeted three levels of cognitive functioning based on the ICE framework (Fostaty Young & Wilson, 2000), which stands for *Ideas*, *Connections*, and *Extensions*. The ICE framework represents the gradual progression and growth of the learner towards deeper understanding. Ideas are the fundamental, distinct pieces of information that make up the building blocks of learning. Connections are the relationships that students can form among discrete ideas, and associating new concepts to prior learning. Extensions constitute creating new learning and applying knowledge to completely new and novel situations (Fostaty Young & Wilson, 2000).

2   Think-Alouds as Our 'Best Fit for Purpose' Method

We chose the think-aloud interview (Ericsson & Simon, 1984) as the initial approach to gathering data as it provided an opportunity to obtain rich, deep, and descriptive information from the participant's perceptions, meanings, and misconceptions in solving multiple-choice questions. This was the most suitable methodology to help us answer the following research question: What procedures do students use to solve multiple-choice anatomical questions? Through think-alouds, we were aiming to uncover the thinking patterns and strategies used by students and obtain rich insights into the choices students make as they encounter those choices. Think-alouds can be a powerful vehicle in making visible metacognitive processes that often remain hidden to learners. Studying metacognition has proved to be difficult as researchers cannot directly infer cognitive processes from observing behavior, and must take into account the specific context and mediating processes in play (Durning et al., 2013).

2.1 Data Collection

We recruited participants from a second-year undergraduate anatomy course offered in the winter semester and conducted think-aloud interviews with 10 participants. This was carried out to develop the framework for our later data collection using a survey. The one-on-one think-aloud interviews ranged from 40–60 minutes in length and were audio-recorded and transcribed. We used concurrent think-alouds which involve verbalizations taking place during the task, rather than articulating reflections after the task has been completed as would be the case in retrospective think-alouds. The focus was on the cognitive processes, rather than the final product, with the goal of making these processes as explicit as possible during task performance. Hence, students were frequently reminded that the purpose of the activity was not to evaluate whether they got the correct answer, but rather to articulate their thought processes as they interpreted the question and arrived at a conclusion. We were looking for patterns in the reasoning process that the participants used when solving the multiple-choice questions. Prior to the think-alouds, all students were asked to complete a practice activity in order to better understand the depth of responses that we were looking for in this study and to make students feel comfortable with this approach. The practice activity consisted of reading the following scenario: "You open the door to your apartment and need to put the milk you just bought in the fridge. What are the steps you take to complete this task?" Participants were asked to read the question and say aloud everything they were thinking as they were reading the question. After this practice and feedback session, participants were asked to read each multiple-choice question and follow a similar process. During the data collection, we were also considering how we might code the responses. We did not have standard questions, because we did not know how students would respond but the goal was to unpack student thinking.

2.2 Navigating Meaning

In order to be able to make sense of the students' thought processes and at the same time offer the 'right' level of probing, we designed a rubric with prompts corresponding to the different strategies that might be adopted by the students. We transcribed the think-alouds and followed the qualitative content analysis protocol (Patton, 1990) to identify operators that students followed when working through the multiple-choice questions. These operators explained the predominant reasoning processes used by the students. Once we became more clear and confident in these emerging procedures, we clustered similar coded units together into categories. This process helped us to compare segments of data and to confirm whether or not the data mapped onto existing categories (Charmaz, 2006). Next, we compared our list of categories to the ICE Framework and mapped the categories to the appropriate level in the ICE taxonomy. Responses to the individual think-aloud sessions were used to generate a survey that was distributed across anatomy courses at Queen's University. We analyzed and categorized reasoning processes that were used by the 82 students who responded to our survey as well as those 10 students who participated in the think-alouds. At the same time, we explored the relationship amongst the level of the question, the strategies that were being used, and the likeliness of students getting the answer correct.

Initially, we had contemplated interviews as an alternative to think-alouds; however, we rejected that format as it was important that the participants immediately verbalized their reaction to the question, rather than being given sufficient time to prepare an answer. Instantaneous feedback is a unique feature of think-alouds and it allowed us to capture thinking processes as they occurred. It also enabled us to see the different approaches students draw upon. Some focused on the connection between the content and their own knowledge: "what do I know about that," while others had a more holistic approach, "when I first read this means I need to choose what the question is demanding as opposed to what I know." Some students realized that the factual questions at the ideas-level were simple recall questions. One of the questions we had at the ideas-level asked the following: Fissures divide the lungs into, followed by four options to choose from ((a) lobules, (b) lobes, (c) alveolar sacs, and (d) segments). Most students instantaneously made comments similar to:

> I just like pick out certain words that kind of cue an answer, so what I noticed is I looked at the question and as soon as I saw "fissures" then I'm like "it has to be lobes" like just because like we have learned that fissures divide the lungs into lobes so I just automatically associate the word fissure with lobes.

Similarly, the other ideas-level questions asked students about trochlea and specifically which of the bones it was a part of. The students responded by noting that they remembered the bones, recalled the definition of trochlea, looked at the answer to refresh their memory, then they picked their answer out of the four options. At the same time, as instructors, we were reflecting on the purpose of those multiple-choice questions and whether our goal should have been to have students apply their learning rather than recall straight facts, then the questions would have been designed quite differently.

We were curious to find out if their problem-solving strategies changed as they encountered connections-type questions. Examples included: (1) The muscles that were most likely damaged if a 20-year-old patient cannot abduct and medially rotate the thigh while running and climbing; and (2) Finding the length of the sarcomere when given the length of the 'I' and 'A' bands. These types of case study questions are asking students to identify pertinent information, understand the context, and associate actions of the muscles with their proper function and intricacies of muscle contraction. As soon as the students started verbalizing their thought process, we were able to identify if connections were made as the think-aloud procedure allowed us to hear some of those associations amongst different ideas. We could hear them say: "First I went through the motions of abduction and medial rotation, like pictured it on my body" and

> I took a couple of seconds to just be like okay don't make an automatic assumption, then I went back and actually read the actual sentence, read out the answers and then I thought of pictures that I saw in the textbook and just knowing that the keywords in this were like "I band A band and sarcomere," then I associated the words with the diagram and I could just see the diagram in my head.

Another question triggered more complex thinking patterns: Kyphosis affects the structure of vertebrae causing forward rounding and abnormal curvature of the spine. Regarding the anatomy of the spine and associated axial skeleton, what may be the functional implications of this bony disorder? Answer options were: (a) shorter stature, (b) change in shape of the thoracic cavity, (c) odd shaped stomach, and (d) two of the above options. When students started to extrapolate and make predictions, we could infer that this type of question was more demanding and at the extensions-level. Many students remarked on the multiple thinking processes needed to answer the question, as exemplified by this quotation:

> the idea is that I am going to have to use a level of higher thinking, I'm going to have to integrate concepts that we have learned regarding the spine and apply it to a case that we haven't seen before.

Students were trying to think of people they knew that had such a condition to fully understand what this meant, and tried to predict what could happen in the future as a result of having this condition. This was highlighted by another student when they stated that:

> It's not something that we like may have explicitly went over, like what effects it has on the whole body, we just know what kyphosis is and what it does to the spine, so you kind of have to like assume from that what effects it has on the overall body, like we wouldn't have talked about the stomach or anything, we just have like pictures of the spine and which portions of the spine, so you would have to go above that and to see how that would look from the outside.

The students' answers revealed the procedures used and allowed us to associate these with a specific level of thinking as defined by the ICE model. It was a challenging process to probe the students as we felt somewhat limited in the amount of prompting we could do without distracting them from the act of thinking. We had to wait for what students had to say and honor their voice, but at the same time we were trying to understand their interpretations without making an assumption. In anticipation of some of these challenges, we created a rubric to help us identify patterns in students' thinking processes and also establish some clarity around what we were hearing (Table 9.1).

TABLE 9.1   Rubric created to capture strategies and prompts in solving multiple-choice questions

Clarifying	Restated or paraphrased the problem stem or one of the multiple-choice options.	What did you think when you first saw the question? What do you think the question is asking?
Comparing language of options	Detected similarities and differences in the language of two multiple-choice options.	What differences or similarities do you see in how the options are worded?
Correcting	Pointed out that they had been thinking incorrectly about the problem earlier in the written think-aloud and now see the correct way to think about the problem.	What don't you understand about this question?

(cont.)

TABLE 9.1 Rubric created to capture strategies and prompts in solving multiple-choice questions (cont.)

Delaying	Considered one of the multiple-choice options and decide that it should not be eliminated. Rather, the quality of that option should be evaluated later, after the other multiple-choice options are considered.	What are the steps you are taking to review the multiple-choice options? Will you come back to that option later?
Recognizing	Noted that a multiple-choice option is correct or incorrect without any rationale.	Noted an option as correct or incorrect.
Adding Information	Provided more information about one of the multiple-choice options, such as additional facts that were omitted or corrections to incorrect statements (i.e., presented incorrectly to serve as distractors).	Is there certain relevant information omitted from that option or presented as incorrect?
Asking a question	Asked a question about the problem stem or multiple-choice options.	Clarifying the question stem or multiple-choice options.
Checking	Explained why an option is correct or incorrect by comparing the option with their knowledge or with the data provided in the problem.	How does it fit in with what you already know?
Predicting	As an early step in the written think-aloud, predicted what they expected the answer to be (i.e., what multiple-choice option they were looking for).	What do you anticipate the answer to be?
Recalling	Retrieved basic facts or concepts from class, notes, or the textbook (i.e., declarative knowledge).	What do you know about this topic?
Visual presentation	Convert the written information to a visual that they have encountered previously	What images/pictures you create in your mind connected to the words you are reading?

3 Revisiting Think-Alouds as 'Best Fit for Purpose' Approach

Amongst the challenges experienced with this approach were: students' tendencies to get distracted and go off topic; their inability to vocalize their thoughts or provide in-depth information; finding the 'appropriate' level of researcher prompting; as well as the labor-intensive analysis process. Think-aloud procedures can be quite time consuming, and the participants need to have a model of what 'thinking aloud' looks like. One of the limitations of our study was not having an opportunity to meet with the students beforehand and properly mentor them on how to 'think-aloud.' The mentoring was done during the actual think-aloud and it might not have been sufficient for some students. As a result, while we identified several strategies used by the students, there might have been other thoughts or procedures that were not captured. Although we used the practice activity, there was a tendency for some participants to go off task, although with some gentle reminders we were able to redirect them to the task at hand. It was difficult to find what the 'right' amount of probing was. We noticed in the cases where we provided more prompts that the participants changed their subsequent performance on the task, which made us question the accuracy of the cognitive processes being investigated. We had to be careful with the amount of information we supplied and how much prompting to provide.

At the same time, in cases where students were shy or distracted, there was a need to supply more information. Although it was critical to understand their thought process, we did not want them to focus more on the verbal reports than the task at hand. We are mindful that the verbalized thoughts are attributed to working memory and do not always capture the automatic thoughts that might not necessarily be vocalized. It could also be possible that some students do not have the conceptual framework or vocabulary for describing the event in a way that helps us understand the processes at play. This poses another limitation for think-alouds. The think-aloud interview approach promised to provide rich, deep, and descriptive data from students as it allowed them to articulate their patterns of reasoning throughout the course of solving multiple-choice questions. This can make visible metacognitive processes that often remain hidden to both the participants and the researcher. In our case, the benefit of using think-alouds outweighed the challenges as only through this methodology would we have been able to uncover patterns in the reasoning process that students used when solving multiple-choice questions. A better understanding of students' decision-making processes can help us as educators redesign our assessment practices and offer better support for student learning.

4 Using Visual Mapping and Dialogue to Expand Concept Elaboration

The second case study used a qualitative paradigm involving three forms of data collection not commonly combined. The scenario was dialogue about a thesis topic among a graduate student, the thesis supervisor, and a research librarian. Visualization in the form of a mind map was used by the student to track the dynamic evolution of key ideas, concepts, and their inter-relationships. In tandem with the map construction, collaborative dialogue was used to unravel and clarify ideas. Sessions for five students (one male, five female) were videotaped and a survey was later distributed to gather feedback on the process.

This research emerged from the authors' practical experience of supporting graduate research at a Faculty of Education. One author is a librarian who assists graduate students in locating research materials. The other is a professor who supervises graduate theses using ongoing meetings to discuss research questions, methodology, and to set goals. The impetus for the study resulted from the librarian's experiences in research consultations using a mind map to record and clarify ideas, concepts, and resources. Students consistently requested their map for future reference triggering curiosity about the value of the interaction and the resulting visual aid. Both authors are instructors and the overarching goal for the study was to understand how to better support student information gathering and subsequent clarification of research topics. The research literature documents the need to support graduate information search processes (Catalano, 2013; Delaney & Bates, 2018; Spezi, 2016) and the mapping approach appeared to be a strategic tool to facilitate negotiating and sharing knowledge associated with these challenges (Hay et al., 2008). Drawing upon these experiences we sought to examine how visualization and dialogue interact to shape and extend student research topics. In particular:

- How do visual mapping and collaborative dialogue help students clarify and extend conceptions of their research?
- What aspects of verbal support enable students to extend their thinking during collaborative dialogue?

Research methods were selected on the basis of their similarity to authentic interactions between a graduate student, librarian, and thesis supervisor, and to mimic the context in which student-researcher interactions typically took place. Rather than adopt an approach providing reflection on a past event, such as a formal interview, the researchers wanted to capture the human and learning dynamics taking place in situ. We intended this approach to promote open and unscripted dialogue with the student enabling them to take the lead in setting conversation directions. Consequently, the study took place in the familiar setting of the library and combined the mind map and conversational style of both the librarian and supervisor.

Three forms of data collection were combined:
- Students independently created a mind map of their thesis topic using a concurrent think-aloud protocol (audio and videotaped with visual map)
- Collaborative dialogue between the student and researchers with continued student construction of the mind map (audio and videotaped with visual map)
- Follow-up survey of students' perceptions of the exercise

4.1   Selection of Research Methods

Our study combined a mind map, participant-researcher dialogue, video capture, and a survey. It was the first time we used the mind map and collaborative dialogue as data capture tools. The next sections of this chapter outline our reasons for choosing these methods and link them to the literature describing their functionality as techniques that help to make learning visible.

4.2   Visualization as Research Method

Capturing data visually was a key consideration in our study. Visual images are used in qualitative research to gather or interpret data and can be pre-existent or generated by the researcher and/or participant during an interview (Drew & Guillemin, 2014; Renfro, 2017). They can take the form of diagrams, videos, drawings, photographs, and maps (Weber, 2008). While interviews provide an opportunity to explore and probe themes of interest as they arise, they rely on mutual and immediate understanding and interpretation. As exchanges take place, previously discussed ideas recede while others claim a focus in the conversation. Given our limited capacity to recall aural information, it may be difficult to remember what was previously discussed and how it relates to the topic at hand. Listeners may not be aware of individual frameworks for prior knowledge and expert understanding nor do they have a way to illustrate shared understanding as it develops. Recording ideas visually offers a mechanism to make ideas transparent and to capture conversation over time, thereby enabling better communication, shared understanding, and depiction of data (Glegg, 2018). The English idiom 'a picture is worth a thousand words' captures the essence of this idea: complex thoughts can be translated into essential ideas through images.

Psychologists of cognition represent information in different forms (e.g., illustrations, diagrams, flow-charts, concept maps) to examine how they affect learning (Nesbit & Adesope, 2006). In this study, we used a free form of visual mapping (mind map) as the students were at an early stage in developing their research proposal. Traditional concept maps are difficult to make because they necessitate the identification and naming of ideas and their multiple relationships within a hierarchical structure that applies formal rules (Eppler, 2006). In his comparison of concept maps, mind maps, conceptual diagrams, and visual metaphors he ranked mind maps as "easy to learn and apply" versus concept maps "not easy to apply by novices; requires extensive training" (Eppler, 2006, p. 206). Mind maps allow a freer form of visual expression in which ideas and relationships are evolving and shifting. As a data collection tool mind maps provided an objective visual and permanent representation of the dynamic evolution of a student's thoughts and served as a focus for the collaborative dialogue. When individuals are asked to draw maps on the same topic at different stages of learning, changes in learning can be made visible (Hay, 2007). The collaborative construction of this type of diagram reveals both the underlying structure of a topic alongside deeper understandings captured during the idea elaboration process (Adesope & Nesbit, 2010).

4.3 Collaborative Dialogue

The use of multiple tools for data collection allowed us to better answer our research questions as each tool had benefits and limitations. Dialogue is auditory, impermanent, and linear while mapping is visual, permanent, and non-linear, while video-taping captured the changes in both. We viewed unstructured dialogue as a form of collaboration that "is the result of a continued attempt to construct and maintain a shared conception of a problem" (Roschelle & Teasley, 1995, p. 70). Although our scenario was naturalistic, the synchronous interaction did require intensive attention (Baker, 2015). One very pertinent observation during our dialogue was an awareness of Vygotsky's (1978) zone of proximal development (ZPD) in action. Vygotsky (1978) focused on the role of social interaction and the use of cultural tools (e.g. language, diagrams, and images) in the learning process. The ZPD refers to the learning that takes place when students interact with and receive support from partners who are more knowledgeable in an area. As the map changed during conversation, we observed knowledge being actively constructed first hand. The map evidenced clarification of new ideas and enhanced understanding of the inter-relationships among them through the extended focused discussion as outlined by Murphy et al. (2009). The reiterative mapping process encouraged revision of ideas and interaction among participants revealing the underlying topic structure and subsequent deeper understanding and co-construction of knowledge, as documented by other researchers (Basque & Pudelko, 2010; Bereiter & Scardamalia, 2012; Wells, 1999, 2002). Given that each interview lasted from 1–1.5 hours, it was important to remain focused on developing ideas without trying to solve specific issues such as decisions about research methods. This meant that researchers had to remain focused on the task at hand and acknowledge when the conversation was moving beyond its purpose, such as making concrete decisions for preferred research methods.

4.4   Visualization and Dialogue in Combination

Visualization combined with dialogue offers a dual approach to communicating shared understanding. Individuals' navigation of the external world is through the information gathered by their perceptual systems (Kellman, 2002). Dual coding theory (Pavio, 1986) argues that when visual and auditory stimuli are perceived simultaneously it is encoded in both the auditory and visual cortices and these are linked (Craik & Lockhart, 1972; Pavio, 1986). Perceptual information is processed in working memory which has a limited capacity for the number of items that can be kept active at one time, that is, the cognitive load (Sweller, 2011). This limitation means that only some of the information is transferred from working memory to long-term memory, the rest being discarded. Information that is processed together results in multiple pathways for long-term memory storage and retrieval, hence the benefit of dual coding (Baddeley, 2000; Pavio, 1986). In generating a mind map, an individual retrieves stored information from long-term memory and creates a visual representation of their conceptual understanding. The map transfers some of the cognitive load from working memory, freeing capacity in working memory for the continual retrieval of other aspects of a complex concept (Baddeley, 2000). The collaborative dialogue functioned in tandem with the map creation to enable the student to return to past ideas, connect new with old, and draw relationships among them as well.

4.5   Concurrent Think-Aloud as Research Method

As described previously, concurrent think-alouds invite students to articulate whatever comes to mind as they carry out a task (Afflerbach, 2000; Ericsson & Simon, 1980). This allows greater insight into individuals' active ongoing cognitive processes, that is, the content of their working memory in comparison to a summary after completing the task (retrospective think-aloud). Our study traced student prior knowledge and depiction of a topic and followed its elaboration during conversation. To differentiate between the two stages, we should have asked that a single black marker be used to illustrate the first map stage and then required other colors to express new ideas. This would have made it easier to distinguish between the independent map and the collaborative one. Fortunately, the transition was captured on videotape. Further discussion about the purpose of a mind map and practice in creating one using an everyday topic would also have helped as some students had little recent experience with the technique.

4.6 *Analysis and Interpretation of the Mind Maps*

The data collection methods appeared to be straightforward at the outset. What was unanticipated was how difficult it would be to code and then integrate three distinct data sets: transcripts of the dialogue, maps of the ideas, and the video of the process as it transpired which revealed moments when a specific aspect of the dialogue caused the student to make a change to the mind map.

Four formats of data were collected for each of the five students: audio transcript, mind map (Figure 9.1 provides an example of a before and after map), videotape, and survey. The analysis was completed in stages. The audio of the student think-aloud and follow-up collaborative dialogue was transcribed verbatim. Transcripts averaged 30 pages and were uploaded into NVivo (Version 11, 2015) for thematic analysis. The intention was to openly code the dialogue for significant categories and emerging patterns (Heath & Cowley, 2004; Glaser & Strauss, 1967). However, initial attempts to code the transcripts did not provide a coherent picture of the data. Each transcript was unique and addressed a different topic. It was difficult to determine what was relevant in the absence of seeing where a change was made to the map. In retrospect, what was missing was a framework for coding. We inadvertently came to this later in the analysis process. Consequently, we abandoned NVivo and switched to independently hand-coding transcripts in an attempt to identify emerging themes. This did not generate a coherent picture, but we could see that what transcripts had in common were discussions around different aspects of the research process. We then attempted a quantitative analysis of the independently generated map in comparison to the expanded map generated by counting map nodes and sub-nodes. However, given the complexity of some of the maps (Figure 9.1), this proved to be a dead-end because it did not inform our research questions regarding how the dialogue and visual mapping enabled clarification of the research topic. In an 'aha moment,' we realized that because we had five separate cases in which each student described a unique topic, it was difficult to find common themes across disparate content. We had failed to consider the interaction between the dialogue and the map as captured on video revealing student-initiated changes in response to the dialogue. This led to an analysis of the videotapes. We viewed each videotape and marked on the transcript whenever a change to the map was made. We then independently examined and highlighted each segment of dialogue that prompted the change. Collaboratively, we discussed the segments that elicited visual additions and categorized the types of dialogue that led them. These were referred to as 'prompts.' Further, re-reading and comparison enabled definitions for two types of prompts: clarifying and knowledge prompts. Clarifying prompts occurred when researchers asked questions to unravel the verbal description or visual representation given by the student. Knowledge prompts occurred when researchers offered information to extend student thinking or analysis. This proved to be the level of analysis needed to produce a meaningful picture of the data.

Following the analysis of the prompts, we returned to examining the data for commonalities across all cases. We identified the need for a coding framework that could be applied across transcripts. In stepping back from the detailed analysis, we decided to apply a standard social sciences model of research stages (Berg, 2001) as each case had this in common. Each researcher independently identified segments of the dialogue by the stages of the research process. Codes were compared resulting in three themes: defining the research question, information gathering and evaluation as part of the literature review, and study methodology. This employed a deductive model of analysis using a template method (Blair, 2015).

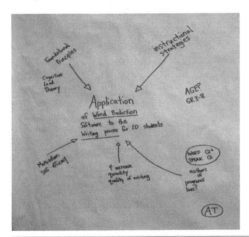

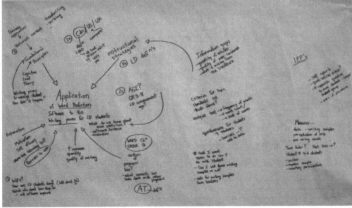

FIGURE 9.1   Student-generated maps. The first map was created independently by the student and the second map is the same map with additions made by the student at the close of the collaborative dialogue

5   Reflection on the Methods: Challenges and Benefits

The benefits of our methods were also the challenges. We were inspired by the notion of capturing learning as it happens, but were unprepared for the complexity of analysis.

Each student brought their own style to the mapping exercise and used a free form of visual representation. The dialogue was responsive to the student's map and the resulting ongoing changes to the map by the student. As we did not follow a script, each transcript was unique with different prompts and varying amounts of time spent on different aspects of the map. While this provided freedom and choice to the student, it resulted in greater difficulty in analysis. The first challenge was working with the different data formats: printed transcript, hand-drawn mind map, live-action video, and survey. Next, there was the need to code and analyze them as an integrated whole which required multiple iterations and approaches. With five distinct cases, we also needed to apply a common framework which was the research process model. Getting beyond the surface level representation in the mind maps was difficult and likely is why NVivo and the initial thematic coding attempts were not successful.

Multiple forms of data collection allowed for triangulation in data analysis. The dialogue prompted changes to the map and these were captured both visually and, over time, on the video enabling us to identify trigger points for student conceptual understanding; the survey data gave student perceptions of the process. Using an open-ended approach, mind maps and unscripted collaborative dialogue afforded each student the opportunity to represent their understanding and conceptualization of the thesis topic. Collaborative dialogue that followed the student's map and think-aloud provided a very rich dataset. Students were very engaged in the process because they generated the map that was the focal point of the collaborative dialogue. They were in control of the process, responding or not as they wished, to the prompts from the researchers that had been elicited by their map. The visual additions to the maps enabled us to capture the moments that had meaning to the students. Having five distinct cases provided unique perspectives on how students' conceptualize the research process. The extensive reiterative re-coding and consequent familiarity with the data eventually allowed us to perceive deeper levels of commonality across seemingly disparate cases. In response to the follow-up surveys, students were very positive stating that the visualization and dialogue enabled them to develop and deepen conceptualization of their topics.

6 Conclusions

This chapter focused on qualitative methods that helped make learning visible for both researchers and participants. In the first case, think-alouds allowed students to deconstruct their problem-solving strategies by articulating their thought processes in action. This enabled the researchers to identify types of strategies that aligned with different levels of sophistication in the multiple-choice questions. It also exposed cognitive biases, assumptions, and attitudes towards multiple-choice questions. In the second case, visualization offered study participants an opportunity to externalize some of their thoughts reducing cognitive load. The mind map served as a truncated form of expression offering a snapshot and consolidation of ideas using single words and phrases, unlike oral exchange in typical sentence format. Mind maps build an overarching picture of a multi-faceted concept and reveal the elaboration of ideas over time. Non-scripted collaborative dialogue changes the power dynamic from a typical interview making the student a conversation partner who directs discussion and consequently remains more engaged with the task.

The choice of data collection methodologies determined the analysis process and is a reminder that we keep the end in mind when selecting which forms of evidence are gathered. Researchers must anticipate how that evidence will inform their specific research questions. Research is an iterative process and this critical reflection on our work has similarly sparked further insights into our choice of methodologies.

References

Adesope, O. O., & Nesbit, J. C. (2010). A systematic review of research on collaborative learning with concept maps. In R. de Cassia Veiga Marriott & P. Lupion Torres (Eds.), *Handbook of research on collaborative learning using concept mapping* (pp. 238–251). Information Science Reference.

Afflerbach, P. (2000). Verbal reports and protocol analysis. In M. L. Kamil, P. B. Mosenthal, P. D. Pearson, & R. Barr (Eds.), *Handbook of reading research* (Vol. III, pp. 171–188). Lawrence Erlbaum.

Baddeley, A. (2000). The episodic buffer: A new component of working memory? *Trends in Cognitive Sciences, 4*(11), 417–423. doi.org/10.1016/S1364-6613(00)01538-2

Baker, M. J. (2015). Collaboration in collaborative learning. *Interaction Studies: Social Behaviour and Communication in Biological and Artificial Systems, 16*(3), 451–473.

Basque, J., & Pudelko, B. (2010). Intersubjective meaning-mapping in dyads using object-typed concept mapping. In R. de Cassia Veiga Marriott & P. Lupion Torres (Eds.), *Handbook of research on collaborative learning using concept mapping* (pp. 187–209). Information Science Reference.

Bereiter, C., & Scardamalia, M. (2012). Theory building and the pursuit of understanding in history, social studies, and literature. In J. Kirby & M. Lawson (Eds.), *Enhancing the quality of learning: Dispositions, instruction and learning* (pp. 160–177). Cambridge University Press.

Berg, B. L. (2001). *Qualitative research methods for the social sciences* (4th ed.). Allyn and Bacon.

Blair, E. (2015). A reflexive exploration of two qualitative data coding techniques. *Journal of Methods and Measurement in the Social Sciences, 6*(1), 14–29. doi:10.2458/azu_jmmss_v6i1_blair

Catalano, A. (2013). Patterns of graduate students' information seeking behavior: A meta-synthesis of the literature. *Journal of Documentation, 69*(2), 243–274. doi.org/10.1108/00220411311300066

Charmaz, K. (2006). *Constructing grounded theory: A practical guide through qualitative analysis*. Sage.

Craik, F., & Lockhart, R. (1972). Levels of processing: A framework for memory research. *Journal of Verbal Learning and Verbal Behavior, 11*(6), 671–684. doi.org/10.1016/S0022-5371(72)80001-X

Delaney, G., & Bates, J. (2018). How can the university library better meet the information needs of research students? Experiences from Ulster University. *New Review of Academic Librarianship, 24*(1), 63–89. doi: 10.1080/13614533.2017.1384267

Drew, S., & Guillemin, M. (2014). From photographs to findings: Visual meaning-making and interpretive engagement in the analysis of participant-generated images. *Visual Studies, 29*(1), 54–67. doi: 10.1080/1472586X.2014.862994

Durning, S. J., Artino, A. R., Beckman, T. J., Graner, J., van der Vleuten, C., Holmboe, E., & Schuwirth, L. (2013). Does the think-aloud protocol reflect thinking? Exploring functional neuroimaging differences with thinking (answering multiple choice) versus thinking aloud. *Medical Teacher, 35*(9), 720–726.

Eppler, M. J. (2006). A comparison between concept maps, mind maps, conceptual diagrams, and visual metaphors as complementary tools for knowledge construction and sharing. *Information Visualization, 5*(3), 202–210. doi.org/10.1057/palgrave.ivs.9500131

Ericsson, K. A., & Simon, H. A. (1984). *Protocol analysis: Verbal reports as data*. The MIT Press.

Ericsson, K. A., & Simon, H. A. (1980). Verbal reports as data. *Psychological Review, 87*(3), 215–251. doi.org/10.1037/0033-295X.87.3.215

Fostaty Young, S., & Wilson, R. J. (2000). *Assessment and learning: The ICE approach.* Portage & Main Press.

Glaser, B. G., & Strauss, A. L. (1967). *The discovery of grounded theory: Strategies for qualitative research.* Aldine Transaction.

Glegg, S. M. (2019). Facilitating interviews in qualitative research with visual tools: A typology. *Qualitative Health Research, 29*(2), 301–310. doi:1049732318786485

Hay, D. B. (2007). Using concept maps to measure deep, surface and non learning outcomes. *Studies in Higher Education, 32*(1), 39–57. doi:10.1080/03075070601099432

Hay, D. B., Kinchin, I., & Lygo-Baker, S. (2008). Making learning visible: The role of concept mapping in higher education. *Studies in Higher Education, 33*(3), 295–311. doi:10.1080/03075070802049251

Heath, H., & Cowley, S. (2004). Developing a grounded theory approach: A comparison of Glaser and Strauss. *International Journal of Nursing Studies, 41*(2), 141–150. https://doi.org/10.1016/S0020-7489(03)00113-5

Kellman, P. J. (2002). Perceptual learning. In H. Pashler & R. Gallistel (Eds.), *Stevens' handbook of experimental psychology 3: Learning, motivation, and emotion* (3rd ed.). Wiley. doi:10.1002/0471214426.pas0307

Murphy, P. K., Wilkinson, I. A. G., Soter, A. O., Hennessey, M. N., & Alexander, J. F. (2009). Examining the effects of classroom discussion on students' comprehension of text: A meta-analysis. *Journal of Educational Psychology, 101*(3), 740–764. doi.org/10.1037/a0015576

Nesbit, J. C., & Adesope, O. O. (2006). Learning with concept and knowledge maps: A meta-analysis. *Review of Educational Research, 76,* 413–448. doi:10.3102/00346543076003413

Patton, M. Q. (1990). *Qualitative evaluation and research methods.* Sage.

Pavio, A. (1986). *Mental representation: A dual coding approach.* Oxford University Press.

Renfro, C. (2017). The use of visual tools in the academic research process: A literature review. *The Journal of Academic Librarianship, 43*(2), 95–99. doi.org/10.1016/j.acalib.2017.02.004

Roschelle, J., & Teasley, S. D. (1995). The construction of shared knowledge in collaborative problem solving. In C. O'Malley (Ed.), *Computer supported collaborative learning* (pp. 69–97). Springer Verlag.

Spezi, V. (2016). Is information-seeking behavior of doctoral students changing? A review of the literature (2010–2015). *New Review of Academic Librarianship, 22*(1), 78–106. doi:1080/13614533.2015.1127831

Sweller, J. (2011). Cognitive load theory. In J. P. Mestre & B. H. Ross (Eds.), *Psychology of learning and motivation* (Vol. 55, pp. 37–76). Elsevier. https://doi.org/10.1016/B978-0-12-387691-1.00002-8

Vygotsky, L. V. (1978). *Mind and psychology.* Harvard University Press.

Weber, S. (2008). Visual images in research. In J. G. Knowles & A. L. Cole (Eds.), *Handbook of the arts in qualitative research: Perspectives, methodologies, examples, and issues* (pp. 42–54). Sage.

Wells, G. (1999). Dialogic inquiry in education: Building on the legacy of Vygotsky. In C. D. Lee & P. Smagorinsky (Eds.), *Vygotskian perspectives on literacy research* (pp. 51–85). Cambridge University Press.

Wells, G. (2002). Dialogue about knowledge building. In B. Smith (Ed.), *Liberal education in a knowledge society* (pp. 111–138). Open Court.

CHAPTER 10

Reflecting on Messy Practice: Action Research on Peer Review of Teaching

Agnes Bosanquet and Rod Lane

Abstract

In this chapter, we offer a glimpse behind the scenes of higher education scholarship in action. We reflect on the unanticipated complexities of a participatory action research project on the peer review of teaching in a university context. Our aim was to promote a culture of ongoing reflection that would lead to quality enhancements in learning, teaching, and curriculum practices. Instead, this was one of the most fraught teaching development and research projects in which we been involved, in over thirty years combined working, researching, and teaching in higher education. Documenting our reflective practice offers a way of working through the complex and messy ethical, theoretical, practical, and affective challenges of this research and teaching development project. We share our learning about the risks and complexities of 'insider research' or researching within our own institution. This chapter has provided an opportunity to reflect on our assumptions, values, integrity, and ethical positioning–in other words, to explore questions of researcher reflexivity.

Keywords

peer review of teaching – participatory action research – reflection – researcher reflexivity

1   Introduction

This chapter offers a glimpse behind the scenes of higher education scholarship in action. The specific project is participatory action research on the peer review of teaching in a university context. It is no exaggeration to say that this was one of the most fraught teaching development and research projects in which we have been involved in a combined thirty years of working, researching, and teaching in higher education. Documenting our reflective practice offers a way of working through the complex and messy ethical, theoretical, practical, and affective challenges of this research project. The use of the term 'messy' here is drawn from Jones' (2011) work using narrative methods to articulate the multiple layers and complexities of academic practice.

There are various theoretical and practical approaches to reflection in higher education contexts. Ryan (2013) notes that academic or professional reflection differs from a purely personal reflection in that it involves a conscious and stated purpose (Moon, 2006), and includes evidence of learning and growing professional knowledge. This type of purposeful reflection ultimately reaches the critical level for deep, active learning to occur.

The reflections in this chapter are structured by Bain, Ballantyne, Mills and Lester's (2002) 4R's framework for reflection:

1. Reporting and responding – describing the activities that took place, making observations, expressing opinions or asking questions;
2. Relating – connecting the event with your own experience, skills and knowledge;
3. Reasoning – explaining the factors shaping these events and actions with reference to relevant theory and literature, considering different perspectives;
4. Reconstructing – reframing or reconstructing future practice or professional understanding.

Our reflections are structured around questions that align with this framework: What were your aims, hopes, dreams going into the project? How did you try to enact these (reporting and responding)? What were the challenges? Ethical, theoretical, practical, affective? Where did these come from and what were the consequences (reporting and responding)? How did events align with your experience, skills, and knowledge? Were the conditions the same or different from what you expected (relating)? What were the factors shaping these events and actions (reasoning)? What have you learned (reconstructing)?

The reflections in this chapter are an example of researcher reflexivity. Reflexive researchers recognize and acknowledge the *context of knowledge construction* and how their backgrounds and positions as researchers shape their research questions, methods, interpretations, and subsequent actions (Malterud, 2001). In our discussion of the research context in this chapter, we share our learning about the risks and complexities of 'insider research' or researching within our own institution. Sikes' (2006) paper, 'On dodgy ground? Problematics and ethics in educational research' is illustrative:

> Insider research is inherently sensitive and, therefore, potentially dodgy in both ethical and career development terms. People considering embarking on insider research have to think very carefully about what taking on the role and identity of researcher can mean and involve in a setting where they are normally seen as someone else with particular responsibilities and powers. (p. 110)

Throughout this project we were indeed, as you will see, on dodgy ground.

2 Level 1: Reporting and Responding

The impetus for undertaking participatory action research was a request from our Faculty's Executive Dean to develop a model for peer review of teaching. This aligned with the University and Faculty strategic plan to promote a culture of "ongoing reflection and communication amongst academics, leading to quality enhancement in learning and teaching." In Agnes' then role as Senior Teaching Fellow, responsible for academic development across the Faculty, she drafted a framework for peer review of teaching. Based on scholarship, notably the work of Sachs and Parsell (2014), the framework included the most well-known form of peer review of teaching, classroom observation (peer review of teaching practices). It also, however, encompassed online teaching (peer review of online teaching practices) and teaching-related activities, such as revision of materials, development of units, assessment review, mapping program learning outcomes (peer review of curriculum practices) at a unit (or subject) and course (or program) level. Using the framework and resources provided, individual staff could make decisions about the purposes and need for peer review: why undertake peer review, and what will be achieved? What is to be reviewed? Who will be the reviewer? How will the peer review take place? How will the results be communicated, and for what purposes?

The peer review approach was chosen for this project because it had the potential to promote collegial conversations, provide alternative sources of feedback, and prompt reflection that could lead to improvements in teaching practice. Effective educators are reflexive about their practice. Reflexive practice involves "active, persistent, and careful consideration of any belief or supposed form of knowledge in light of the grounds that support it and the further consequences to which it leads" (Dewey, 1933, p. 9). Reflexive educators understand their experiences in the social context and use this knowledge to develop their practice (Stîngu, 2012). The peer review process provided an opportunity for academics in the Faculty to look through a different lens at the impact and effectiveness of the work they do and suggest ways of doing things better.

To be effective as a formative tool, a non-judgmental approach peer review was required. The review processes also needed to be flexible and fit for purpose. Academics differ in their areas of interest and focus. Some staff may wish to focus on their resource development, while others focus on their ability to engage students, design assessment tasks, etc. The review process was made flexible so that some staff could provide feedback on a single lecture/tutorial or take part in observation and feedback over a period of time. The peer-review initiative was not implemented as a 'one-size fits all' approach. We needed an approach that catered for the diverse needs and interests of staff in the Faculty.

The implementation of peer review of teaching was supported by leaders in each Department, who formed a working party to revise and ratify the framework, evaluate peer review of teaching resources and promote the use of specific templates and exemplars, raise awareness and build capacity within Departments by piloting peer review practices, and share experience, knowledge, and inspiration, including practicing a peer review of teaching activities as a team. Peer review was implemented in a range of ways through assessment moderation, mentoring for tutors, program review, teaching, and curriculum development projects.

We envisaged a process of mutual learning, increased critical reflection, and tangible benefits attached to support and guidance such as career advancement (Barkham, 2005; Hughes, Boyd, & Dykstra, 2010; Lindgren, 2006). Hendry, Bell, and Thomson (2014) go further in emphasizing the learning opportunities of peer observation of teaching, defining it as "the process of a university teacher watching another colleague's teaching, *without* necessarily judging or being required to give feedback" (p. 318).

We nonetheless recognized risks and challenges associated with peer review of teaching. We consciously included casual (adjunct or sessional) staff to participate in peer review of teaching, but were mindful of the uneven distribution of power between experienced and inexperienced staff members (Darwin & Palmer, 2009; Lindgren, 2006). Hendry et al. (2014) offer a note of warning: "If not conducted under supportive conditions, academics may perceive that peer observation of teaching is: invasive, only a snapshot of teaching, subjective and time-consuming … and too focussed on performance" (p. 277).

TABLE 10.1 Peer review of teaching plan

	Unit level	Program level
Peer review of online practices	– Via [open access online units] and collegial conversations – Unit Convenors and teaching staff (including tutors) act as reviewer and reviewee – Review online unit	– Via [open access online units] and collegial conversations – Program teams/teaching staff (including tutors) led by Program Directors review online units across program – Review online units, compare across program

Peer review of curriculum practices	– Via [open access online units], Unit Guides, Webforms, Handbook and collegial conversations
	– Unit Convenors and teaching staff (including tutors) act as reviewer and reviewee
	– Review at least three of:
	  – learning outcomes
	  – teaching methods and strategies (e.g. collaborative and active learning, integration of technology)
	  – assessment
	  – grading and feedback (e.g. rubrics, examples of marked student work, moderation)
	  – class preparation
	  – reading list/recommended resources
	  – student evaluation
		– Via [open access online units], Unit Guides, Webforms, Handbook and collegial conversations
		– Program teams/teaching staff (including tutors) led by Program Directors review curriculum across programs
		– Review at least three of:
		  – program structure and mapping
		  – program learning outcomes
		  – teaching methods and strategies (e.g. collaborative and active learning, integration of technology)
		  – assessment
		  – grading and feedback (e.g. rubrics, examples of marked student work, moderation)
		  – class preparation
		  – reading lists/recommended resources
		  – student evaluation

(cont.)

TABLE 10.1   Peer review of teaching plan (cont.)

	Unit level	Program level
Peer review of teaching practices	– Via peer observation of teaching (f2f, recorded or online) and collegial conversations – Unit Convenors and teaching staff (including tutors) act as reviewer and reviewee – Review f2f or online teaching and at least two of: – Teaching philosophy – Teaching development and support for tutors – Student outcomes – Effectiveness of teaching strategies for identified priority areas (e.g. student feedback, employability, retention)	– Via peer observation of teaching (f2f, recorded or online) and collegial conversations – Program teams/teaching staff (including tutors) led by Program Directors review teaching across programs – Templates provided to review f2f or online teaching and at least two of: – Teaching philosophies – Teaching development and support for tutors – Student outcomes – Effectiveness of teaching strategies for identified priority areas (e.g. student feedback, employability, retention)

Rod was a member of the working party who enthusiastically embraced the possibilities of peer review of teaching. Together, we decided to make the Department of Educational Studies an exemplar of good practice and use peer review of teaching as a springboard for curriculum development projects. As Chair of the Department Learning and Teaching Committee, Rod recognized the potential benefits of teaching staff working together to reflect on and improve practice. Time and research pressures often led to academics to work in silos. They rarely made time to discuss their teaching practice with colleagues or to obtain feedback on their teaching. This is in contrast to their research work where they regularly sought and received feedback. A supportive and collegial peer review process had the potential to break down silos and promote conversations about evidence-based and innovative teaching.

A secondary aim was to build a research group to investigate the process of peer review and its impact on curriculum design, pedagogy, and student learning outcomes. This was part of a larger goal to ensure there was a nexus between research and teaching within the Department, researching teaching practice, and using the data collected to refine and enhance pedagogy. Research was planned to take place at two levels: firstly, group members would identify core curriculum and teaching issues to investigate (e.g. teaching methods, program-based assessment, grading and moderation practices, development of units, etc.) and provide each other with feedback informed by their own professional experiences and the literature. It was hoped that this would prompt staff to modify their practice.

Participants would also have the option of publishing the results of their peer review as an action-research project. At a broader level, research aimed to investigate all stages of the review cycle including the identification of issues for investigation and the processes of observation, feedback, reflection, and refinement of practice. This included a meta-analysis of the outcomes of the peer review process.

We planned a process of participatory action research (PAR) for the project. The fundamental aim of action research is to link action and research, that is, practice and theory. This assumes partnerships between participants involved in reflection. Although there are multiple models of action research, most share spiral steps of planning, acting, observing, and reflecting in a repeated cycle. Action research is essentially a collaborative partnership in which all project members are considered participant observers (Wadsworth, 2011). There is also an assumption that change results from the action research process. The PAR approach appeared ideal for this project as it enabled communities of inquiry and action to evolve, and empowered participants to collaborate as co-researchers to explore questions that emerge as significant to their practice (Kemmis, McTaggart, & Nixon, 2014). The approach was attractive as it had the potential to distribute leadership amongst the academics in the team and to break down perceived power relationships.

In the Department of Educational Studies, we planned to implement peer review of teaching in three phases. The first phase consisted of workshops on peer review of teaching. Open to all teaching staff in the Department of Educational Studies, a three-part workshop series introduced staff to peer review and assisted them to set up the process. Subsequent workshops provide a scholarly context for peer review of teaching, support to develop learning and teaching projects in response to feedback, and to present ideas for teaching and curriculum development projects emerging from the feedback. The second phase invited volunteers to participate in an action research project to identify the impacts of peer review on learning and teaching quality in the Department; investigate participants' views of the peer review process, and evaluate the usefulness of the scaffolds and resources provided to support the peer review process. This phase proved more complicated than we anticipated and is still

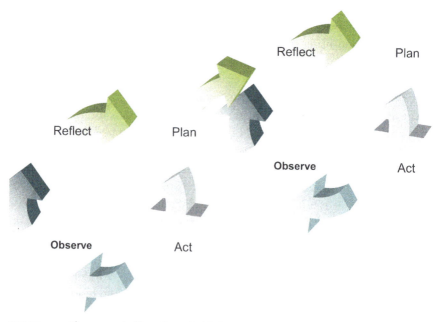

FIGURE 10.1   The PAR cycle (from Kemmis, McTaggart, & Nixon, 2014, p. 19)

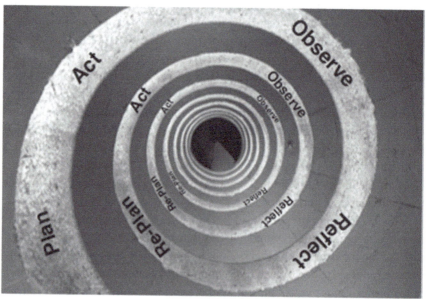

FIGURE 10.2   The action research spiral (from Kemmis, McTaggart, & Nixon, 2014, p. 19)

in progress. Finally, an anticipated outcome of the peer review process is that participants will wish to review their teaching methods, assessment, grading and moderation practices, curriculum development.

It was intended that we would have funding available to support individual teaching and curriculum projects, but this was complicated. The funding of individual projects was intended to provide staff with buyout time and resources they required to complete their reviews and respond to the feedback in a meaningful way to create sustained changes in their teaching practice. Initial funding for these individual projects was promised, but did not eventuate. Despite repeated assurances and, when these came to nothing, much time and effort preparing funding applications, there was no dedicated funding to support peer review of teaching initiatives. Our attention shifted to thinking about other sources of funding and ways of delivering the project outcomes without funding. Some individual projects are ongoing.

Undertaking the action research project started with an application for approval to the Human Research Ethics Committee. The first workshop on peer review of teaching was scheduled to run a fortnight after the submission of the ethics application. Unfortunately, we did not receive approval in time. We intended to run the workshop with no mention of the action research component of the project. A senior member of the Faculty rang Rod to cancel the workshop because we did not have ethics approval. Rod explained that we could run the workshop without mentioning the action research, but to no

TABLE 10.2 Components of the peer review of teaching project

Workshops on peer review of teaching	Workshops on peer review of teaching: open to all teaching staff in the Department of Educational Studies, a three-part workshop series to introduce staff to peer review and assist them to set up the process; provide support to develop learning and teaching projects in response to feedback; and reflect on the experience of peer review. The resources from these workshops were made available on a Moodle site.
Voluntary action research projects	Voluntary action research projects to: identify the impacts of peer review on learning and teaching quality in the Department of Educational Studies; investigate participants' views of the peer review process, and evaluate the usefulness of the scaffolds and resources provided to support the peer review process
Teaching development research projects	Teaching development research projects: An anticipated outcome of the peer review process is that participants will wish to review their teaching methods, assessment, grading and moderation practices, curriculum development, etc.

TABLE 10.3   Structure of the workshop series

Workshop 1	Introduction – Why?, What?, What's Next?
Peer review	Peer review process undertaken
Workshop 2	Responding to feedback. Participants propose to undertake a teaching development project.
L & T Projects implemented	
Workshop 3	Evaluating the Peer Review Process
Interviews	Impact of the project on interviewee and interviewer (June, 2018). Draft publications from projects due

avail. On reflection, the distinction between the teaching development workshops and the action research study was not clearly articulated in the ethics application. But the response demonstrated a lack of understanding of the model of peer review being employed in the project. The aim was to encourage and support conversations around quality learning and teaching and for colleagues to provide formative feedback. Review was not being used as an accountability tool or a vehicle for evaluating and appraising staff. There was also an implied distrust in our ability to manage the complex ethics of the project. The cancellation of the workshop at the last minute was heavy-handed, and our immediate reaction was of shock, anger, and embarrassment.

Once we had an opportunity to regain equilibrium, Agnes emailed the academic responsible for canceling the workshop:

> I am just following up about the cancellation of the peer review of teaching workshop that I was co-facilitating with Rod Lane this afternoon. It was unfortunate to cancel this without discussion as it is a key aspect of the Faculty's teaching strategy. The workshop and the research project could have been easily managed separately. Rod and I had discussed the fact that we did not have ethics approval and had removed the research component from the workshop, except to indicate that it was pending ethics approval.
>
> We can address any other concerns about the research once we have a written response from the ethics committee. This type of institutional research often needs consideration in relation to the nuances of professional relationships, and we welcome feedback on how to address issues of power relations and perceived coercion. The peer-review model developed by a Faculty working party with representatives from each Depart-

ment is focused on developing collegial and developmental conversations about learning and teaching. Through the action research project outlined in the ethics application, we wanted to make this a scholarly and reflective activity.

In a written response from the Ethics Committee, one of the key concerns was perceived coercion in the recruitment of participants to the action research project. The Committee had "serious reservations primarily about the recruitment, given the relationship between the investigators and the potential participants. The overall impression is that the potential for coercion is too high with the present procedures." In our application, the Head of Department was named as a member of the research group. The ethics committee felt that this may make staff feel obliged to be involved in the project or be judged for not participating especially casual staff.

> The primary concern about this project is that given one of the investigators is the Head of Department, how will coercion be managed? ... Are casual staff involved as well as permanent? Casual staff may be quite vulnerable in terms of wanting to make a good impression on department staff in order to continue working in the department. There may also be staff who have the named investigators as their [performance development review] mentors, for example, and may feel pressured to participate, especially if they have identified difficulties in their teaching. (Ethics Committee Written Response)

The issues raised by the Ethics Committee are indeed a concern in university learning and teaching research projects. In Australia, as elsewhere, the higher education workforce is highly casualized (May, Strachan, Broadbent, & Peetz, 2011). Casual staff, also known as adjuncts, contingent, non-tenure track, and sessionals, now dominate the higher education sector. The negative impacts of casualization for individuals are well documented: multiple jobs; high teaching workloads, limited or no research time, low pay, lack of job security, marginalization in decision-making, last-minute appointments, and minimal professional learning opportunities (Harvey, 2017). Note in relation to the comments of the Ethics Committee that casual teaching staff do not participate in performance development reviews, so do not have access to this mentoring opportunity.

The perception of peer review as a performance measurement, and possibly punitive processes, was precisely what we, perhaps naively, wished to challenge and reconstruct through the project. Once the Head of Department's name was removed from the application, the ethics application was approved with minor amendments to make clear the distinctions between the different components of the project, and within a few days and the workshops were rescheduled.

Our experience in obtaining ethics approval for participatory action research is similar to that of Parsell, Ambler, and Jacenyik-Trawoger (2014) in many respects, who share our institutional affiliation. Like their research, ours utilizes the method of participatory action research, focuses on teaching in higher education, and is concerned with peer review of teaching. Their experience highlights the messiness of insider research:

> Concerns about dependent relationships, coercion to participate, access to information and conflict of interest make decisions about research complex. Everyday activities and relationships are suddenly transformed when they become part of a formalized research process. Positivist research attempts to accommodate ethical concerns in the same way it attempts to achieve objectivity: by occupying a disinterested and detached high ground. Such a position is unavailable to researchers aiming to drive institutional change. They necessarily occupy an engaged and normatively committed position. By attempting to change a practice, environment or institution, one is making a stand against the present practice, environment or institution … By its very nature, action research moves beyond the mere discovery of knowledge to attempts to change the very system under investigation. Thus, participatory action research necessarily involves a commitment to how a system should operate. (Parsell, Ambler, & Jacenyik-Trawoger, 2014, pp. 170–172)

In our project, we attempted to challenge the conception that peer review processes in higher education need to be evaluative and hierarchal in nature. In contrast, we hoped to create a culture within the department that was collegial and formative. Our vision for a collaborative and transformative culture of learning and teaching driven by peer review remains incomplete.

3   Level 2: Relating

In most accounts of this research project, our context and past experience as researchers of higher education would be rendered invisible, along with the complexity of receiving ethical clearance to undertake the study. But for the purposes of exploring researcher reflexivity, our positioning as qualitative researchers impacts on our research (Malterud, 2001).

At the beginning of the project, Agnes was in a new role as Senior Teaching Fellow, a new Faculty academic development role. This position was created following an organizational change process that saw the closure of the central academic development unit and the loss of many academic and administrative jobs. This was a period of upheaval, individually and institutionally, with a loss of support and expertise in higher education teaching and curriculum development experienced across the university. Compounding this period of professional uncertainty, Agnes' 11-year-old daughter was very ill, with repeated hospitalizations and a 20-week absence from school. The emotional ups and downs of the project were an added stressor. One example: Agnes left her daughter in the hospital to come to work and facilitate the first workshop. As described above, it was canceled at short notice.

Prior to the project, Agnes' experiences with peer review of teaching were positive. She has had her teaching peer-reviewed by colleagues who were students (in postgraduate higher education) and by colleagues who were co-teachers. She has also acted as a reviewer for colleagues within Education and other disciplines. Sometimes this was initiated because the teacher wanted to respond to student feedback or go for promotion. In most cases, the focus was on improving the student experience. Peer review of teaching was very much a collegial and formative process, rather than an evaluation of someone's performance. Agnes also has had the privilege of co-supervising a PhD candidate whose research was focused on academics' experiences of peer review of teaching.

Rod was also in a new role as Deputy Head of Department (Learning and Teaching) in a large, recently restructured Education department. His focus was on creating a community through non-threatening conversations about teaching that involved teachers from previously separate departments and new staff members. Our backgrounds and the ideologies that shape our teaching and learning are revealing of how we approached the peer review of a teaching participatory action research project.

Agnes has a background in the discipline of Critical and Cultural Studies. As a student, she was inspired by teachers who challenged the way she saw the world and raised awareness of the taken-for-granted in everyday life. Starting as a tutor 17 years ago, she followed this lead and focused on developing students' thinking processes by asking questions rather than delivering content. On completion of her PhD in 2010, she shifted discipline to Higher Education but took this approach to teaching with her. Her work as an academic developer responsible for professional development, and as a teacher in postgraduate higher education, has a social reform agenda, with learning as a collective process of change. The role of the teacher is, as Skelton (2005) puts it, to "disturb the student's current epistemological understandings and interpretations of reality by offering new insights" (p. 33). To put it simply: Agnes wants her students to make their world a better place in a small way.

Rod's specialization in assessment has its origins in his experience as a secondary school geography teacher. As an academic, he aims to ensure preservice teachers develop the knowledge and skills to enhance student learning. Achieving this requires more than merely teaching students *about* effective assessment, pedagogy, and critical reflection, it demands careful *modeling* and *active student engagement with* these practices. To foster this engagement, he adopts an 'assessment *as* learning' (Earl, 2007) approach in his teaching. Through a range of assessment methods, including electronic portfolios, simulations, and action research, future teachers are actively engaged in monitoring their own learning; providing and responding to feedback; critically reflecting on their progress towards learning goals and using the insights gained from this process to make ongoing improvements to their practice. The development of these skills empowers pre-service teachers as reflective practitioners and independent lifelong learners.

This peer review of teaching action research project was Agnes and Rod's first collaborative project as teachers and researchers. We were enthusiastic about the possibility of a genuinely collaborative and empowering peer review process that produced real change. Our enthusiasm, perhaps naïvely, led us to overestimate the institutional support for the project and underestimate many of the structural and institutional barriers to achieving our vision. These enabling and constraining factors are outlined below.

4 Level 3: Reasoning

There was a broader sector-wide context that meant a focus on measuring the quality of higher education learning and teaching was timely. As noted above, there was a University-wide push to make peer review of teaching a priority, and the Faculty wanted to make it compulsory across all departments and programs. The framework emphasizes peer review of teaching as a formative process. Much of the context and the drivers of peer review of teaching, by contrast, had expectations of summative purposes, including quality evaluation and assurance, career progression, and professional recognition (awards, fellowships, etc.). Many of the reasons that peer review of teaching is increasingly important across the sector reinforce this understanding.

In Australia, and across the world, higher education systems are marked by increased regulation and reporting in the context of increased globalization, massification, and marketization (Vidovich, 2002). Shifts in public policy directions influenced by neoliberalism and New Public Management principles are felt at all levels of higher education, from macro (national/sectoral) and meso (institutional) to micro (institutional unit and individual). The accountability regimes that Australian universities currently work under are manifold, with an increased emphasis on efficiency, effectiveness, quality, and performance of higher education systems and institutions, accompanied by the development of metrics, regulatory reporting, quality audits and standards for qualifications, institutional operations (including governance) and (in some disciplines) learning outcomes (Stensaker & Harvey, 2011).

Peer review of teaching is an element in professional accreditation, benchmarking, and regulatory frameworks for quality assurance of academic programs. In Australia, the Higher Education Standards Framework (2015) requires all higher education institutions to undertake external referencing and/or peer review of all aspects of academic programs, from approval to curriculum design to delivery. The framework articulates threshold standards that universities are required to meet in order to operate as higher education institutions. This is monitored by the independent regulatory body Tertiary Education Quality and Standards Agency (TEQSA), who are particularly focused on external benchmarking activities.

Accountability and regulatory systems operate in this way at the macro and meso levels and are becoming more apparent at the micro level (Stensaker & Harvey, 2011). The academic work of individuals, especially research output which is readily quantified, is subject to the measurement of defined metrics (e.g. specific annual targets for research funding, number of publications and citations, grant income) (Tyler & Wright, 2004). Teaching is increasingly the focus of attention. This external context has driven practice within our university, where peer review of teaching aligned with University and Faculty strategies for learning and teaching, program reviews, new promotions criteria that more explicitly recognize the scholarship of teaching, and a university-wide curriculum redevelopment project.

We were aware of this context for measuring quality in higher education at the outset. Agnes represents the Faculty at a University level community of practice (CoP) on peer review of teaching. This CoP is currently drafting a discussion paper for Academic Senate, with a view to proceeding with the formulation of relevant policies, procedures, and guidelines as deemed appropriate, and to serve as a framework for organizing resources, support, and implementation of a range of peer feedback practices for professional learning and recognition across the University. There is overlap between peer review of teaching and other university-wide projects currently underway including program lifecycle, program review, shared governance, quality indicators, and curriculum standards. We failed to perceive, however, the impact the external and institutional context would have on our peer review of teaching action research project. The neatness of the alignments between University, Faculty, Department, and individual goals should have sounded a warning bell – how often are the needs of multiple institutional levels the same? How frequently are the needs of teaching and research entirely in sync?

Volkwein's (1999) typology for the purposes and roles of institutional research, and the conflicts researchers face, has helped us understand some of the competing agendas and tensions that emerged between peer review for improvement and peer review for accountability. At different levels – individuals, teaching teams, the department and faculty and the university – competing values, expectations, and motivations meant different understandings of the formative and summative purposes of peer review of teaching were operating simultaneously. According to Gosling's (2002) model, many of our colleagues and leaders hold evaluative and/or developmental understandings of peer review of teaching, which can be performance-based, hierarchical, and managerial. This was at odds with the formative and collaborative approach to peer review that we aimed to put in place.

Finally, Winter's (2009) work on 'schisms' in academic identities and fractured work environments that result from attempts to align academics with institutional ideologies and values has offered a useful way to reflect on these differing values and contexts. Winter (2009) distinguishes between the "identities of 'academic manager' (values congruent with the managerial discourse) and 'managed academic' (values incongruent with the managerial discourse)" (p 121). An academic manager is defined by Winter (2009) as a professorial position, middle or line manager, who aligns themselves with institutional norms and values (examples of which might include students as consumers or economic rationalism). On the other hand, a managed academic is described as having a limited influence on decision-making, being disengaged with the institution, and holding a greater commitment to their discipline and professional identity (which might be determined by discipline scholarship, intellectual curiosity, a community of practice, or student learning) (Winter, 2009).

The work of Winter (2009) and Volkwein (1999) provides us with a theoretical lens for making sense of our 'messy' experiences and assists us to identify the wider contextual factors enabling and constraining the project. The following section summarizes our professional learning from the project and our plan for future practice.

5 Level 4: Reconstructing

This chapter has provided an opportunity to reflect on our assumptions, values, integrity, and ethical positioning–that is, questions of researcher reflexivity.

We are now in a position to critique the validity of the assumptions we made when designing the action research project "in light of the grounds that support [them] and the further consequences to which [they] lead" (Dewey, 1933, p. 9). With the benefits of hindsight, we consider the implications of our experiences future practice and professional understanding.

A key lesson from this experience was not to underestimate the influence of institutional ideologies and values, and the broader higher education sectoral context, on the everyday work of academics. When planning the project, we assumed that the University and Faculty's strategic goals to promote a culture of "ongoing reflection and communication amongst academics" would make funding relatively easy to obtain. This is rarely the case in higher education learning and teaching projects, and projects should not be designed and introduced based on a promise that they will be funded.

Engaging the whole department in the project was a key challenge. The workshops were advertised and put in staff calendars; however, they were only attended by 10–15 staff. Many who attended already had positive perceptions of peer review, were enthusiastic, and had undertaken some form of peer review in the past. The staff we wanted to engage, those more resistant to the peer review process, were less likely to attend. This limited the extent to which the project could shape the culture in the department.

In the future, we will be more cautious about the framing of ethics applications in learning and teaching projects, specifically action research projects. In this case, it means making explicit that formative peer review is a tool for promoting reflection and personal professional development. In PAR initiatives like this, it is essential to have a clear distinction between the research and professional development components of the project and to carefully consider the positional authority of research participants.

Our perspective of peer review as a formative, collaborative, and transformative process was at odds with the conception of peer review as a part of the accountability and quality assurance agenda. Universities are complex organizations, and it is not unusual for competing values, expectations, and motivations to operate across different levels. In this case, the difference was stark with competing rather than complementary conceptions of peer review of teaching.

An important lesson from the project focuses on designing for and measuring impact in learning and teaching interventions. Several academics involved in the PAR project followed the steps in the framework, modified their practice, and believed that they had improved through the process. However, there was little evidence that these modifications had shifted learning experiences and outcomes for students. This could be addressed in the future by ensuring that measures of impact were built into all stages of the project.

Our peer review of teaching action research project is ongoing. Perhaps the most significant outcome of this complex, incomplete, and messy project is the learning experience it has provided for us as researchers of teaching practices in higher education.

References

Bain, J. D., Ballantyne, R., Mills, C., & Lester, N. C. (2002). *Reflecting on practice: Student teachers' perspectives*. Post Pressed.

Barkham, J. (2005). Reflections and interpretations on life in academia: A mentee speaks. *Mentoring and Tutoring, 13*(3), 331–344.

Darwin, A., & Palmer, E. (2009). Mentoring circles in higher education. *Higher Education Research & Development, 28*(2), 125–136.

Dewey, J. (1933). *How we think: A restatement of the relation of reflective thinking to the educative process*. Prometheus Books.

Earl, L. (2007). Assessment as learning. In W. D. Hawley (Ed.), *The keys to effective schools: Educational reform as continuous improvement* (pp. 85–98). Sage Publications.

Gosling, D. (2002). *Models of peer observation of teaching.* Learning and Teaching Support Network (LTSN) Generic Centre. [Online]

Harvey, M. (2017). Quality learning and teaching with sessional staff: Systematising good practice for academic development. *International Journal for Academic Development, 22*(1), 1–6.

Hendry, G. D., Bell, A., & Thomson, K. (2014). Learning by observing a peer's teaching situation. *International Journal of Academic Development, 19*, 318–329.

Hughes, C., Boyd, E., & Dykstra, S. (2010). Evaluation of a university-based mentoring program: Mentors' perspectives on a service-learning experience. *Mentoring Tutoring Partnership in Learning, 18*(4), 361–382.

Jones, A. (2011). Seeing the messiness of academic practice: Exploring the work of academics through narrative. *International Journal for Academic Development, 16*(2), 109–118.

Kemmis, S., McTaggart, R., & Nixon, R. (2014). *The action research planner: Doing critical participatory action research*. Springer.

Lindgren, U. (2006). Mentoring in the academic world. In C. Cullingford (Ed.), *Mentoring in education* (pp. 153–165). Ashgate Publishing Limited.

Malterud, K. (2001). Qualitative research: Standards, challenges, and guidelines. *The Lancet, 358*, 483–488.

May, R., Strachan, G., Broadbent, K., & Peetz, D. (2011). The casual approach to university teaching: Time for a re-think? In K. Krause, M. Buckridge, C. Grimmer, & S. Purbrick-Illek (Eds.), *Research and development in higher education: Reshaping higher education* (Vol. 34, pp. 188–197). Higher Education Research and Development Association of Australasia.

Moon, J. A. (2006). *Learning journals: A handbook for reflective practice and professional development*. Routledge.

Parsell, M., Ambler, T., & Jacenyik-Trawoger, C. (2014). Ethics in higher education research. *Studies in Higher Education, 39*(1), 166–179.

Ryan, M. (2013). The pedagogical balancing act: Teaching reflection in higher education. *Teaching in Higher Education, 18*(2), 144–155.

Sachs, J., & Parsell, M. (Eds.). (2014). *Peer review of learning and teaching in higher education: International perspectives*. Springer.

Sikes, P. (2006). On dodgy ground? Problematics and ethics in educational research. *International Journal of Research & Method in Education, 29*(1), 105–117.

Skelton, A. (2005). *Understanding teaching excellence in higher education: Towards a critical approach*. Routledge.

Stensaker, B., & Harvey, L. (Eds.). (2011). *Accountability in higher education: Global perspectives on trust and power*. Routledge.

Stîngu, M. M. (2012). Reflexive practice in teacher education: Facts and trends. *Procedia-Social and Behavioral Sciences, 33*, 617–621.

Tertiary Education Quality and Standards Agency (TEQSA). (2015). *The Higher education standards framework*. Australian Government Publishing Service.

Tyler, D., & Wright, R. D. (2004). It's a shame about audit. *Australian Universities' Review, 47*(1), 30–34.

Vidovich, L. (2002). Quality assurance in Australian higher education: Globalisation and 'steering at a distance.' *Higher Education, 43*, 391–408.

Volkwein, J. F. (1999). The four faces of institutional research. *New Directions for Institutional Research, 104*, 9–19.

Wadsworth, Y. (2011). *Do it yourself social research*. Routledge.

Winter, R. (2009). Academic manager or managed academic? Academic identity schisms in higher education. *Journal of Higher Education Policy and Management, 31*(2), 121–131.

CHAPTER 11

Concluding Comments

Nancy E. Fenton and Whitney Ross

Ellis (2010) describes autoethnography as about making oneself vulnerable – exposing one's strengths, weaknesses, innermost thoughts, and opening it up for others to criticize.

In similar ways, this volume is designed to open a space for researchers as they take up their journeys across teaching and learning landscapes that can be at times unsettling – filled with false starts, impasses, and surprises. The intentional framing of reflection on praxis in this volume is meant to make accessible a space for researchers to expose aspects of their journey that might not otherwise fit neatly into 'traditional' methodology chapters or essays, but are nonetheless instructive – issues, events, thoughts, and learnings that deserve to be highlighted rather than buried in a footnote.

As a methodology, qualitative research holds high expectations of its practitioners insisting upon face-to-face, heartfelt, encounters – in other words, opening up a person's experiences of joy, suffering, and identity, and a recognition that each of us is unique in our effort to make sense of ourselves in the social context in which we live. This approach takes intellectual and moral courage, risk-taking, and artful representation of what we learn (Luttrell, 2010). In this volume, we showcase the work of authors who bring novel methodologies to bear on their research questions with the singular purpose of delving deeply into the experiences of educators and students. In the process, they do take risks, and in doing so, share the successes and failures of their journey along the way.

Writing a concluding chapter to this book implies more closure than we set out to achieve – in a way, this volume is a call to open the windows into the world of innovative qualitative methods that will inevitably provide new approaches to exploring the embodied nature of teaching and learning experiences within a broader web of sociocultural relations. Stepping into this space means, as researchers, we need to be vulnerable and more than likely encounter the "messiness, uncertainty, multi-voiced texts, as well as cultural criticisms more often, just as reflective forms of fieldwork and analysis will also be more common" (Denzin & Lincoln, 2016, p. 26). The research in this book offers insights and exposes the 'trials and tribulations,' making transparent the efforts researchers' have taken in navigating this messy space (Forber-Pratt,

2015, p. 12). We believe this collection serves a critically important role in challenging teaching and learning researchers to offer 'witness' to their research process, to be open, flexible, and adaptable to accommodating unexpected unique challenges they confront in their work.

1   Reflections on Praxis

These same things we, as researchers, grappled with within our own research. In keeping with the spirit of the book and each of the chapters before, we begin with our own reflections on praxis related to the research study we conducted together using collaborative autoethnography (CAE) with educational leaders. Adamson and Muller (2017) view CAE as languages of different stages; while Allen-Collinson (2013) see this approach as providing discursive spaces for voices too often muted or forcibly silenced within more traditional forms of research. Our investigation involved cooperatively building a 'conversational narrative' (Ochs & Capps, 2001, p. 2) with faculty members who were inaugural fellows in a new teaching & learning fellowship program.

> A narrative is a personal perspective on a journey experienced uniquely but not without travel companions. Today, I realize that there is very little left of my life if I imagine it with learning taken out, I am perhaps, not really a teacher at all, but someone who just keeps on learning in company. My teaching is my research into what I do, who I am, and how I know. (Faculty participant & co-researcher)

The stories of teaching leadership, described in the individual quote above, reflect the depth as well as the rich texture that is generated by the collective work and multiple voices of Collaborative Autoethnography. Using this approach strengthened our interrogation of 'what teaching leadership means' – it created a unique synergy that we believe individual researchers could not have achieved alone. Our decision to adopt CAE research came in stages and was driven mostly by an interest to explore both individual and collective ideas of teaching leadership. The idea of employing a novel method to interrogate a complex, social phenomenon, such as teaching leadership, was an exciting venture to consider. This was especially exciting given our prior experiences of conducting stand-alone interviews and focus groups, which in comparison did not seem adequate enough to pierce the surface of such complex experiences. As researchers, we were breaking new ground and keen to experiment with CAE research because of its flexibility and evolving nature, which enabled us the freedom to adopt reflexivity strategies to make the research more transparent and enhance the quality of it.

CAE has a unique capacity to give voice and power to everyday experiences. We were drawn to this method for its ability to enhance trusting relationships through deep listening or witnessing, collegial feedback, and mentorship (Chang, 2008). As a method, its approach advanced the dialogue between researchers through individual and group conversations that added a rich texture and multiple perspectives to interrogate the social phenomena of teaching and leadership. We learned that the broader, extended engagement allowed for a collective exploration of research subjectivity (Chang, Ngunjiri, & Hernandez, 2013, p. 25) that achieved deeper learning of self and others. As co-researchers, we discovered the method served a more equitable voice in the research process and provided a solid structure to support 'witnessing' (Lapadat, 2017) by flattening the power dynamics of the team since all co-researchers were vulnerable in sharing their experiences.

In recent years, Autoethnography (AE) has become a popular method in social sciences and is an approach to qualitative inquiry that combines characteristics of autobiography and ethnography (Ellis, Adams, & Bochner, 2011). In AE, the researcher recounts their own personal experience coupled with an analysis of the cultural context with which the experience resides (Bocher & Ellis, 1995; Lapadat, 2017). AE is reflexive and positions the researcher within the study, in that the author of an autoethnography is both subject and researcher (Coffey, 2002).

Just as autoethnography grew out of and in parallel with the practice of self-reflexivity, this collaborative approach to autoethnography that engages multiple researchers emerged concurrently with a solo approach. Multi-voiced approaches to AE research have employed various labels and methodological permutations. Lapadat et al. (2009, 2010) use the label collaborative autoethnography (CAE) to describe their approach to writing, telling, interrogating, analyzing, and collaboratively engaging and writing up research on personal life challenges and on negotiating personal and professional identities. Denzin (2013) describes CAE as "the co-production of an autoethnographic text by two or more writers, often separated by time and distance" (p. 125). Similarly, and more recently, Chang et al. (2013) have popularized the label CAE for AE qualitative research that combines the AE study of self with ethnographic analysis of the sociocultural milieu within which researchers are situated.

CAE is a qualitative method where researchers work in community to gather individual reflections then analyze and interpret their data collectively to gain a richer, more meaningful, embodied understanding. In our study, this individual-collective heuristic approach enabled faculty co-researchers to embrace the permeability of the binary construct of the researcher and researched and re-embody within a social context. Eloquently shared by one faculty co-researcher:

Since commencing this journey – the Fellowship path, I think I am a much more reflective educator, more prone to think critically, and to interpret the meaning of course materials and customize to my students and their settings that I was consciously aware of previously. I trust my professional judgment more than previously.

2 Reflections on the Field of Teaching & Learning

In the introductory chapter, we emphasized that this volume is less a 'how-to' book, and more a book that focuses on the doing of research. Each chapter's inclusion of a portion on praxis highlights the practice of 'doing research' and making visible the central role that research relationships play. Embedded in each chapter are honest reflections on the process and progress of each author's expression of research on teaching and learning in action. We, as editors, place praxis at the center of this work, and in this sense, praxis is focused on the 'liminal spaces' in between the doing of research (Simmons et al., 2013) – falling between the cracks of writing about theory, writing about methodology, and writing about research implications. In terms of a learning space, liminal spaces are more aptly characterized as a "more liquid, simultaneously transforming and being transformed by the learner [researcher] as he or she moves through it" (Meyer & Land, 2005, p. 380). In this volume, contributors cast light upon what and how they learn with themselves and about others, while actively engaging and deeply listening to their participants in the broader contexts in which they inhabit, while at the same time they wrestle with and make sense of it all during and after 'doing research' (Lave & Wenger, 1991).

Traditional qualitative research acknowledges the centrality of rapport between researcher and informant. Most references to establishing rapport discuss the need to establish trust in the field with informants, and at the same time to remain detached and 'neutral' to avoid biasing the data collected (Ulichny & Schoener, 2010). Recently, however, more critical and postmodern qualitative researchers in the field have critiqued the traditional, detached stance precisely because it leads to objectifying and 'othering' the participants, while also hiding the identity of the much-implicated researcher (Fine, 1994; Lather, 1991; Oakley, 1981; Van Maanen, 1988). Researchers in the field of teaching and learning have increasingly placed themselves more consciously in the field of inquiry since "data do not provide a window on reality" (Charmaz, 2010, p. 197). Rather, as Charmaz (2010) notes, the "discovered reality arises from the interactive process and its temporal, cultural, and structural contexts" (p. 197), and researchers and participants frame that interaction and confer meaning upon it. This volume champions qualitative approaches as a means toward these ends by underscoring:

> The stories people tell constitute the empirical material that interviewers need if they are to understand how people create meanings out of events in their lives. To think of an interviewee as a narrator is to make a conceptual shift away from the idea that interviewees have answers to researchers' questions and toward the idea that interviewee s are narrators with stories to tell and voices of their own. (Chase, 2010, p. 218)

This book is ample evidence that Gergen's (2000) urgings for qualitative researchers to be more methodologically imaginative have begun to gain traction within teaching and learning. Yet, at the same time, there is a need to ensure Denzin and Lincoln's (1994) cautionary note that the quest for creativity also comes at the cost of encountering "tensions, contradictions, and hesitations" (p. 15).

The foregoing chapters embrace earlier calls for more embodied approaches. More and more researchers, in teaching and learning are bringing creative qualitative methods and new paradigms of inquiries to the questions that arise from within the teaching and learning landscapes. These chapters highlight methods that step into the old expression of 'a picture can paint a thousand words,' offer critical reflexivity about the writing-self (Richardson, 2003, p. 931) in different contexts as a valuable analytic practice, bring collaborative action research strategies for addressing the complexities of teaching, and combine mixed approaches to systematically analyze how networks and conversations of educational leaders happen. As researchers, it means accessing approaches from many different disciplines (Denzin & Lincoln, 2000, p. 4). For participants, it means asking them to be more vulnerable in deeply human ways through sharing their emotions and experiences. While new and novel approaches take us out of our comfort zones and require us to cross epistemological and methodological boundaries, the opportunities these methods ultimately open up involve deeper connections to engage and dialogue with those we encounter.

CONCLUDING COMMENTS

For the most part, the semi-structured interview has dominated as a method of choice for many decades, but more recently there has been increasing dissatisfaction with its capacity to generate information that speaks to what is really going on. No matter the approach, most researchers agree an interview provides insights into knowledge accumulated in a unique context at a unique point in time – a snapshot view of what the world looks like here and now. This disconnected, isolated understanding of the complexity of the life being lived has long been one of the criticisms leveled at the research interview (Becker & Geer, 1957). In this collection, many alternative methods are considered to complement the interview in order to achieve greater transparency of self on the part of participants, researchers, or both. These interview methods take into account Becker's criticism –for example, by a practitioner [interview subject] partnering with a researcher to investigate a particular issue together (Spradley, 2016) or by extracting the interview from the twosome relationship through visualization and dialogue so that it aligns into an everyday context. Strangely enough though, there remains a degree of doubt and suspicion for researchers to decide on something other than traditional social scientific research methods in higher education. Experiences described by authors in this volume and by others who share their struggles of finding reviewers who trust their process represent experiences in living in 'creative tension' (Palmer, 2011). Despite these criticisms, the standard interview has stood the test of time and is still a widely used qualitative research method in part because is it logistically easy to use to study the meaning systems and narratives of participants.

When considering novel approaches, it also means there are sticky moral questions that can entangle researchers as they work to transform a research proposal into an application for ethics committee approval. A key challenge, if not a constraint, is how ethical theory plays out in the field in the real world of research. In several chapters, the authors tease out the implications of the research ethics approval process in what they describe as an increasingly rule-bound system, which governs how university researchers conduct themselves and their participants in the field. Halse and Honey (2010) argue, "research ethics policy positions research participants as the 'object' of the research and assumes that these 'subjects' form an identifiable, knowable constituency whose members share particular characteristics that distinguish them from others" (p. 125). This notion is challenged by some authors as they take up methodologies to explore intensely interactive, personal encounters and relationships, which resist such comfortable categorizations. For instance, Raffoul, Hamilton, and Andrews' use of portraiture for understanding the embodied practice of educational leadership legitimizes the 'interpretative witness of the portraitist.' In doing so, it exposes the messiness of power dynamics as 'subjects' ultimately emerge as research partners. In such cases, where power, authority, or social capital differences sit on shifting sands, the responsibilities of researchers to stand with participants in the uncertainty becomes paramount.

Perhaps a good point to close this volume aligns with one made in Chapter 1 that it is an exciting time to be practicing qualitative research on teaching and learning. As authors in this volume openly shared, the practice of qualitative research is conflict-ridden, but in helpful ways. That is, "researchers must reconcile the abstract and the concrete, and be prepared to resolve glitches and dilemmas they encounter in the field" (Luttrell, 2010, p. 5). Since we borrow from different disciplines, with different research designs and evaluation cultures, it is critical more than ever that we as educational researchers understand the nuances and assess its rigor. These disciplines vary in their embrace of epistemological stance and their emphasis on description and interpretation and their prominence of qualitative research methods.

The diversity of research included in this book is a testament to the courage of authors to explore new approaches by pulling threads from different disciplines to connect with their participants to achieve more fully immersive experiences. As a collective journey, this volume has included authentic portraitures, elicited illustrations, the use of video-elicited reflections, constructions of poetic representations, and collaborations and partnerships with participants. An emphasis on praxis provides an open window into how researchers critically explore the complexities of teaching and learning through listening, dialoguing, partnering, and embracing more intimate and embodied ways of understanding their participants' experiences. As Dewsbury (2003) suggests, it is something akin to witnessing:

> I am thinking here about the folded mix of our emotions, desires, and intuitions within the aura of places, the communication of things and spaces, and the spirit of events. Such folds leave traces of presence that map out a world that we come to know without thinking. (p. 1907)

In sum, these chapters challenge us to move away from assuming the world can be simply understood through what we can gather at a unique point in time with a standard interview and venture into, at times, unknown territories to capture unexpected insights.

3 Looking Ahead

Research on teaching and learning continues to inform and affect how aspects and concepts of learning and teaching are comprehended, assessed, and reevaluated. Such assessments are inextricably linked to practice. How research in teaching and learning can influence what practice is, and will be, is a critical issue moving forward for learning and teaching in higher education.

Finally, as we look ahead at the methodological richness that is open to research on teaching and learning in higher education, the challenge in this quest for methodological creativity is to balance it against an ongoing commitment to advancing teaching and learning. Denzin and Lincoln (2006) write that, "we are in a new age where messy, uncertain, multi-voiced texts, cultural criticisms, and new experimental works will become more common, as will more reflective forms of fieldwork, analysis, and inter-textual representation" (p. 26). These novel methodological approaches ask researchers to be vulnerable, to take more risks, to engage in struggle, and be more courageous. As a result, the window of opportunities they peer through will generate more meaningful journeys for both teachers and students.

References

Adamson, J., & Muller, T. (2017). Joint autoethnography of teacher experience in the academy: Exploring methods for collaborative inquiry. *International Journal of Research & Method in Education, 41*(2), 207–219. doi:10.1080/1743727X.2017.1279139

Allen-Collinson, J. (2013). Autoethnography as the engagement of self/other, self/culture, self/politics, selves/futures. In S. Holman, S. Jones, T. E. Adams, & C. Ellis (Eds.), *Handbook of autoethnography* (pp. 281–299). Left Coast Press.

Becker, H. S., & Geer, B. (1957). Participant observation and interviewing: A comparison. *Human Organization, 16*(3), 28–32.

Bochner, A. P., & Ellis, C. (1995). Telling and living: Narrative co-construction and the practices of interpersonal relationships. In W. Leeds-Hurwitz (Ed.), *Approaches to communication* (pp. 201–213). Guildford.

Chang, H., Ngunjiri, F. W., & Hernandez, K.-A. C. (2013). *Collaborative autoethnography*. Left Coast Press.

Charmaz, K. (2010). Grounded theory: Objectivist and constructivist methods. In W. Luttrell (Ed.), *Qualitative educational research: Readings in reflexive methodology and transformative practice* (pp. 184–207). Routledge.

Chase, S. (2010). Narrative inquiry: Multiple lenses, approaches, voices. In W. Luttrell (Ed.), *Qualitative educational research: Readings in reflexive methodology and transformative practice* (pp. 208–236). Routledge.

Coffey, A. (2002). Ethnography and self: Reflections and representations. In T. May (Ed.), *Qualitative research in action* (pp. 313–331). Sage.

Dewsbury, J. D. (2003). Witnessing space: Knowledge without contemplation. *Environment and Planning A, 35*, 1907–1932.

Denzin, N. K., & Lincoln, Y. (2000). Introduction: the discipline and practice of qualitative research. In N. Denzin & Y. Lincoln (Eds.), *Handbook of qualitative research* (2nd ed., pp. 1–28). Sage.

Denzin, N. K. (2013). Interpretive autoethnography. In S. Holman, S. Jones, T. E. Adams, & C. Ellis (Eds.), *Handbook of autoethnography* (pp. 123–142). Left Coast Press.

Denzin, N. K., & Lincoln, Y. S. (Eds.). (1994). *Handbook of qualitative research*. Sage.

Ellis, C., Adams, T. E., & Bocher, A. P. (2011). Autoethnography: An overview. *Historical Social Research-Historische Sozialforchung, 36*, 273–290. Retrieved from http://nbn-resolving.de/urn:nbn:de:0114-fqs1101108

Fine, M. (1994). Working the hyphens: Reinventing the self and other in qualitative research. In N. Denzin & Y. S. Lincoln (Eds.), *Handbook of qualitative research* (pp. 70–82). Sage.

Forber-Pratt, A. J. (2015). "You're going to do what?" Challenges of autoethnography in the academy. *Qualitative Inquiry, 21*, 821–835. doi:1077800415574908

Gergen, M. M., & Gergen, K. J. (2000). Qualitative inquiry: Tensions and transformations. In N. Denzin & Y. Lincoln (Eds.), *Handbook of qualitative research* (2nd ed., pp. 421–447). Sage.

Halse, C., & Honey, A. (2010). Unraveling ethics: Illuminating the moral dilemmas of research ethics. In W. Luttrell (Ed.), *Qualitative educational research: Readings in reflexive methodology and transformative practice* (pp. 123–138). Routledge.

Lather, P. (1991). Deconstructing/deconstructive inquiry: The politics of knowing and being known. *Educational Theory, 41*(2), 153–173.

Lave, J., & Wenger, E. (1991). *Situated learning: Legitimate peripheral participation*. Cambridge University Press.

Luttrell, W. (Ed.). (2010). *Qualitative educational research: Readings in reflexive methodology and transformative practice*. Routledge.

Meyer, J. H. F., & Land, R. (2005). Threshold concepts and troublesome knowledge (2): Epistemological considerations and a conceptual framework for teaching and learning. *Higher Education, 49*, 373–388.

Oakley, A. (1981). Interviewing women: A contradiction in terms. In Helen Roberts (Ed.), *Doing feminist research* (pp. 30–62). Routledge & Kegan Paul.

Ochs, E., & Capps, L. (2001). *Living narrative*. Harvard University Press.

Lapadat, J. C. (2017). Ethics in Autoethnography and collaborative autoethnography. *Qualitative Inquiry, 23*(8), 589–603. doi:10.1177/1077800417704462

Lapadat, J. C. (2009). Writing our way into shared understanding: Collaborative autobiographical writing in the qualitative methods class. *Qualitative Inquiry, 15*(6), 955–979. doi:10.1177/1077800409334185

Lapadat, J. C., Black, N. E., Clark, P. G., Gremm, R. M., Karanja, L. W., Mieke, M., & Quinlan, L. (2010). Life challenge memory work: Using collaborative autobiography to understand ourselves. *International Journal of Qualitative Methods, 9*, 77–104. Retrieved from http://ejournals.library.ualberta.ca/index.php/IJQM/article/view/1542

Richardson, L. (2003). Writing: A method of inquiry. In Y. S. Lincoln & N. K. Denzin (Eds.), *Turning points in qualitative research: Tying knots in a handkerchief* (pp. 379–396). AltaMira Press.

Simmons, N., Abrahamson, E., Deshler, J., Kensington-Miller, B., Manarin, K., Morón-García, S., & Renc-Roe, J. (2013). Conflicts and configurations in a liminal space: SoTL scholars' identity development. *Teaching & Learning Inquiry, 1*(2), 9–21. doi:10.2979/teachlearninqu.1.2.9

Spradley, J. P. (2016). *Participant observation*. Waveland Press.

Ulichny, P., &. Schoener, W. (2010). Teacher-researcher collaboration from two perspectives. In W. Luttrell (Ed.), *Qualitative educational research: Readings in reflexive methodology and transformative practice* (pp. 123–138). Routledge.

Van Maanen, J. (1998). *Tales of the field: On writing ethnography*. University of Chicago Press.

Index

action 7, 21, 39, 41, 42, 47, 48, 76, 81, 82, 89, 90, 95, 97, 100, 104, 114, 136–139, 148, 158, 164, 169, 174
action research 3, 8, 9, 133–143, 145–149, 152, 173, 175, 179–190, 196
analysis 4, 6, 7, 16, 35, 39, 45, 46, 48, 49, 52–55, 57, 60, 61, 64, 66, 80, 98, 108–110, 120, 124, 125, 136, 139, 141, 144, 156, 161, 166–169, 192, 194, 199
approach 2–4, 6–9, 17, 23, 27, 29, 34, 35, 43, 47, 53–55, 58, 61, 67–69, 76, 78, 79, 94–96, 98, 99, 101, 102, 107, 109–114, 118, 119, 121, 122, 125, 126, 134–136, 152, 155–157, 161, 162, 165, 168, 174–176, 179, 185, 186, 188, 192–199

change 4, 7, 24, 36, 37, 39, 55, 57, 58, 61, 83, 85, 90, 100, 103, 113, 115, 124–126, 136–138, 143, 147, 149, 158, 164, 166, 168, 169, 179, 181, 184–186
clinical 6, 16, 18–23, 29
collaboration 8, 67, 69, 104, 136, 137, 139, 145, 146, 164, 198
complexity 2, 3, 7–9, 60, 61, 64, 65, 94, 97, 99, 107, 108, 112–114, 126, 137, 166, 168, 174, 184, 196–198
concept 2, 4, 6, 7, 28, 41, 53, 55–58, 64, 67, 68, 141, 155, 158, 160, 162–165, 169, 198
context 1–4, 7, 8, 16, 18, 22, 27, 36, 37, 41, 57–61, 63, 64, 66–69, 81, 85, 86, 89, 94–99, 101–104, 110, 112, 115, 122, 126, 135, 146, 156, 158, 162, 174, 175, 179, 184, 186–189, 192, 194–197
conversation 7, 21, 22, 25, 53–55, 58–64, 76, 86, 95, 98, 99, 119, 123, 163–165, 175, 177, 178, 182, 183, 185, 193, 194, 196
critical 3–8, 16, 18, 26, 27, 31, 35, 37, 48, 52, 53, 67, 82, 86, 87, 90, 96, 100, 102, 104, 111, 126, 136, 141, 142, 146, 147, 149, 161, 169, 174, 185, 186, 195, 196, 198, 199

dialogue 7–9, 17, 21, 30, 31, 70, 76, 77, 80, 90, 97, 98, 118, 127, 134, 162–169, 194, 196, 197

education 3, 4, 6–8, 15–18, 23–28, 31, 35–38, 42, 45–49, 54, 57, 58, 63, 75–81, 86–90, 104, 109–111, 124, 126, 127, 133, 137, 141, 162, 173, 174, 183–187, 189, 190, 197, 199
emotion 7, 17, 22, 29, 30, 78, 82, 84–86, 89, 95, 196, 198
ethics 6, 8, 60, 65, 79, 134, 139, 142, 149, 174, 181–184, 189, 197
experience 6, 18, 22, 23, 26, 27, 28, 30, 31, 35–37, 50, 44, 46, 47, 49, 53, 54, 69, 77, 78, 80, 82–84, 87–89, 95–103, 108, 116, 121, 148, 149, 162, 165, 174, 176, 184–186, 189, 190, 194

faculty 6, 35, 37, 38, 55, 57–60, 63, 65, 66, 94, 136, 137, 138, 147, 149, 162, 175, 176, 181, 182, 185–189, 193, 195
future 8, 21, 44, 69, 94, 110, 113–118, 121

goal 68, 87, 100, 101, 141, 143, 148, 155–157, 162, 178

individual 5, 7, 23, 24, 30, 38, 42, 43, 45, 46, 53, 55, 57–60, 61, 65, 66, 69, 81, 88, 95–98, 100, 103, 104, 112, 114, 149, 157, 163–165, 175, 181, 183, 187, 188, 193–195
insight 25, 48, 54, 61, 111, 112, 165
interview 3, 7, 19, 20, 25, 27, 29, 38, 53, 61, 63–65, 67, 68, 79, 81–83, 86, 108, 112–115, 118–127,139, 140, 145, 152, 155, 161, 162–164, 169, 197, 198

knowledge 2, 16, 17, 20, 30, 35–37, 41, 42, 49, 54, 58, 69, 78, 89, 94–100, 102, 103, 109, 110, 112, 114, 123–127, 135, 137, 149, 155, 157, 160, 162–167, 174–176, 184, 186, 197

leader 6–8, 53, 55, 58, 59, 68, 94–105, 176, 188, 193, 196
leadership 6, 7, 52–55, 58, 59, 61, 62, 87, 89, 90, 93–101, 103, 179, 193, 194, 197
learn 1, 2, 6, 9, 21, 26, 29, 35, 39, 49, 58, 78, 103, 104, 108, 134, 137–139, 143, 146, 152, 155, 162, 192, 195

longitudinal 4, 8, 60, 68, 107–115, 118, 119, 120, 122, 124–127

methodology 5–8, 53, 66–68, 76, 77, 79, 80, 86, 87, 89, 108, 109, 113, 114, 121, 122, 141, 143, 145, 155, 161, 162, 167, 192, 195
model 7, 9, 36, 46, 47, 57, 64 , 67, 76, 94–96, 101, 134, 141, 143, 146, 149, 159, 161, 167. 168, 175, 179, 182, 186, 188

narrative 4, 7, 8, 16, 60, 93–103, 107, 108, 112–115, 117–127, 147, 152, 174, 193, 197
narrative research 7, 8, 101, 114
network 4, 6, 7, 52–68, 95, 96, 196

partnership 1, 54, 64, 67–69, 101, 134, 143, 145, 148, 149, 179, 198
peer 6, 9, 17, 28, 30, 36, 38, 39, 42, 43, 45, 55, 59, 81, 83, 173, 175–190, 199
photo-elicitation 4, 6, 15–21, 23–30
poetic 7, 78, 88
poetic representation 4, 7, 75–80, 82, 86–90, 198
portraiture 4, 7, 93, 96–101, 103, 104, 197, 198
power 6, 7, 16–18, 23–26, 29, 47, 67, 89, 96, 101, 111, 118, 123, 169, 175, 176, 179, 182, 194, 197, 198
practice 1, 4–9, 17, 22–29, 34, 36, 37, 39, 45–47, 49, 54, 58, 64, 77, 78, 81, 89, 90, 93–101, 103, 104, 134–139, 142, 144, 145, 146, 148, 153, 156, 161, 165, 173–176, 178, 179, 181, 184, 186–188, 198, 194, 195, 196, 198, 199,
process 5, 8, 9, 17, 18, 42, 43, 45–49, 63, 66, 69, 76–80, 82, 86, 94, 96, 99–104, 112–114, 124–126, 136–149, 152, 153, 155–159, 161, 162, 164, 166–169, 176, 178–182, 184–186, 189, 195–197

qualitative 3–5, 8, 9, 17, 24, 25, 27, 31, 39, 54, 58, 60, 64, 68, 76, 79, 80, 87, 88, 107, 110, 112, 113, 118, 124, 125–127, 142, 155, 156, 162, 163, 169, 184, 192, 194–198

reflection 1, 2, 4–6, 8, 9, 17, 19, 22, 24, 27, 34–36, 39, 40–43, 45–48, 84, 87, 89, 95–98, 101, 121, 136–138, 143, 144, 149, 152, 162, 168, 169, 174–176, 179, 186, 189, 192
relationship 1, 7, 20, 23, 26, 28, 43, 55, 65, 68, 76, 80–82, 89, 90, 97, 100, 104, 111, 112, 118–121, 126, 134, 136, 137, 145, 147, 155, 157, 162, 164, 165, 179, 182–184, 194, 195, 197
research 1–9, 16–31, 34–38, 43, 45, 47–49, 53, 54, 57–60, 65–70, 75–85, 87–90, 94–96, 98–104, 108–115, 117–119, 124–127, 133–149, 152, 154, 155, 162–169, 173–175, 179–190, 192–199
researcher 2–9, 16–18, 22, 25–31, 35, 42, 49, 53, 54, 58, 60, 64, 67–69, 76–78, 80, 83, 86–90, 94, 100–102, 109–115, 120, 124–127, 134, 136–139, 141–145, 147–149, 155, 161–169, 174, 175, 179, 184, 188, 190, 192–199
review 6, 9, 79, 83, 98, 137, 139–141, 144, 145, 160, 167, 173, 175–180, 183, 187
role 4, 7, 30, 36, 40–42, 44–47, 57, 61, 67, 76, 77, 82, 87, 95, 116, 118, 119, 125, 137, 141–146, 152, 153, 164, 175, 185, 193, 195

self reflection 6, 35, 36, 39, 42, 43, 45, 47, 48, 138
social 3, 4, 6, 7, 23, 24, 26, 52–55, 57–60, 65–68, 87, 89, 95, 97, 101, 110, 111, 114, 115, 118, 138, 142, 149, 164, 167, 175, 185, 192–195, 197, 198
social network theory 55, 59, 66
story 7, 57, 76, 77, 98–102, 142
strategy 2, 4, 6, 9, 15–18, 20–31, 81, 97, 117, 134–136, 138, 141, 152, 155–162, 169, 175, 177, 178, 182, 187, 189, 194, 196
student 1, 2, 4, 6–9, 16–29, 31, 35–49, 54, 59, 64, 65, 67, 68, 76, 77, 79–85, 87, 90, 94, 96, 103, 108, 111, 116, 117, 120, 121, 126, 135, 137, 139, 147, 152, 153, 155–159, 161, 162, 163, 165–169, 178, 185, 189, 192, 194, 199
supervisor 21–23, 29, 35–47, 49, 68, 117, 120, 162, 163

teacher 6, 7, 26, 27, 28, 35–49, 68, 69, 76, 77, 80–84, 88–90, 103, 108, 110, 113, 115, 123, 145–147, 176, 185, 186, 193, 199
teaching 1–9, 16, 17, 23–29, 35–37, 39–48, 53–55, 57–64, 66, 68, 69, 80–82, 87, 94, 96, 104, 108, 109, 133–135, 137, 138, 141, 142, 146–149, 173–190, 192–196, 198, 199
theory 3, 5, 8, 39, 43, 45, 48, 55, 57, 59, 66, 102, 134–136, 165, 174, 179, 195, 197
trust 7, 16, 31, 57–68, 75–86, 88–90, 99, 100, 111, 118, 195, 197

visual   6, 9, 16–18, 22, 23, 25–31, 53, 55,
    58, 59, 61, 63, 65, 67, 160, 162–166, 168,
    169
visual-elicited reflection   6, 34
visual mapping   9, 162, 163, 166
visualization   9, 162, 163, 165, 168, 169, 197

work   1, 4, 5, 7–9, 17, 28, 30, 35, 39, 54, 59, 64,
    66, 67, 76, 77, 79, 81, 83–87, 89, 90, 95,
    97, 99, 100, 102, 109, 110, 113, 114, 116, 118,
    121, 123, 134, 135, 141, 142, 146, 147, 149,
    152, 157, 165, 169, 174–176, 178, 182, 185,
    187–189, 192–195, 197

Printed in the United States
By Bookmasters